Rebels and King's Men

Rebels and King's Men

Bertie County in the Revolutionary War

Gerald W. Thomas

Raleigh
North Carolina Department of Cultural Resources
Office of Archives and History
2013

North Carolina Department of Cultural Resources
Susan W. Kluttz
Secretary

Office of Archives and History
Kevin Cherry
Deputy Secretary

Historical Publications Section
Donna E. Kelly
Administrator

Cover: Image of American Patriot, *Harper's Weekly,* July 15, 1876.

Printed by Edwards Brothers Malloy Inc.

Contents

Maps and Illustrations

Tables

Foreword

Gerald W. Thomas has written *Rebels and King's Men: Bertie County in the Revolutionary War* as the third installment of his military works about his native county published by the North Carolina Office of Archives and History. The first two were *Divided Allegiances: Bertie County during the Civil War* (1996) and *Destitute Patriots: Bertie County in the War of 1812* (2012).

Rebels and King's Men traces the Revolutionary War service of and provides rosters for Continental Line soldiers, minutemen, and militia from Bertie County. Mr. Thomas identified 485 men who served in some capacity during the war. This number does not represent the total number of men from the county who actually served, since nearly all records that would document the total number have over the years been unintentionally destroyed or lost. However, the number identified still represents over twice as many as those who subsequently served in the War of 1812 (241).

Events leading up to the Revolutionary War affected activities in Bertie County. Passage of the Stamp Act and other regulatory provisions curtailed the recording of land transactions and holding court. A militia was raised to march against the Regulators, but it never saw action. Representatives from Bertie were elected to all five provincial congresses, and a committee of safety was established.

In the early stages of the war, men were raised for county militia and minutemen companies and not Continental regiments. Troops were assembled, and supplies were often provided by local citizens in the county. Recruiting efforts continued, and men were strongly encouraged to volunteer rather than be drafted. They were often paid small bonuses for enlisting of their own volition.

As the title of the book implies, in addition to the "rebels" (Patriots), there was a small contingent of "king's men" (Loyalists) in Bertie County and the surrounding area. A conspiracy among the Tories formed against the Whigs. These treasonous individuals took an oath to support the Anglican Church, oppose the militia draft, and support Loyalists. In a six-county area that included Bertie, many conspirators worked to thwart Whig activities. When caught, they were banished in lieu of death and forfeited all of their property.

When recruiting was successful among the Patriots and troops were raised, the men had to fight in close quarters. Many died from wounds in battle or from disease caused by poor living conditions in camp, particularly at Valley Forge. Some were captured as prisoners and ultimately paroled. All of those who fought from Bertie County, and the rest of the nation, made tremendous personal sacrifices in the name of liberty and freedom.

Gerald Thomas graduated from East Carolina University and worked for the federal government before retiring several years ago. He meticulously searched all available sources, both primary and secondary, to compile a record of the Bertie County men who served in the Revolutionary War. His exhaustive documentation is second to none, as is evidenced in his two previous publications. The Office of Archives and History is honored to bring his work to fruition in this printed edition, and as a Kindle e-book.

Assisting in the production of this volume was Robert M. Topkins (former staff member of the section) who edited and indexed the book. Susan Trimble designed the layout and the cover (assisted by Bill Owens), and typeset the volume. Lisa Bailey proofread the text, and I added illustrations and oversaw all aspects of production.

Donna E. Kelly, Administrator
Historical Publications Section

Publication of this book was made possible by the support of the North Carolina Society of the Cincinnati.

Preface

On Wednesday, June 10, 1970, a slender, fair-complexioned Bertie County country boy drove the family car into Windsor and stopped by his mother's place of employment. The lad had graduated from Bertie Senior High School six days earlier, and having made no definitive plans for his post-high-school endeavors, was privately considering "what" he was going to do in the immediate future. In a brief conversation, the boy advised his mother that he was going to the local post office to "talk" with the army recruiter who was in town that day. At the time the United States was bogged down in a highly unpopular war in Vietnam, about which, on this same day, Edwin Starr released a blatant, anti-war song, "War." Also on June 10, in Vietnam over two dozen Americans died while serving their country and government. The mother pleaded with the lad, "Please, don't sign up [for service in the army]." A couple of hours later, the lad returned for a second visit with his mother. She suffered that sickening feeling every mother surely experiences when a son or daughter breaks the news that he or she has decided to serve in the nation's military during wartime. The young man advised his mother that he had "signed up" to serve in the army. He was scheduled to leave town one week later on a Trailways bus for Raleigh and the state's military induction center. In the early afternoon of June 17, 1970, the lad stepped aboard a bus at the Trailways station in Windsor, sat down at a window, and waved goodbye to his weeping mother. Two days later, the boy took the oath of allegiance to the United States at the Raleigh center and enlisted in the United States Army; by midnight he was at the United States Army Basic Training Center, Fort Jackson, South Carolina.

I was the lad who "signed up" on June 10, 1970, and left home a week later. At the time the event meant no more than the immediate action it executed—a teenaged boy had enlisted in the army. Now, over four decades later and having conducted this study, I realize that I had actually "followed in the footsteps" of many of my ancestors who, for almost two centuries, had enlisted for military service in Windsor during times of war, beginning with the Revolutionary War. Certain members of my lineal ancestors, or immediate relatives of my lineal ancestors, had served in the military during nearly all of the nation's conflicts [Revolutionary War, War of 1812, Civil War (both Union and Confederate armies), World War I, and World War II].

My lineal ancestry in Bertie County dates back prior to the Revolutionary Period (1764–1789). My ancestors who resided in the county during the Revolutionary War experienced anxiety, uncertainty, worries, strife, and sacrifices, as did thousands of other North Carolinians who lived during that era in our nation's history. As such, my interest and desire to learn about the experiences of Bertie County's citizens during the War for Independence motivated me to conduct several years of research and document my findings in this study. Particularly, at least eighteen of my lineal ancestors and close relatives of those ancestors served in the Continental army and/or detached militia units from the county.

For the most part, the citizens of Bertie County affiliated themselves with the Whig Party and generally supported the party's political positions, including colonies-wide, anti-British measures before the war. The term "Whig" has had different uses throughout American history, but during the American Revolution, Patriots used it to symbolize their opposition to the tyrannies of the English Crown. However, while the majority of Bertie County's citizens were pro-Whig, within the county a number of persons—Loyalists who were commonly termed "Tories"—maintained their avid support for King George III in the midst of wartime turmoil and consternation. During 1777 and 1778, Bertie County justices exiled those Loyalists who refused to take the statutorily mandated oath of allegiance to North Carolina. Other county residents became caught up in a 1777 subversive conspiracy to overthrow the new state government and to create chaos and civil violence within the Albemarle Sound-Roanoke River region. Their plans, however, never materialized into action since their secret society was ousted, and regional Whig officials hauled dozens of the conspirators into county courts, effectively publicizing and crushing the plot.

Throughout the war Bertie County's sons served in significant numbers in the North Carolina Continental Line and detached companies of the county's militia. Due to the destruction of numerous War Department records and the lack of essential information in surviving documents and rolls, the precise number of Bertie County men who actively served in the Continental army and detached militia units cannot be ascertained. Indeed, the identities of dozens of county men who marched away from Windsor as army recruits or detached militiamen cannot be documented—the details of their services and sacrifices are lost to history. For example, in early January 1779, Capt. Thomas Pugh arrived at Kinston with a detached militia company comprised of eighty-five Bertie County men. I was able to identify only one rank-and-file member (Pvt. James Ward) of the company. Furthermore, in

June 1780, Col. Andrew Oliver reported to Gov. Abner Nash that there were 18 volunteers and 112 draftees in Bertie County ready for service. Presumably, some, if not all, of the men saw military service. But I found no record(s) to document the identities of the 130 men. Similarly, records do not exist to document the identities of all the members of a half dozen other companies of detached militia with Bertie County members.

Sufficient records exist to confirm that soldiers and militiamen from the county served in both the northern and southern theaters of operations. County natives were present at the Battles of Brandywine and Germantown, Pennsylvania; Monmouth, New Jersey; Sullivan's Island, Eutaw Springs, Stono Ferry, and Camden, South Carolina; Brier Creek, Georgia; and Guilford Courthouse, North Carolina. Some men were killed in battle. Poorly clad and provisioned soldiers from the county endured the brutal winter of 1777–1778 at Valley Forge, Pennsylvania, as members of Gen. George Washington's beleaguered Continental army. A number of Bertie County men perished at the camp during that horrible time, succumbing to disease and illness. County sons withstood the British siege of Charleston, South Carolina, and surrendered en masse with their comrades on May 12, 1780. In short, Bertie County's warriors contributed significantly to the nation's cause for war and independence.

Generally, I have organized the contents of this book chronologically, but not strictly so from the beginning of chapter 1 to the conclusion of chapter 5. I concluded that the material herein presented in chapters 3 through 5 was most logically conveyed by topic (as described below). Chapter 1 chiefly covers the events of the decade-plus period that led up to the war. The chapter also briefly covers the evolution of local politics and the establishment of the new town of Windsor as the societal and governmental center of the county. Furthermore, it includes a short account of the Regulator movement in the backcountry of North Carolina for which Bertie County militiamen were placed in readiness to respond during the pre-war era. Chapter 2 addresses events following the commencement of hostilities at Lexington and Concord, Massachusetts (April 1775) through December 1776—the date of the establishment of the North Carolina state government and the adoption of the state constitution. Chapter 3 solely focuses on the Loyalist elements of Bertie County who were exiled from the state in 1777 and 1778, as well as the "John Llewelyn" anti-government conspiracy, which included secret supporters and participants from Bertie County. Chapter 4 is dedicated to the experiences of Bertie County men who served in North Carolina's Continental Line regiments, including a significant number of men who, in the early summer of 1778, were drafted from the county's militia regiment to serve for nine months with Gen. George Washington's main army. (Appendix 1 presents a compiled roster of the men whom I identified as serving in the Continental army.) Chapter 5 concentrates on the service of Bertie County's detached militia companies, including a couple of units (Capts. Allen Ramsay and Elisha Rhodes's companies) that included members from neighboring counties (Hertford and Gates counties, respectively). (Appendix 2 conveys a roster of Bertie County militiamen whom I identified.)

Concerning the rosters (appendixes 1 and 2), a meager few muster rolls, pay-rolls and enlistment rolls exist at the State Archives and the National Archives in Washington, D.C. to document the service of Bertie County's Continental soldiers and detached militiamen. Other persons who have researched North Carolina during the Revolutionary War and prepared formal histories have encountered the same regrettable constraint. Therefore, I have diligently reviewed and analyzed available, pertinent records at both of the aforementioned institutions, primary records at the Bertie County courthouse in Windsor, and various secondary sources to compile the rosters. Of particular note, the State Archives holds thousands of Revolutionary War vouchers of which, I am confident, include documents for military pay owed to Bertie County soldiers and militiamen. Unfortunately, the vouchers predominantly do not differentiate the county of residence (during the war) of the payees or the purposes of the amounts owed (such as military pay, payment for provisions, commodities, firearms, other tangible items, etc.). Despite my effort to use the vouchers to identify Bertie County citizens who served in the Continental Line and detached militia, I found the attempt to be futile due to the lack of necessary details. Consequently, the rosters do not contain the names of all men who actively served in the army and/or detached militia, but they are as accurate as possible, given the lack of detailed records and selected deficiencies in available sources.

Due to space limitations in this print edition, the service histories for the individual soldiers and officers were not included. The Kindle e-book edition of this work includes a link to the service histories and the copious endnotes that identify the sources used in compiling the data. It is found at www.ncpublications.com/bertie.html. In most cases the rosters do not present complete service histories for the included individuals. Furthermore, the Note on Appendixes conveys to the reader limitations and constraints encountered in preparing the rosters. However, I am of the opinion that the rosters as presented here and in the e-book edition will enable future historical and genealogical researchers to build upon them and perhaps conclusively document additional men from the county who served and sacrificed during the Revolutionary War.

And finally, I am ever so grateful and appreciative to the officials and staff members of the North Carolina Department of Cultural Resources, Historical Publications Section, for publishing this study, as well as my two previous efforts—*Divided Allegiances: Bertie County during the Civil War* (1996) and *Destitute Patriots: Bertie County in the War of 1812* (2012). Without their assistance and support, I am not certain that the studies would have ever been published.

Gerald W. Thomas

A WIDENING RIFT

O n Thursday, August 25, 1774, John Campbell, a highly respected and influential businessman, planter, and legislator of Bertie County, assembled in New Bern with seventy other men from the counties and principal towns of the colony of North Carolina. Those men, elected as members of North Carolina's First Provincial Congress, were about to launch the colony on an unsure and daunting path toward statehood and independence from the ties of the British king and Parliament. Important business faced the men: they were impelled to designate several persons to represent North Carolina at the forthcoming Continental Congress, a first-ever convention of delegates from the American colonies scheduled to begin in Philadelphia during September. That body was slated to assemble and discuss various options available to the Americans concerning British infringements.[1]

This moment in North Carolina's existence had been building for more than a decade—a period during which an ever widening rift and deteriorating relationships developed between the British government and its thirteen colonies in North America. The period was for North Carolina a time of escalating anti-British sentiment, protests, and public demonstrations. Campbell and the other members of the provincial congress had no way of knowing with certainty that North Carolina's forty-five-year period of royal rule was rapidly coming to an end. During that period the majority of the people residing in the northeastern region of the colony, including Bertie County, were of British descent. The region had been settled predominantly by persons who migrated from southeastern Virginia in the late 1600s and 1700s. Many of the settlers were descendants of the yeoman farmer class in England, who, having been (or their parents having been) indentured servants, agreed to labor for periods of time to repay whoever advanced the money for their passage to Virginia. Once their terms of indenture were served, they were at liberty to work for themselves and strike out on their own. Desiring to avoid any stigma that might have been attached to their previous social status, many of the former servants departed Virginia and started new lives in North Carolina.[2]

The decade of the 1760s in Bertie County was a time of political, social, and economic definition. The county's leaders were occupied with defining the county's economic and political structure. Central to their efforts was establishing Windsor as the county's center of local government, commerce, and social and political interaction. In 1759 North Carolina's colonial assembly had established Hertford County from an expanse that had been included within Bertie, Chowan, and Northampton counties, thereby rendering Bertie County's geographical area as it essentially exists today. While people of English descent continued to migrate to Bertie County, mainly from southeastern Virginia, the county's Native American residents—the Tuscarora Indians—for the most part departed. In 1763 and 1766 most of the Indians who resided in the Indian Woods sector of the county (a reservation that had been established in 1717) migrated north to settle with other Iroquoian peoples, predominantly in New York. By 1767 slightly more than one hundred members of the Tuscarora tribe continued to reside on the reservation. In January 1768 the colonial assembly passed an act authorizing the establishment of the town of Windsor on 100 acres of land along the Cashie River owned by William Gray. Six years later the assembly directed that the county's courthouse, prison, pillory, and stocks be constructed in Windsor. The assembly further directed that the county's court was to be held quarterly in Windsor beginning June 1, 1774, thereby effectively establishing Windsor as the county seat.[3]

While residents of Bertie County endeavored to advance their parochial interests, relationships between the American colonies and Great Britain devolved toward confrontation, primarily as a result of a continuum of parliamentary statutes that many colonists considered overbearing and unjust. On October 7, 1763, King George III signed the Proclamation of 1763, a law that prohibited any British settlements west of the Appalachian Mountains and required people who had already settled in those regions to return east in an attempt to ease tensions with the Indians. Six months later, on April 5, 1764, the British Parliament passed the Sugar Act to offset the war debt incurred by the British during the French and Indian War and to help pay the expenses of maintaining the colonies and newly acquired territories. The measure increased

George III (1738–1820) became king of Great Britain in October 1760. During his reign Great Britain became the dominant European power in North America; but more than ten years of civil and political tumult and rebellion in the thirteen American colonies precipitated the Revolutionary War, which culminated in the loss of those colonies to the British Empire. King George III remained the British monarch until his death in January 1820. Image from the Prints and Photographs Division, Library of Congress, Washington, D.C.

the duties on imported sugar and other items, such as textiles, coffee, wines, and indigo (dye). It doubled the duties on foreign goods reshipped from Great Britain to the colonies and also forbade the import of foreign rum and French wines. Later in 1764 Parliament passed a measure to reorganize the American customs system to better enforce British trade laws, which had often been ignored in the past.[4]

By the spring of 1764, smoldering colonial opposition to the British statutory measures ignited, initially in Massachusetts. During a town meeting in

Boston in May 1764, James Otis, an influential local lawyer and political activist, raised the issue of taxation without representation and urged a united colonial response to the recent acts imposed by the British. A few months later Otis published a pamphlet titled, *The Rights of the British Colonies Asserted and Proved*, which asserted that rights are not derived from human institutions but from nature and God, and thus arguing that government does not exist to please monarchs but rather to promote the general well-being of the entire society. Shortly thereafter, Boston merchants began a boycott of British luxury goods. In early September 1764 Parliament passed the Currency Act, which prohibited the colonists from issuing any legal tender paper money. The act, which threatened to destabilize the entire colonial economy of both the industrial North and the agricultural South, united the colonies in opposition. The act also contained a provision for the British to establish a vice admiralty court in Halifax, Nova Scotia, to provide jurisdiction over all of the American colonies in trade matters.[5]

The laws Parliament enacted prior to 1765 to deal with various aspects of life in the American colonies placed varying degrees of hardship upon those who resided there, but the most despised and financially burdensome statute was yet to come. On March 22, 1765, Parliament passed the Stamp Act, which imposed the first direct tax on the American colonies. British officials intended to use taxes collected per the act's provisions to offset the high costs of their country's military presence in America. The law specifically named more than fifty types and categories of documents, issuances, and transactions that were to require the payment of duties. Thus, for the first time in the 150-year history of the British colonies in America, the Americans were to pay taxes not to their own local legislatures but directly to England. Under the act, all printed materials were taxed. The colonists swiftly united in opposition, led by the most influential segments of colonial society—lawyers, publishers, landowners, and merchants (those most affected by the act). The act's provisions were to go into effect on November 1, 1765.[6]

The Stamp Act was vastly different from its predecessors in its financial impact upon residents throughout North Carolina. For example, printed materials—including legal documents (such as deeds, bills of sale, and affidavits) and other paper issuances (newspapers, magazines, pamphlets, and so on)—were required to be printed on British stamped paper and embossed with a stamp. The cost of the paper and stamps was a direct British tax—an added expense to each individual who consummated a business transaction, required a legal document, or purchased a printed product.[7]

On October 7, 1765, the American colonists, aroused and united against the forthcoming implementation of the Stamp Act, convened the intercolonial Stamp Act Congress in New York. Representatives from nine colonies attended; but inasmuch as Gov. William Tryon neglected to call together the colony's assembly to ascertain whether or not to dispatch a delegate to the gathering, no one from North Carolina attended the conclave. The congress prepared for delivery to King George III and the British Parliament a "Declaration of Rights and Grievances," requesting that the Stamp Act and other measures be repealed. The document asserted that only colonial legislatures could tax colonial residents and that taxation without representation violated the colonists' basic rights. North Carolina residents subsequently affirmed their support for the congress's position. Nonetheless, the provisions of the Stamp Act went into effect on November 1, 1765. New Yorkers promptly erupted in violent protest at the governor's residence. Most daily business and legal transactions in the colonies ceased as the colonists refused to use the stamps.[8]

Reaction to the law across North Carolina, particularly in the more heavily populated eastern region, was intense. Some persons proclaimed that they would resist the enforcement of the act and the collection of the taxes to their deaths. Public demonstrations filled the streets in the port towns of Edenton, New Bern, and Wilmington. The most vocal and vehement opposition occurred in and about Wilmington, the colony's chief port, near the mouth of the Cape Fear River. Angry crowds gathered to resist the enforcement of the act, nearly bringing on a state of civil war. On November 20, 1765, the Wilmington *North Carolina Gazette* reported that in the early evening of October 19, nearly five hundred persons gathered in Wilmington and hanged an effigy of a "certain Honourable Gentleman" who had expressed support for the Stamp Act. They burned the effigy in a "large Bonfire." Afterward, they reportedly visited every house in the town, rounded up all the "Gentlemen," and escorted them to the fire, where they drank until midnight, proclaiming "LIBERTY, PROPERTY, AND NO STAMP-DUTY." Twelve days later "a great Number of People again assembled" in Wilmington, where they publicly demonstrated for liberty of the colonies. Lastly, the paper reported that on Saturday, November 16, about 300 to 400 people—"with Drums beating and colours flying"—met William Houston, the British stamp distributor, upon his arrival in the town. They adamantly inquired whether he intended to execute the duties of his office, to which he responded that he "should be very sorry to execute any Office disagreeable to the People of the Province." But the mob, not content with such a declaration, carried him into the courthouse, where he signed a resignation. As soon as Houston had complied with their desire, members of the mob placed him in a chair and paraded him around the court-house, streets, and squares of the town before proceeding with him to his lodging, where they cheered him and consumed "the best Liquors to be had." For the remainder of the evening, the mob treated Houston "very genteely."[9]

In early January 1766 Governor Tryon proclaimed to North Carolina's residents that "the Stamp papers for use of this Province" were available at the Cape Fear River. He cautioned the residents that "no person may plead ignorance," that the required papers were available, and anyone properly authorized to distribute the papers could receive them from the commander of the British sloop of war *Diligence* at the port of Brunswick (then an active port on the Cape Fear River).[10]

Attempted imposition of the Stamp Act's provisions by royal authorities further increased tensions and animosity in eastern North Carolina, particularly within the Wilmington-Brunswick-Cape Fear region. The printer of Wilmington's *North Carolina Gazette* informed his readers that he was "in a very disagreeable situation" and was endeavoring "with great difficulty" to sustain his newspaper, recognizing that in essence the province was deprived of the liberty of the press—one of the "darling" privileges of which "Englishmen boast."[11]

British authorities began to seize private citizens' vessels loaded with goods "for want of stamped Clearances." Residents from a number of locales about the Cape Fear River were "greatly dissatisfied" with the royal officers' heavy-handed actions and defiantly assembled at Wilmington on February 18, 1766. They appointed "officers" to take command of the worsening situation and to act on their behalf. With pending prosecutions of the owners of the seized sloops imminent, the residents—asserting that they were "free and natural born subjects of [King] George the third"—declared that they were ready and willing, at the expense of their lives and fortunes, to oppose "the oppressive and arbitrary" Stamp Act. On February 19 more than a thousand people marched to Brunswick, where they hoped to obtain a redress of their grievances from the commanding officer of British naval forces in the area. On the following day the residents met with the officer and the collector of the port to discuss their concerns. By the afternoon, through a conciliation "happily" reached, the two royal officials promised that the port would, for the future, be freed from the particular restrictions of the Stamp Act—at least until the British surveyor general of the customs arrived—and that merchant vessels were to be cleared as usual.[12]

On the next day the residents (many of whom were armed), having learned that the comptroller of the customs was present at Governor Tryon's residence (in Brunswick), sent for him to meet with them. The comptroller, however, refused to depart the residence. A party of men then marched directly toward the governor's abode, where they were halted near the house by a royal guard. A member of the party was dispatched once more to encourage the comptroller to meet with the people, lest they be prompted to undertake "the disagreeable necessity of entering" the governor's house. To this ultimatum the comptroller capitulated and agreed to meet with the people. The dispatched party, with the comptroller and other customs officers in accompaniment, then joined the main body of people in the town. The residents "drew up in a large circle" and positioned the comptroller and customs officers in the center. Obviously intimidated, the officers in unison made an oath that they would not, directly or indirectly, in any manner sign or execute any stamped papers until the Stamp Act had been accepted by the province. The officers further decreed that all clerks of the courts, lawyers, and other officials were bound to the oath they had just concluded. Satisfied, the assemblage of people immediately dispersed and returned to their homes.[13] The Stamp Act would not be enforced in the province of North Carolina. Civil violence had been avoided through public demonstration and intimidation. The Cape Fear mobs had prevented the enforcement of the Stamp Act in the province, thereby precluding Parliament from taxing the colony, at least for the short term.

Within Bertie County the turmoil associated with the Stamp Act curtailed the recording of land conveyances and court proceedings. During the eight-month period from July 1765 through February 1766, only two deeds for land transfers were consummated and recorded on the county's books. Furthermore, no quarterly court sessions were held for the November 1765 and February 1766 terms.[14]

Throughout the other twelve colonies, opposition and, in certain instances, violence, toward the Stamp Act continued. Finally, on March 18, 1766, King George III signed a bill repealing the act after much debate in the British Parliament. The American statesman Benjamin Franklin had appeared before Parliament and argued for repeal, direly warning of a possible revolution in the American colonies if the Stamp Act was enforced by the British military. News of the repeal reached the colonies in April, prompting exuberant celebrations and a relaxation of the boycott of imported British trade goods that had been instituted.[15]

Even though the British government had repealed the detested Stamp Act, it duly alerted the Americans that it had not relinquished its statutory authority over the colonies. On the day it repealed the Stamp Act, Parliament passed the Declaratory Act, which decreed that the British government had "total power" to legislate any laws governing the American colonies in all cases whatsoever.

On June 29, 1767, Parliament exercised its self-decreed taxing authority over the colonies and passed the Townshend Revenue Acts ("Townshend Acts"), which imposed a new series of taxes on the colonists to offset the costs of administering and protecting the American colonies. Items taxed included imports such as paper, tea, glass, lead, and paints. The act also established a colonial board of customs commissioners in Boston. Before the end of the year, Bostonians rose up to oppose the taxes levied by the Townshend Acts by imposing a boycott of British luxury items.[16]

Furthermore, attempted forced implementation of the so-called Quartering Act, enacted in March 1765, was creating turmoil and animosity in the northern colonies. The measure required the colonists to lodge British troops and supply them with food—in essence, imposing an additional tax upon the Americans. In December 1765 British army general Thomas Gage, commander of all British military forces in America, asked the New York Assembly to force the colonists in that province to comply with the act by housing and supplying his troops. The assembly refused to comply with Gage's request. Tension between New Yorkers and British troops increased until violence erupted between the soldiers and armed colonists in August 1766. In December 1766 the British Crown suspended the New York legislature after it once again voted to refuse to comply with the Quartering Act.[17]

In February 1768, amid ever escalating tensions with Britain throughout the colonies, Samuel Adams of Massachusetts prepared a circular letter in which he espoused opposing taxation without representation. Adams called for the colonies to unite in their actions against the British government. The Massachusetts legislature sent the letter to legislative assemblies throughout the colonies and also instructed them on the methods the Massachusetts general court was employing to oppose the Townshend Acts. Two months later, England's secretary of state for the colonies, Wills Hill, the earl of Hillsborough, ordered colonial governors to stop their own assemblies from endorsing Adams's letter. Hillsborough also ordered the Massachusetts governor to dissolve the general court if that province's assembly did not revoke the letter. By the end of the month, the assemblies of New Hampshire, Connecticut, and New Jersey had endorsed the document.[18]

In May a British warship armed with fifty cannon sailed into Boston harbor in response to a call for help from customs commissioners who were constantly being harassed by Boston agitators. Shortly after the ship's arrival, Bostonians detained a customs official and locked him in the cabin of the *Liberty*, a sloop owned by John Hancock. Boston merchants thereupon unloaded imported wine without paying any duties. British customs officials then seized

Thomas Gage (1721–1787), British general, commanded all British forces in North America for more than a decade (1763–1774). He subsequently served as the royal military governor of Massachusetts (1774–1775) but was unsuccessful in stemming the tide of colonial rebellion at the outbreak of the American Revolution. Image from the Prints and Photographs Division, Library of Congress.

Hancock's sloop, which prompted threats of violence from Bostonians. Fearing for their safety, the officials fled to an island off Boston and requested the intervention of British troops. In early August Bostonians and New Yorkers agreed to boycott most British goods until the Townshend Acts were repealed. Then, in September at a town meeting in Boston, residents were urged to arm themselves. Later in the month, British warships sailed into Boston Harbor; then two regiments of British infantry landed in Boston and set up permanent residence to keep order.[19] The future looked ominous to the colonists.

In the fall of 1769, with events in the northern colonies captivating the attention of King George III and Parliament, North Carolina's colonial assembly "asserted its wonted spirit and independence" in a series of resolutions opposing direct taxation by the British Parliament. On November 6 Governor Tryon reactively dissolved the assembly. Nevertheless, the members gathered and decided to reject the purchase of any items from British sources.[20] North Carolina colonial legislators were publicly exhibiting their rebellious temperament.

Events in 1770 continued to exacerbate emotions and relations, particularly between northern colonists and the British. In January violence erupted between New Yorkers and British soldiers over the posting of broadsheets by the British; several persons were wounded. Then, on March 5, a throng of Bostonians harassed British soldiers, who fired their muskets at point-blank range into the crowd, killing three instantly, mortally wounding two others, and injuring six. After the incident, the royal governor of Massachusetts, Thomas Hutchinson, at the insistence of Samuel Adams, withdrew British troops out of Boston to nearby harbor islands. Later in the year colonial lawyers John Adams and Josiah Quincy successfully defended the captain, although six of his men were acquitted. Two other soldiers were found guilty of manslaughter, branded, and released. In April the British government repealed the Townshend Acts, eliminating all duties on imports into the colonies except for tea. Moreover, the British chose not to renew the Quartering Act. Despite the British concessions, tension remained strong.[21]

Concurrently with the continually deteriorating relations between the American colonies and their British rulers, sectional tensions flared between certain factions of North Carolina's population. Yeoman farmers in the colony's backcountry, known as the Regulators, rebelled against royal officials. The Regulators, dissatisfied elements of the colony's Piedmont region, were suspicious and resentful of political leaders, primarily from the eastern region of the colony. Those leaders, in essence, dominated and controlled the affairs of the colony.[22] Furthermore, the Regulators protested the corrupt and extortionate practices of sheriffs and court officials. By the mid-1760s the "Regulator movement" was well established, particularly in Orange, Granville, Halifax, and Anson counties, and was gaining momentum within other regions of the colony. Public protest began evolving into vehement threats and violence toward appointed officials, who naturally became concerned for their personal safety. The movement represented a significant organized challenge to local government elements within the colony.[23]

Bertie County's militiamen seemed destined to help quell the unrest. Governor Tryon designated the county's militiamen to potentially assist in subduing the turmoil associated with the insurrectionary Regulator movement then taking place within the backcountry region of the colony. On April 27, 1768, Tryon—in response to appeals by his friend Edmund Fanning, an Orange County militia officer, royal judge, and target of the Regulators' ire—directed

Edmund Fanning (1737–1818), a colonial official and land speculator, became the target of the Regulators' ire because they believed he epitomized corrupt and abusive officials. Distrustful of his close relationship with Gov. William Tryon, the disgruntled Regulators destroyed his home and belongings. Fanning later moved to New York to be Governor Tryon's personal secretary. Image from Benson J. Lossing, *The Pictorial Field-Book of the Revolution*, 2 vols. (New York: Harper and Brothers, publishers, 1859), 2:368.

the commanders of a number of militia regiments, including Thomas Whitmell, colonel of the Bertie County regiment, to be ready to march with such numbers of men and officers as might be required by Fanning or the commanding officer of the Orange County militia. The governor, also a target of the Regulators' ire, was preparing to suppress "in the most effectual manner" the "several riotous and tumultuous Assemblies" taking place in Orange

County. The Orange County Regulators believed Judge Fanning epitomized political corruption.[24]

Also on April 27, Tryon wrote to Fanning, advising him that he fully understood the precarious situation that had arisen in Orange County. The governor stated that he hoped Fanning and other county officials would not carry matters to the extreme before the militia regiments could be ready to march and address the "Exigencies of the miserable state" of Fanning's home area. Tryon provided Fanning a copy of his directive to the commanders of the militia regiments, which empowered Fanning to call out the Orange County militia and the regiments of the several designated counties to "oppose and repel all Insurrections" as Fanning deemed necessary. Tryon felt that his show of force would "be sufficient to bring the many deluded [Regulators] to a proper Sense, both of their Errors and their Duty."[25]

Furthermore, Tryon, with the consent of the governor's council, simultaneously issued a proclamation to the "Riotous and disorderly persons" in Orange County who had "confederated together" to oppose the government, assembled themselves in a "tumultuous Manner in Arms," and "committed several outrages" in violation of the laws of their country. He commanded and required all persons who were involved in the insurrections to immediately disperse and retire to their respective homes and submit themselves to the laws of the country. In conclusion, he proclaimed that all persons who refused to obey his directive would be subject to "all lawful means for suppressing" their actions by all civil and military officers.[26]

On May 1 Fanning issued a public "advertisement" to the citizens of Orange County in which he published Tryon's proclamation and expressed his "hearty concern" for the "miserable situation" within the county. He appealed to the residents to disperse and behave themselves "in an orderly and peaceable manner" by duly obeying the laws. He proclaimed the "integrity" of his soul and that he had acted in the "true Interest and happiness" of Orange County. Further, he declared that he did not believe that the public had "ever been cheated or wronged" by the county's public officials. Then he sternly noted that he did not "intend to suffer any injury [to] myself but I intend to use my endeavors to enforce an obedience to His Majesty's Laws & Governments." Otherwise, he had orders from Governor Tryon to call to his aid the militia regiments of Anson, Bertie, Cumberland, Granville, Halifax, Johnston, Mecklenburg, and Rowan counties. He had duly warned the "daring Insurgents."[27]

The crisis eased, and Fanning never requested the assistance of the Bertie County and other counties' militia. Four months later Fanning was set to be tried in Orange County court; however, his popularity with his fellow citizens made a fair trial impossible. Judge Alfred Moore, presiding, ruled that according to common law the evidence against Fanning did not meet the level of certainty that was legally required.[28]

The Regulators were aroused, and their movement continued to gain momentum and followers over the next several years. Finally, on March 19, 1771, Governor Tryon ordered the militia commanders of twenty-nine counties to raise volunteers "to march against the Insurgents." Tryon called for 2,550 militiamen, of whom he designated fifty to be drawn from Bertie County's regiment.[29] On April 3 Tryon ordered Col. Thomas Whitmell of the Bertie County militia and the commanders of eight other counties to march to Hillsborough the forces that they previously had been ordered to raise. Tryon directed that each detachment be marched "by the most convenient route" to Hillsborough and to arrive by May 6. There, the units were to join other North Carolina detachments that Tryon had ordered to the rendezvous. The county commanders would receive further instructions once they and their men reached Hillsborough.[30]

Ten days later Tryon transmitted funding warrants to Whitmell and seven other colonels, recipients of the governor's April 3 instructions. The warrants (in the amount of £150 each, except one for £300 to Col. Richard Henderson of Rowan County) were to be drawn upon the colony's treasury, and the funds were to be used to pay bounties to the militiamen and defray other expeditionary expenses. The county detachments were to provide their own provisions until they reached Hillsborough.[31] Once they reached the rendezvous location, Thomas Hart, an Orange County merchant and militia officer who had contracted with Governor Tryon, was to furnish rations to the troops. Each man was to be provided one pound of pickled pork and one pound of flour, or alternatively, one and one-half pounds of fresh beef and a similar amount of corn meal, each day.[32]

The Regulators, growing increasingly agitated, threatened to disrupt the colony's assembly in New Bern. Governor Tryon called out elements of the province's militia, totaling about a thousand men (substantially less than the 2,550-man force he had ordered to be readied for action in March), and marched to the heart of the Regulator country. On May 16, 1771, the governor's force soundly trounced armed Regulators at Alamance Creek in Orange County (now Alamance County), about eight miles south of present-day

William Tryon (1729-1788), royal governor of North Carolina, served as the colony's top leader from late March 1765 through the late spring of 1771. He served during times of controversy and conflict, leading the province through the Stamp Act crisis (October 1765 to May 1766) and the War of the Regulation (late 1760s until May 16, 1771). In March 1771 he ordered Col. Thomas Whitmell to designate a fifty-man contingent of the Bertie County militia to prepare to march to the colony's backcountry to assist in subduing a group of dissatisfied yeoman farmers known as "Regulators." Nevertheless, the Bertie County citizen soldiers were never called to participate in that campaign, which culminated on May 16, 1771, when Tryon's royal militia force defeated the Regulators at Alamance Creek, a few miles south of present-day Burlington. Image provided courtesy of the State Archives, North Carolina Office of Archives and History, Raleigh.

Burlington. The battle climaxed over a decade of social unrest, violence, and disorder and ended the so-called War of the Regulation.[33]

Throughout 1772 into 1774, the undercurrent of tension between the colonies and the British government continued. In November 1772 Samuel Adams called a Boston town meeting during which the participants appointed a twenty-one-member committee of correspondence to communicate with other towns and colonies. Shortly thereafter, the Bostonians endorsed three radical proclamations asserting the rights of the colonies to self-rule. Four months later the Virginia House of Burgesses appointed an eleven-member committee of correspondence to communicate with the other colonies regarding common complaints against the British. Within a few months, New Hampshire, Rhode Island, Connecticut, and South Carolina appointed their committees. North Carolina's legislature appointed the colony's first committee of correspondence on December 8, 1773. The committees were responsible for taking the sense of their parent bodies' views on particular issues, committing those views to a written form, and then disseminating the documents to other similar groups. During the pre-Revolutionary War era, news was generally disseminated in hand-written letters that were carried aboard ships or by couriers on horseback. The colonists, severe critics of British imperial policy in America, employed the process to spread their interpretations of current events.[34]

On May 10, 1773, the British Parliament passed the Tea Act, which imposed a three-pence-per-pound import tax on tea arriving in the colonies. The statute also gave the nearly bankrupt British East India Company a virtual monopoly on tea by allowing it to sell directly to colonial agents, bypassing any middlemen and thus underselling American merchants. In October Pennsylvania colonists held a mass meeting in Philadelphia in opposition to the tea tax and the East India Company monopoly. The Philadelphians formed a committee that forced British tea agents at that town's port to resign their positions. In November a town meeting held in Boston endorsed the actions taken by the Philadelphians in October. Bostonians then tried, but failed, to persuade their British tea agents to resign. A few weeks later, three ships loaded with tea sailed into Boston Harbor. On November 29 and 30, Bostonians held mass meetings to decide what measures should be taken regarding the tea aboard the three ships then docked in the harbor. The colonists decided to send the tea on one ship back to England without paying any import duties. Thomas Hutchinson, the Massachusetts royal governor, opposed this measure and ordered harbor officials to prevent the ship from sailing out of the harbor unless the tea taxes had been paid. On December 16, about 8,000 Bostonians gathered to hear Samuel Adams tell them that Governor Hutchinson had reiterated his command not to allow the ships out of the harbor until the tea taxes were paid. That night colonial activists disguised as Indians boarded the ships and dumped their cargoes of tea into the harbor. The evening's event became commonly known as the "Boston Tea Party."[35]

An angry British Parliament reacted in late March 1774 by passing the first of a series of Coercive Acts (called "Intolerable Acts" by the colonists) in response to the rebellion in Massachusetts. The Boston Port Bill effectively shut down all commercial shipping in Boston harbor until Massachusetts paid the taxes owed on the tea dumped into the harbor in December and reimbursed the East India Company for the loss of the tea. On May 12 Bostonians at another town meeting called for a boycott of British imports in response to the Boston Port Bill. The following day, British general Thomas Gage arrived in Boston and replaced Hutchinson as royal governor. Four regiments of British troops soon arrived in Boston. Massachusetts was now under military rule.[36]

Within a week, colonists in Providence, New York, and Philadelphia began calling for an intercolonial congress to overcome the Coercive Acts and discuss a common course of action against the British. On May 20 the British Parliament enacted the next series of Coercive Acts, which included the Massachusetts Regulating Act and the Massachusetts Government Act, which virtually ended any self-rule by the colonists there, as well as the Administration of Justice Act, which protected royal officials in Massachusetts from being sued in colonial courts. The Massachusetts colonists were squarely in the sights of the British government and were beginning to bear the brunt of retaliatory statutes. On June 2 Parliament passed a new version of the 1765 Quartering Act, requiring all of the American colonies to provide housing for British troops in occupied houses and taverns and in unoccupied buildings. On June 22 the Quebec Act established a centralized government in Canada controlled by the Crown and the British Parliament. The Quebec Act greatly upset American colonists by extending the southern boundary of Canada into territories claimed by Massachusetts, Connecticut, and Virginia.[37]

On August 25, 1774, John Campbell and the other delegates to North Carolina's First Provincial Congress convened at New Bern amid extreme tensions and apprehensions within the American colonies. For three days the delegates read and discussed letters from other colonies' committees of correspondence, debated proposed resolutions, and elected three representatives—Richard Caswell (Dobbs County), Joseph Hewes (Chowan County), and William Hooper (New Hanover County)—to attend the forthcoming Continental Congress. On Saturday, August 27, the provincial congress reached consensus on twenty-five resolutions. The delegates fully recognized that they were dutiful and loyal subjects to King George III, but that "in the present alarming state of British America" most of their "essential rights" had been "invaded by powers unwarrantably assumed by the Parliament of Great Britain." Therefore, they publicly declared their sentiments as a unified body, "lest [their] silence should be construed as acquiescence" to the burdens that the

British rulers had imposed upon them. Principally, the delegates collectively resolved that:

• they claimed nothing more than the rights of Englishmen and that they would constantly endeavor to maintain those rights to the utmost of their power consistently with the loyalty that they owed the king and the British constitution;

• no subject should be taxed but by his own consent, freely given or by his legal representatives;

• as British subjects residing in North America, they did not have, nor could they have, any representation in the Parliament of Great Britain, and therefore, any act of Parliament imposing a tax upon them was illegal and unconstitutional;

• the duties imposed by several acts of the British Parliament upon tea and other articles consumed in America for the purpose of raising revenue were highly illegal and oppressive;

• the inhabitants of Massachusetts had distinguished themselves in "a manly support of the rights of America in general," and the cause in which they suffered was the cause of every honest American who deserved the blessings held forth by the British constitution;

• the Boston Port Act effectually destroyed trade and deprived merchants and manufacturers of their honest subsistence;

• they would not, directly or indirectly, after January 1, 1775, import from Great Britain any East India goods or any merchandise whatever, medicines excepted;

• unless American grievances were redressed before October 1, 1775, they would not after that day directly or indirectly export tobacco, pitch, tar, turpentine, or any other article whatsoever, to Great Britain, nor would they sell any such articles as they perceived could be exported to Great Britain;

• the people of North Carolina would break off all trade, commerce, dealings, and commercial intercourse with any American colony, city, or town, or individual who refused, declined, or neglected to adopt and carry into execution such general plan as might be promulgated by the Continental Congress;

• they approved the proposal to hold a "General Congress" in Philadelphia in September for the purpose of deliberating the present state of British America and to take such measures as may be deemed prudent to describe with certainty the rights of Americans; and

• the three delegates appointed to attend the Continental Congress on the part of North Carolina express their "most sincere attachment to our most gracious sovereign King George the third, and our determined resolution to support his Lawful authority in this Province," but at the same time they could not "depart from a steady adherence to the first law of Nature, a firm and resolute defence of our persons and properties against all unconstitutional encroachments whatever."

The delegates asserted their rights to all the privileges of British subjects, particularly that of paying no taxes or duties but with their own consent. They proclaimed that the North Carolina legislature had the exclusive power of making laws to regulate the colony's internal polity, subject to the king's disallowance. Furthermore, they espoused that, should the British Parliament continue to exercise the power of levying taxes and duties on the colonies and making laws to bind them, in all cases whatsoever such laws must be highly unconstitutional and oppressive to the colonists since they did not have a fair and equal representation in the British Parliament. Anticipating the probable position of the forthcoming Continental Congress, they conveyed to the three representatives who were to attend the congress that North Carolina "most sincerely and ardently desire[d]" to restore a "lasting harmony, and good understanding with Great Britain." However, they declared that the three representatives agree with a majority of representatives from the other colonies on "all necessary measures, for promoting a redress of such grievances" as were to come under consideration by the Continental Congress.[38]

On September 5, 1774, the First Continental Congress convened in Philadelphia at Carpenters' Hall. North Carolina's representatives had not arrived when the congress opened. William Hooper and Joseph Hewes arrived in Philadelphia by September 14 and took their seats at the conclave. Richard Caswell arrived three days later.[39] Fifty-six representatives from twelve of the thirteen colonies (only Georgia was not represented) attended the congress.[40]

For the next seven-plus weeks, the congress met to consider the colonies' options to resolve their grievances with the British. It expressed the colonists' unequivocal opposition to the Coercive Acts, declaring that the laws were "not to be obeyed." It promoted the formation of local militia units and asserted the colonists' rights to "life, liberty and property." It published a list of the colonists' rights and grievances and petitioned King George III for redress of those grievances. When the congress adjourned on October 26, it had achieved two primary accomplishments: it consummated a compact among the colonies to boycott British goods effective December 1, 1774, and further declared that if the "Intolerable Acts" were not repealed, the colonies would cease exports to Britain after October 10, 1775; and it announced that a second Continental Congress would be held in May 1775 in the event the colonists' petition to King George III was unsuccessful in halting enforcement of the Intolerable Acts.[41]

Meanwhile, on October 25, 1774, as the First Continental Congress was concluding its deliberations, in Edenton, North Carolina—immediately across the Chowan River from Bertie County—a group of more than fifty women held their own "tea party." The women, in a patriotic display, declared that they could not be indifferent to whatever affected the peace and happiness of the county. They signed an agreement to do everything they could to support the American cause.[42]

Throughout the winter of 1774–1775 and the early spring of 1775, the British made no moves to capitulate to the Americans' demands. Tensions between Britain and the colonies increased further as the scheduled date for the meeting of the second Continental Congress approached. On February 11 John Harvey, a resident of Perquimans County and moderator of North Carolina's First Provincial Congress, issued a call for a second such body to meet in New Bern on April 3. The agenda for the proposed conclave was to elect delegates to the Continental Congress. On March 6 royal governor Josiah Martin (who had replaced William Tryon in August 1771) issued a proclamation urging North Carolinians to eschew the "illegal assembly." Martin intensely desired that North Carolina send no representatives to the forthcoming Continental Congress. He therefore designated that the "lawful" colonial assembly convene on April 4.[43]

Certain citizens in Great Britain viewed the tumultuous and deteriorating relations between the colonies and the mother country as a crisis. Some citizens seemed to support the colonies' move to break away from Great Britain's rule. One British individual, writing to a friend who resided in North Carolina, declared: "let the Americans be united, and they shall obtain the glorious prize; but if they divide, they are irretrievably ruined."[44] North Carolina's Whig leaders assuredly intended, during this period of crisis, to unite the province in efforts and spirits with the twelve other colonies.

On Monday, April 3, North Carolina's Second Provincial Congress convened in New Bern. The counties and principal towns of the colony had elected ninety-three men to attend the session; however, only fifty-six of them (60 percent of those elected) were present when the congress was called to order. Two of Bertie County's representatives—John Campbell and John Johnston—were present on Monday. The county's third representative, David Standley, appeared at the session two days later. Eventually five other representatives would join the congress before it adjourned. For five days the attending representatives met, during which time they approved the proceedings and

A Society of Patriotic Ladies, at Edenton in North Carolina. This print is a satirical depiction of women pledging to boycott English tea in response to the Continental Congress resolution in 1774 to boycott English goods. Image from the British Cartoon Collection, Library of Congress.

resolutions reached by the First Continental Congress. They appointed Richard Caswell, Joseph Hewes, and William Hooper—the same men who had attended the First Continental Congress—to represent North Carolina at the "General Congress," to be held at Philadelphia in May. While the representatives clearly took steps to further North Carolina's involvement and contributions to the causes of the united American colonies, they also expressed their "most earnest wishes and desires" that harmony would be restored between Great Britain and the American colonies "on honorable and Constitutional Principles." They concluded their deliberations by resolving that the colonists, subjects of King George III, had "an undoubted Right at any time to meet, and petition the Throne for a redress of Grievances, and that such rights includes [*sic*] a further Right of appointing Delegates for such purpose." In their view, Governor Martin's March 6 proclamation—issued to forbid the meeting of the provincial congress—and his subsequent command that the ongoing meeting was to disperse were "illegal and an infringement of [the representatives'] just rights, and therefore ought to be disregarded as wanton and Arbitrary Exertions of power."[45]

On Tuesday, April 4, Governor Martin convened the colonial assembly, made up predominantly of the same men who were attending the Second Provincial Congress. The latter body met at nine o'clock each morning, adjourned an hour later, and reconvened as the colonial assembly. John Harvey served as moderator of the provincial congress and as Speaker of the assembly. Martin was confronted with an awkward and trying situation. Clearly the delegates to the two gatherings were contemptible toward the governor; they had disobeyed his proclamations and convened the provincial congress and as representatives in the royal assembly had expressed their approval of the actions of the Continental Congress. By Saturday, April 8, the governor was thoroughly disgusted with the whole affair and abruptly dissolved the assembly. A royal assembly would never again meet in North Carolina.[46]

The "gloomy aspect" for North Carolina in particular and for America in general was "truly alarming." The province's citizens—whether loyal to King George III or supportive of the rebellious Whig Patriots—faced an "uncertain situation." Andrew Miller, a former legislator, merchant, and firm Loyalist of Halifax County, wrote to his friend Thomas Burke, a devout Whig leader from Orange County (and future governor of North Carolina), that, in his view, "the Infant State of the Colonys" precluded them from being able to "subsist without the Protection of some Maritime Power such as Britain." Miller suggested to Burke that the colonies would do "well to Submit to the power of [British] Legislation . . . except as to Taxation . . . for a while" until they would be able to manufacture more substantial stores of cloth, gunpowder, and other war items, as well as to enroll "increased" numbers of troops. Miller concluded that "We are not in a Condition to Combat with Britain."[47]

Two weeks after Governor Martin summarily dismissed the colonial assembly, "very shocking" news reached North Carolina: British soldiers and Massachusetts minutemen had engaged each other on April 19, first at Lexington and later at Concord. The news likely reached residents in Bertie County on Thursday, May 4, having been received in the morning of that day by officials in neighboring Chowan County.[48] The political and economic differences between the British and the American colonists had culminated in an armed confrontation. At Lexington a nervous Massachusetts minuteman or British soldier had touched off a shot, and the American Revolutionary War had commenced.

Notes

1. John Campbell, a native of Coleraine, Ireland, served in the North Carolina colonial assembly in 1744, 1754, 1767, and 1773. He was elected Speaker of the assembly in 1754 and filled that position for two successive years. He was appointed commissioner of the Port of Roanoke (Edenton) in 1752, assistant judge in 1756, and mail contractor in 1757. His business attributes were keen. Gov. Arthur Dobbs in 1760 referred to Campbell as the "most eminent Trader" in the province of North Carolina. In 1774 there were thirty-five counties in the colony of North Carolina. Alan D. Watson, *Bertie County: A Brief History* (Raleigh: North Carolina Division of Archives and History, 1982), 15, 65; William L. Saunders, ed., *The Colonial Records of North Carolina*, 10 vols. (Raleigh: State of North Carolina, 1886–1890), 9:xxxi, 1041–1043. The provincial congresses were extralegal unicameral legislative bodies formed between 1774 and 1776 by the people of the province of North Carolina independent of the British colonial government.

2. Royal rule began in July 1729 when King George II purchased North Carolina and South Carolina from the eight Lords Proprietors. (The Lords Proprietors—Edward Hyde, George Monck, William Craven, John Berkeley, Anthony Ashley Cooper, Sir George Carteret, Sir William Berkeley, and Sir John Colleton—were British noblemen who had acquired title to the territory through a charter from King Charles II in 1663.) In essence, the Crown's purchase of the Carolinas replaced the relatively weak and inefficient administration of the proprietors with a more assertive imperial government. William S. Powell, *North Carolina: A History* (Chapel Hill and London: University of North Carolina Press, 1977), 22–24, 36–37 (hereafter cited as Powell, *North Carolina*); *Dictionary of North Carolina Biography*, s.v. "Caswell, Richard"; Watson, *Bertie County*, 63; Saunders, *Colonial Records*, 1:20–33; 3:32–47.

The thirteen American colonies were: Connecticut, Delaware, Georgia, Maryland, Massachusetts, New Hampshire, New Jersey, New York, North Carolina, Pennsylvania, Rhode Island, South Carolina, and Virginia.

3. Walter Clark, ed., *The State Records of North Carolina*, 16 vols. (11–26) (Raleigh: State of North Carolina, 1895–1906), 23:503–504, 755–756, 958–959; 25:507–509; Saunders, *Colonial Records*, 2:283; Watson, *Bertie County*, 6–7.

The formal boundary between Bertie and Hertford counties was permanently settled in 1907. Prior to the North Carolina General Assembly's designating Windsor to be the center of Bertie County's local governmental functions, such activities were held at Cashy, an area known today as Hoggard's Mill. David Leroy Corbitt, *The Formation of the North Carolina Counties, 1663–1943* (Raleigh: Division of Archives and History, North Carolina Department of Cultural Resources, 1987), 26–27; Watson, *Bertie County*, 5; Harry Lewis Thompson, "The Lost Town of 'Cashy' " (unpublished research report dated October 1961, Search Room, State Archives, Raleigh).

4. Barbara Bigelow and Linda Schmittroth, *American Revolution Almanac*, ed. Stacy A. McConnell (Detroit, San Francisco, London, Boston, Woodbridge, Conn.: UXL, imprint of the Gale Group, 2000), 41, 43–47; Bud Hannings, *Chronology of the American Revolution* (Jefferson, N.C., and London: McFarland and Company, Publishers, 2008), 7; Jeffrey J. Crow, *A Chronicle of North Carolina during the American Revolution, 1763–1789* (Raleigh: Department of Cultural Resources, Division of Archives and History, 1975), 5.

France and Great Britain fought four wars between 1689 and 1763, which, among other objectives, included efforts to extend their possessions in North America, principally over the fur trade. The French and Indian War, fought between 1754 and 1763, was the final and most important conflict. It resulted in an Anglo-French treaty (1763), the terms of which granted Great Britain the Canadian territories and France's possessions east of the Mississippi River, as well as the Spanish territory of Florida. Spain received all French lands west of the Mississippi and the Isle of Orleans at the mouth of the river. *World Book Encyclopedia*, 2000 edition, s.v. "French and Indian Wars."

5. Bigelow and Schmittroth, *American Revolution Almanac,* 31, 46.

6. Bigelow and Schmittroth, *American Revolution Almanac*, 45–47; Crow, *A Chronicle of North Carolina*, 6; Hannings, *Chronology*, 9; Powell, *North Carolina*, 52.

7. Crow, *A Chronicle of North Carolina,* 6; Hannings, *Chronology*, 9.

8. Hannings, *Chronology*, 9–10; Bigelow and Schmittroth, *American Revolution Almanac*, 47; Harry McKown, "November 1765: The Stamp Act Crisis in North Carolina," www.lib.unc.edu/ncc/ref/history/nov2006/, website, University of North Carolina at Chapel Hill Libraries. Representatives from the following colonies attended the congress: Massachusetts, Connecticut, Rhode Island, New York, New Jersey, Pennsylvania, Delaware, Maryland, and South Carolina. Georgia, New Hampshire, and Virginia, in addition to North Carolina, did not send representatives.

9. Saunders, *Colonial Records*, 7:123–125; Powell, *North Carolina*, 53–54.

10. Saunders, *Colonial Records*, 7:168.

11. Saunders, *Colonial Records*, 7:168a–168b, 169–174.

12. Saunders, *Colonial Records*, 7:168c–168d.

13. Saunders, *Colonial Records*, 7:168c–168e.

14. Stephen E. Bradley Jr., comp., *The Deeds of Bertie County, North Carolina, 1757–1772* (Keysville, Va.: the compiler, 1992), various pages. The author reviewed the cited publication for land transactions dated and/or recorded from July 1765 through June 1766. One deed was dated July 1765; another, September 1765. Seven deeds were dated March 1766, and twelve bore the date June 1766.

15. Bigelow and Schmittroth, *American Revolution Almanac*, xvi; Hannings, *Chronology*, 9–10; Linda Schmittroth and Mary Kay Rosteck, *American Revolution Biographies*, ed. Stacy A. McConnell, 2 vols. (Detroit, San Francisco, London, Boston, Woodbridge, Conn.: UXL, imprint of the Gale Group, 2000), 1:114, 119.

16. Bigelow and Schmittroth, *American Revolution Almanac*, xvi; Hannings, *Chronology*, 10; Schmittroth and Rosteck, *American Revolution Biographies*, 1:155, 159, 2:451, 457–458.

17. Hannings, *Chronology*, 9; Schmittroth and Rosteck, *American Revolution Biographies*, 1:138, 141–142; The History Place, American Revolution, www.historyplace.com/unitedstates/revolution.

18. Hannings, *Chronology*, 11; The History Place. See also Saunders, *Colonial Records*, 7:686–689.

19. Schmittroth and Rosteck, *American Revolution Biographies*, 1:198, 200–201; Hannings, *Chronology*, 11–12; The History Place.

20. Saunders, *Colonial Records*, 8:xiv, 104–105; Hannings, *Chronology*, 12.

21. Bigelow and Schmittroth, *American Revolution Almanac*, 58–62; Hannings, *Chronology*, 14. The altercation of March 5, 1770, became commonly known as the "Boston Massacre."

22. Powell, *North Carolina*, 50.

23. William L. Saunders, in the preface of volume 8 of his *Colonial Records of North Carolina*, provides a summary of the Regulator Movement. See Saunders, *Colonial Records*, 8:iii–xlviii. For a detailed study of the Regulator Movement, see Carole Watterson Troxler, *Farming Dissenters: The Regulator Movement in Piedmont North Carolina* (Raleigh: Office of Archives and History, North Carolina Department of Cultural Resources, 2011).

24. Saunders, *Colonial Records*, 7:718–719. While Tryon's correspondence does not mention the colonel of the Bertie County militia by name, the author, relying upon various entries in Bertie County's court minutes made during the subject period, determined that Thomas Whitmell served in that capacity. *See* Weynette Parks Haun, comp., *Bertie County, North Carolina, County Court Minutes, 1763 thru 1771, Book III* (Durham: the compiler, 1978), 7, 95.

25. Saunders, *Colonial Records*, 7:717–718.

26. Saunders, *Colonial Records*, 7:720–722.

27. Saunders, *Colonial Records*, 7:739–740.

28. "Edmund Fanning, (1737–1808)," www.northcarolinahistory.org, The North Carolina History Project, website, The John Locke Foundation, Raleigh.

29. Tryon issued orders to the militia commandants of the following counties: Anson, Beaufort, Bertie, Bladen, Bute, Carteret, Chowan, Craven, Cumberland, Currituck, Dobbs [present-day Lenoir and Greene], Duplin, Edgecombe, Granville, Halifax, Hertford, Hyde, Johnston, Mecklenburg, New Hanover, Northampton, Onslow, Orange, Perquimans, Pitt, Rowan, Tryon, Tyrrell, and Wake. Saunders, *Colonial Records*, 8:696–697.

30. On April 3, 1771, Tryon sent his instructions to the militia colonels of Bertie (Thomas Whitmell), Bute, Chowan, Edgecombe, Granville, Halifax, Hertford, Northampton, and Tyrrell counties. Saunders, *Colonial Records*, 8:702.

31. Saunders, *Colonial Records*, 8:706–707.

32. Saunders, *Colonial Records*, 8:707.

33. Tryon's return of the forces under his command six days after the battle (May 22, 1771) shows militiamen (1,068 officers and men) from Craven, Carteret, New Hanover, Onslow, Johnston, Orange, Beaufort, and Dobbs counties, plus artillerymen, rangers, and light horsemen (cavalry) present prior to the battle. More than 265 men—from Wake County and a contingent of light infantry—had joined Tryon's force on May 20, four days after the battle. There is no indication that any Bertie County militiamen participated in the battle. Furthermore, it appears that Tryon did not call out militia from most of the counties that he had ordered to organize troops in March and April. Saunders, *Colonial Records*, 8:677; Powell, *North Carolina*, 50.

34. Hannings, *Chronology*, 15; Saunders, *Colonial Records*, 9:740–741; The History Place.

35. Hannings, *Chronology*, 16; Bigelow and Schmittroth, *American Revolution Almanac*, 64–66.

36. Hannings, *Chronology*, 17–18; Bigelow and Schmittroth, *American Revolution Almanac*, 67–70.

37. Hannings, *Chronology*, 18; The History Place.

38. Saunders, *Colonial Records*, 9:1041–1049.

39. Worthington Chauncey Ford, ed., *Journals of the Continental Congress*, 34 vols. (Washington, D.C.: Government Printing Office, 1904–1937), 1:13–14, 30–32.

40. Ford, *Journals of the Continental Congress*, 1:13–124. The author reviewed the daily journal entries to identify delegates who attended the congress and then calculated the number.

41. Ford, *Journals of the Continental Congress*, 1:41, 102, 107, 112, 119, 120–124.

42. Powell, *North Carolina*, 60.

43. Crow, *A Chronicle of North Carolina*, 17, 19; Saunders, *Colonial Records* 9:1125–1126, 1144–1146; R. D. W. Connor, *History of North Carolina: The Colonial and Revolutionary Periods (1584–1783)* (Chicago and New York: Lewis Publishing Company, 1919), 338.

44. Saunders, *Colonial Records*, 9:1165.

45. Saunders, *Colonial Records*, 9:1178–1185. The author computed the number of persons elected to attend the congress, as well as the number of those actually in attendance, from information contained in the minutes of the congress.

46. Powell, *North Carolina*, 60–61; Saunders, *Colonial Records*, 9:1187–1205. The author's analysis of information relative to the representatives to the colonial assembly and the provincial congress contained in the *Colonial Records* indicates that seventy-three individuals were elected to attend the colonial assembly, of whom fifty-three attended. Of the fifty-three who attended, forty-five (85 percent) also participated in the concurrent provincial congress.

47. Saunders, *Colonial Records*, 9:1173, 1205–1206. In consideration of Miller's Loyalist proclivities, his letter to Burke seems paradoxical, suggesting a forestalling of colonial action against Great Britain until larger stores of military items could be accumulated. Burke represented Orange County in the Second through Fifth Provincial Congresses. Miller, who had a contractual relationship with Burke, may have attempted to soften Burke's anti-British positions. As a result of Miller's Loyalist views, North Carolina later confiscated his landholdings and other property. See Saunders, *Colonial Records*, 9:1179, 10:166, 500, 970; and Clark, *State Records*, 11:715, 13:878, 17:371, 24:262–263, 424.

48. Minutemen were members of teams of select individuals from the colonial militia during the American Revolutionary War. They provided a more mobile and rapidly deployable force than did general militia units, and they enabled the colonies to respond immediately to war threats—hence the name. Generally younger and more adaptable than the overall militia, minutemen served essentially to provide early response to enemy incursions and other crises. Although the terms militia and minutemen are sometimes used interchangeably today, in the eighteenth century there was a decided difference between the two. Militias were men in arms most often formed to protect their towns from invasion and ravages of war. Minutemen comprised smaller, more elite forces, which were required to be able to assemble quickly and be readily mobile.

　　Accounts of the affairs at Lexington and Concord reached Edenton about mid-morning on May 4, delivered by an express rider from Nansemond County, Virginia. Chowan County and Edenton officials immediately dispatched a rider to deliver the papers to Craven County officials, with a request for the recipients to "disperse the material passages" throughout their region. The accounts reached Beaufort County, New Bern, and Bath on May 6; Onslow County and New River on May 7; Wilmington and Brunswick on May 8; and Little River at the boundary between North and South Carolina on May 9. On the latter date, Henry Montfort, a prominent resident and political leader of Halifax County, wrote from the town of Halifax to Thomas Burke: "We have just rec[eive]d some very shocking accounts from Boston. The Regulars and the Bostonians Have Had an Engagement, the former were Intirely defeated with the loss of 1200 men, and 800 taken prisoners. This you may rely on as a fact, as we Have had very authentic accounts." Saunders, *Colonial Records*, 9:1235–1238, 1245.

SPIRIT OF INDEPENDENCE

As news of the hostilities in Massachusetts spread throughout North Carolina, certain residents became "much alarmed" at Great Britain's "intentions" toward the province, concluding that North Carolinians could "expect the worst." Some local militia commanders began mustering and drilling their troops for potential service; however, no efforts were immediately initiated colony-wide to organize and ready North Carolina's citizen soldiers. This circumstance bothered Joseph Hewes, the Chowan County resident who was in Philadelphia attending the Continental Congress. On May 11, 1775, Hewes wrote to his close friend Samuel Johnston, also of Chowan County, that he had learned that all of the provinces were "in Arms Except No[rth] Carolina." With events rapidly transpiring throughout the colonies, Hewes confided to his friend: "I tremble for No. Carolina, every County ought to have at least one [militia] Company formed & exercised, pray encourage it. Speak to the people, write to them, urge strongly the necessity of it, I had rather perish Ten thousand times than they should give up the matter now in the time of tryal." Twelve days later Hewes again wrote to Johnston and reiterated his view: "[W]e must draw the Sword. . . . It is highly necessary that North Carolina should be put[t]ing her self in a State of defence, a Company of Militia ought to be formed in each County and Trained frequently."[1] Obviously Hewes was prompting the influential and respected Johnston to utilize his standing in the colony to persuade leaders in the various counties to organize their militia units.

North Carolina's militia organization and command hierarchy were based on the laws existing under the auspices of royal authority. Accordingly, during instances of insurrection and crisis the province's overall militia responded to instructions and orders from the governor.[2] Gov. Josiah Martin was at great odds with a number of the influential men of North Carolina and its constituent counties, some of whom were officers in the militia. On May 31, 1775, Martin, for reasons involving personal security, fled from his office in New Bern amid increasing turmoil in that town and relocated to Fort Johnston, near Wilmington. Martin's flight left no overall authority to command the colony's militia. Furthermore, Martin's exodus effectively signified the end of royal authority in North Carolina.[3]

By the middle of June, Richard Caswell, Joseph Hewes, and William Hooper jointly concluded that North Carolinians urgently needed to ready their militia companies for potential service. The three men were daily engaging and communicating with congressional delegates from the other colonies, thereby being apprised of military efforts instituted in other locales. The Continental Congress was moving the colonies to a defensive posture, particularly the northern colonies, about which the delegates were of the opinion that a British invasion, potentially launched from Canada, was forthcoming.[4] On June 19 Caswell, Hewes, and Hooper dispatched to the inhabitants of North Carolina a circular letter in which they declared that all Americans should be anxious for their approaching fate from the designs of the British. In a warlike tone, the men advised that the colonists needed to take steps "to ward off or alleviate the impending Calamity." They reported that the northern provinces—Connecticut, Massachusetts, New Hampshire, and Rhode Island—had already enlisted bodies of troops "preparing for the last Extremity and determined to live free or not at all." They further noted that New York, New Jersey, Pennsylvania, and the provinces to the south had armed and equipped forces "to avert the Calamity." From their perspective, all the provinces except North Carolina had taken necessary actions. Attempting to spur North Carolinians to action, Caswell, Hewes, and Hooper penned these words:

> North Carolina alone remains an inactive Spectator of this general defensive Armament. Supine and careless, she seems to forget even the Duty she owes to her own local Circumstances and Situation. Have you not Fellow Citizens a dangerous Enemy in your own Bosom and after Measures which the Minister has condescended to in Order to carry into Execution his darling Schemes do you think he would hesitate to raise the hand of the servant against the master? . . .
>
> Have we not been informed that the Canadians are to be embodied and the Indians bribed to ravage the Frontiers of the Eastern Colonies? Has not

[British] General [Guy] Carlton already given a specimen of his power by forming a Canadian Regiment of Men inimical to our Liberty and Religion? Can you think that your Province is the singular object of ministerial favour and that in the common crush it will stand secure? Be assured it will not. . . .

It becomes the duty of us in whom you have deposited the most sacred trusts to warn you of your danger and of the most effectual means to ward it off. It is the Right of every English Subject to be prepared with Weapons for his defence. We conjure you by the Ties of Religion Virtue and Love of your Country to follow the Example of your sister Colonies and to form yourselves into a Militia. The Election of the officers and the Arrangement of the men must depend upon yourselves. Study the Art of Military with the utmost attention, view it as the Science upon which your future security depends.

Carefully preserve the small quantity of gunpowder which you have amongst you; it will be the last Resource when every other means of Safety fail you—Great Britain has cut you off from further supplies. We enjoin you as you tender the safety of yourselves and Fellow Colonists as you would wish to live and die free that you would reserve what Ammunition you have as a sacred Deposit. He in part betrays his Country who sports it away, perhaps in every Charge he fires he gives with it the means of preserving the life of a fellow being.

We cannot conclude without urging again to you the Necessity of arming and instructing yourselves to be in readiness to defend yourselves against any violence that may be exerted against your Persons and Properties. In one word fellow subjects the Crisis of America is not at a great distance. . . . Everything depends upon your present Exertion and prudent perseverance, be in a state of Readiness to repel every stroke that though you must wound and endanger her, strengthen the hands of civil Government by resisting every Act of lawless power, stem Tyranny in its commencement, oppose every effort of an Arbitrary Minister and . . . preserve the liberty of the Constitution.[5]

A week later the Continental Congress recommended that all North Carolinians "who wish well to the liberties of America . . . [and] for the defence of American liberty . . . embody themselves as militia, under proper officers." The congress further declared that should the North Carolina Provincial Congress conclude that a body of forces was necessary to support the American colonies and ensure the safety of North Carolina, then the Continental Congress would "consider them as an American army, and provide for their pay."[6]

Within North Carolina a number of communities—Bute, Rowan, and Tryon counties and the town of Wilmington—individually initiated measures

Josiah Martin (1737–1786) was the last royal governor of North Carolina. Arriving in the colony in August 1771, he succeeded William Tryon in the governorship. While attempting to implement instructions and policies from the Crown, Martin became the victim of acute conflict with his constituents. Amid concurrent meetings of the colonial assembly and the Second Provincial Congress in April 1775, Martin dissolved the assembly, thereby ending royal rule in North Carolina. Martin fled New Bern at the end of May 1775. Image provided courtesy of the State Archives.

to strengthen their local defensive postures by amassing gunpowder, lead, flints, and weapons, to the extent such items could be procured. The northeastern counties, with the exception of Currituck and Pasquotank, busily armed and trained militia in the late spring of 1775.[7] While awaiting a colony-wide initiative to organize the militia, the inhabitants of various sectors were taking it upon themselves to do what they could to support their militiamen and secure their communities.

Col. Thomas Whitmell, former Bertie County sheriff, Indian commissioner, and legislator, commanded the Bertie County militia.[8] No muster rolls or pay rolls exist to document the musters separately held by Bertie County companies or the regiment overall; however, feasibly Whitmell would have begun mustering and drilling the Bertie troops similarly to the militia

Samuel Johnston (1733–1816) of Chowan County was a prominent voice for the Patriot cause in northeastern North Carolina. He was a member the First and Second Provincial Congresses. Following the death of John Harvey (moderator of the first two congresses), Johnston served as moderator of the Third Provincial Congress, thereby functioning as the virtual governor of North Carolina. Image provided courtesy of the State Archives.

commanders of the neighboring counties in the Albemarle Sound region. Furthermore, by middle to late June, Bertie County officials realized that the county's militiamen, if called into service, were short of gunpowder for their arms. Therefore, the officials raised a significant sum of money to purchase gunpowder but, unfortunately, found that none was available to acquire.[9]

By July the political situation in North Carolina was more acute and critical. The province's legislative assembly was scheduled to convene in New Bern on July 12; however, Governor Martin—who by then had fled from Fort Johnston and taken refuge aboard a British warship in the Cape Fear River—canceled the session. John Harvey, moderator of the previous two provincial congresses, had died in May, and the responsibility for calling the next congress fell to Samuel Johnston. Various persons from across the colony petitioned Johnston to hold a "third" provincial congress. Certain segments of the populace who supported confronting the British (i.e., the "Whigs") were already preparing for war in a number of locations within the colony. Another segment, known as "Tories" (Loyalists), were equally adamant in supporting King George III, particularly within counties heavily populated by persons not of English descent. North Carolina's Patriot leaders clearly needed to convene, inasmuch as the situation in certain locations was "truly alarming," bordering on civil conflict and further exacerbating the volatile circumstances. On Wednesday, July 19, approximately five hundred militiamen under the command of Cornelius Harnett, John Ashe, and Robert Howe (prominent civil leaders from counties in the province's southeastern region) took possession of and burned Fort Johnston to the ground.[10] War had come to North Carolina.

On July 10 Samuel Johnston wrote to the sheriffs of North Carolina's counties, requesting them to summon the freeholders (i.e., landowners) of their counties to meet and elect delegates to the next provincial congress. Johnston advised the sheriffs that the congress would meet at Hillsborough on August 20. He recommended that each county elect at least five delegates, since "affairs of the last importance" to the province were to be submitted for their deliberation. The people of North Carolina were now obliged to manage the province's interim government as best as they could.[11]

Between the date of Johnston's letter and the middle of August, David Standley, sheriff of Bertie County, oversaw the election of the county's delegates to the congress. Bertie County residents elected eleven delegates, all respected persons of the community: Thomas Ballard, William Brimage, William Bryan, John Campbell, Peter Clifton, William Gray, Charles Worth Jacocks, Jonathan Jacocks, John Johnston (brother of Samuel Johnston), Zedekiah Stone, and Standley. Only Bryan, Gray, C. W. Jacocks, Johnston, and Stone journeyed the 150-plus miles to Hillsborough and attended the congress.[12]

Samuel Johnston, true to his notice of July 10, convened the Third North Carolina Provincial Congress in the frontier town of Hillsborough on Sunday, August 20. Unfortunately, however, many of the delegates were apparently still in route to the convention. Since a majority of the members was not present, Johnston adjourned the congress until the morning of the following day. On Monday 184 delegates appeared for the congress, including Bertie County's five representatives. In accordance with parliamentary procedure, the delegates' first order of business was to elect officers. The delegates unanimously chose Samuel Johnston for president and Andrew Knox (Perquimans County) for secretary. They then got down to the critical business for which they had assembled. Immediately, they established two committees—one to investigate the conduct of a number of persons currently in custody, whose "dangerous practices" were counter to the movement toward liberty; and the second to confer with the province's inhabitants who entertained religious or political reservations with respect to the "common Cause of America" and to "induce them by Argument and Persuasion, heartily to unite" with the delegates for protection of their "Constitutional rights and privileges." On Tuesday and Wednesday the delegates turned their attention primarily to several resolutions adopted by the Continental Congress in the fall of 1774. Of most importance, the members "highly approve[d]" of the Continental Association adopted by the general congress on October 20, 1774. The Association established a systemic, total boycott of British commerce by means of non-importation, non-exportation, and non-consumption accords. The boycott was to be enforced within each community by a committee(s) that would monitor merchants and publish the names of those who defied the boycott, confiscate contraband goods. and encourage public frugality.[13]

The delegates deliberated and passed various resolutions relevant to furthering North Carolina's liberty and constitutional freedom. They also signed testaments in which they professed their allegiance to King George III. Even so, their testaments clearly conveyed that they "absolutely" believed that the British authorities did not have the right to impose taxes on the American colonies. They further asserted that the people of North Carolina, singularly and collectively, were bound to abide by the acts and resolutions of the Continental and provincial congresses. All five of Bertie County's delegates—Bryan, Gray, Jacocks, Johnston, and Stone—signed the testaments.[14]

North Carolina's military preparations moved to the forefront of the congress's agenda in the ensuing days. Specifically, the congress deliberated about what sums of money were necessary for procuring arms and ammunition, a dire issue. The Continental Congress had pronounced that a colonies-wide army should be embodied with three million dollars to be "emitted" to support it. The North Carolina body unanimously resolved that the residents of the province would pay their "full proportion" of the expense for the army. The delegates—acknowledging the hostilities in Massachusetts, that British reinforcements were expected there daily, and that Governor Martin was "very active" in attempting to weaken the efforts of North Carolina—resolved that North Carolina "be immediately put into a state of defence." Additionally, the congress affirmed that it was "absolutely necessary for the support of the American Association and safety of the Colony" to raise a military force as resolved by the Continental Congress. To that end, they directed that one thousand troops be immediately raised and organized within the province.[15]

Military Districts of North Carolina, 1775

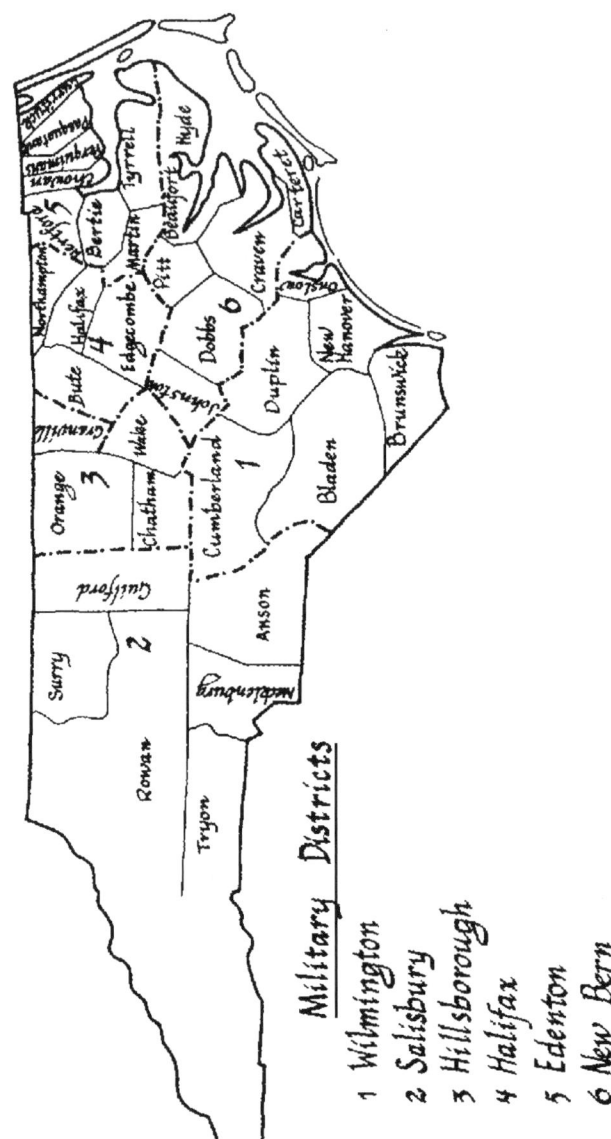

In order to manage and direct military affairs across North Carolina, the Third Provincial Congress organized the province into six military districts. Bertie County was part of the Edenton District. Map by Linda Reeves from the State Archives, North Carolina Office of Archives and History, Raleigh.

The congress directed that the designated troops be organized into two regiments, each consisting of 500 men. The regiments were to be raised and organized as units of the Continental army pursuant to a resolve of the Continental Congress on June 26, 1775. Detachments of the regiments were to be stationed in the districts of Wilmington (400 men), Salisbury (200 men), New Bern (200 men), and Edenton (200 men). The regiments were to take their orders from the provincial congress or the newly authorized provincial council (at times when the congress was not meeting). The congress appointed James Moore (Duplin County) colonel of the First Regiment and Francis Nash (Halifax County) lieutenant colonel. Robert Howe (Brunswick County) was appointed colonel of the Second Regiment, and Alexander Martin (Guilford County) was named lieutenant colonel. Bertie County residents Whitmill Pugh and John Oliver received appointments as ensigns in the Second Regiment, but Pugh, having previously been designated to serve in the company of Capt. Michael Payne of Chowan County, resigned his commission prior to October 20.[16]

The congress established six military districts across North Carolina, namely: Edenton, Halifax, Hillsborough, New Bern, Salisbury, and Wilmington. Bertie County was included in the Edenton District, along with Chowan, Currituck, Hertford, Martin, Pasquotank, Perquimans, and Tyrrell counties. It directed that a ten-company regiment of minutemen (500 rank-and-file members) be raised in each district. The field officers (colonel, lieutenant colonel, and major) for each regiment were to be recommended by officials within the subject regiment's district and appointed by the provincial congress. The congress designated that two companies (100 men, rank and file) be raised in Bertie County.[17] In addition to Bertie County's two companies, the provincial congress also authorized two companies for Chowan County and one company each for Currituck, Hertford, Martin, Pasquotank, Perquimans, and Tyrrell counties. The minutemen units were authorized for six months.[18]

Field officers for each district were to appoint a suitable person or persons in each county to enlist the minutemen. The person(s) appointed to enlist the troops were authorized to accept volunteers who came into the county from other locales, but they were to restrict their particular recruiting activities to their designated county. The recruiters could also give preference to enlisting those men who possessed their own arms. Once the authorized companies were complete, the constituent members were to choose their company officers (captain, lieutenants, and ensigns). Each captain was to notify the chairman of the county's committee of safety that his company was completed; the committee was to review the company to ensure that it was comprised of "able and proper men." The county committee was responsible for furnishing arms to those members of the company who did not have weapons. The committee was authorized to "borrow such guns as are fit for Service." Owners of the borrowed arms were entitled to compensation—ten shillings a year for a "good" smoothbore shotgun or musket and twenty shillings per year for a rifle.[19]

As soon as the minutemen companies of each district were enlisted and approved, they were to be organized into a regiment at or near their district headquarters (Edenton, in the case of the two Bertie County companies). The companies, individually, and the regiment, as a unit, were to train successively for fourteen days. Thereafter, each company was to muster in its home county "at least once a fortnight [two weeks]" on such days and at such places as the captain directed. The adjutant for each district was directed to attend musters in the different counties of his district. Further, the provincial congress authorized a bounty of twenty-five shillings for each private and noncommissioned officer to buy a hunting shirt, legging or splatter dashes (protective garments to repel mud, water, and debris from the lower legs of soldiers), and black garters, the designated uniform for the province's minutemen.[20]

The congress, having established the basic organizational structures and composition of the province's minutemen, militia, and two Continental regiments, addressed the surely-to-arise issue of commensurate ranks and command hierarchy. It stipulated that officers of a particular rank in the regular service (army) would assume rank over officers of the same rank in the "minute service." Similarly, minute service officers would take rank over militia officers. The congress also decreed that minutemen were not to come under the command of the militia, or vice-versa, unless drawn into service together.[21]

The colonel or commanding officer of each county's militia was empowered to order two general regimental musters annually, while the captains were to muster their companies monthly. The adjutant of each county was directed to attend all general and company musters and was to be paid eight shillings for each day that he attended a muster.[22]

The congress appointed the following individuals as field officers of the minutemen in the Edenton District: Edward Vail (Chowan County), colonel; Andrew Knox (Perquimans County), lieutenant colonel; Caleb Nash (Pasquotank County), major. It appointed the following men to be field officers of the Bertie County militia: Thomas Whitmell, colonel; Thomas Pugh, lieutenant colonel; James Moore, first major; and Arthur Brown, second major.[23]

The provincial congress had become the central governing body for North Carolina, but it was necessary for the delegates to constitute a subordinate body to oversee and manage the colony's affairs when the congress was not meeting. Therefore, the congress authorized a thirteen-person (a president and twelve members) provincial council. The membership was comprised of two persons from each of the six military districts. The congress empowered the provincial council to transact all business and manage such matters as the council should judge expedient to strengthen, secure, and defend North Carolina within the auspices of any act or resolution of the congress. The council was further specifically authorized to draw funds on the colony's treasury, apply the funds to necessary public needs, and account for the funds appropriately to the congress. The council was to meet at the Johnston County Courthouse every three months beginning in October 1775. It was authorized to meet more often and at other locations if necessitated by affairs and situations within the colony.[24] The delegates elected the individuals listed in the table above to the provincial council.

In addition, the congress authorized equivalent-size committees of safety in each of the six military districts. Those committees, under the purview of the provincial council, were to meet at least every three months at the principal

TABLE 1

Members of the North Carolina Provincial Council, September 1775[25]

President/Members	Military District
Cornelius Harnett*, president	Wilmington
Whitmel Hill**, Thomas Jones	Edenton
Samuel Johnston***, Samuel Ashe	Wilmington
Abner Nash, James Coor	New Bern
Willie Jones, Thomas Eaton	Halifax
Samuel Spencer, Waightstill Avery	Salisbury
Thomas Person, John Kinchen	Hillsborough

*Harnett was elected president of the council at its first meeting on October 18, 1775. See Saunders, *Colonial Records*, 10:283.
**Hill was originally a resident of Bertie County but relocated to Martin County.[26]
***Johnston hailed from Chowan County, but Saunders, *Colonial Records*, 10:214, indicates that he was elected to the council for the Wilmington District.

towns of their respective districts. Members of the district committees were to be elected. The committees were authorized to direct the operations of their respective district militia and such other forces as were employed for the safety, protection, and defense of the colony. Additionally, committees of safety consisting of fifteen persons each were authorized for the towns of Edenton, New Bern, and Wilmington. The provincial council and the subordinate committees of safety were authorized to direct and control all military affairs and arrangements of the colony's forces—subject, however, to the control of the provincial congress (when in session).[27]

Two Bertie County men—William Gray and John Johnston—were elected members of the District of Edenton Committee of Safety. The eleven other members were: Luke Sumner (Chowan County), Thomas Benbury (Chowan County), Gideon Lamb (Currituck County), Joseph Jones (Pasquotank County), Miles Harvey (Perquimans County), Lawrence Baker (Hertford County), Kenneth McKenzie (Martin County), Stevens Lee (Tyrrell County), Charles Blount (Perquimans County), Isaac Gregory (Pasquotank County), and Day Ridley (Hertford County).[28]

Lastly, the provincial congress resolved that each county in the province should establish a committee of safety to be composed of at least twenty-one members. Each county committee was to meet at its respective courthouse on the first day of each quarterly court session. The county committees were to execute all orders from the committees of safety and the provincial council. Furthermore, each county committee was responsible for superintending compliance with the boycott per the Continental Association, as well as abiding with all resolves, orders, and directions from the Continental Congress and the North Carolina Provincial Congress.[29]

Samuel Johnston adjourned the unicameral congress on Sunday, September 10, after three weeks of arduous deliberations. The congress had established itself as the highest governing body in North Carolina in lieu of the abdicated governorship. The Third Provincial Congress was the first executive governing body in North Carolina that was free of British rule. It had established a governing structure to guide the colony as it and the other twelve provinces undoubtedly were about to challenge the British with arms. The congress laid the foundations for North Carolina's Continental Line units and a structure to marshal the colony's militia and minutemen.[30]

The provincial council convened for the first time on October 18, 1775, at the Johnston County Courthouse. Its agenda was principally focused on completing military-related business from the provincial congress. The council decided that each of the one thousand soldiers to be raised for the province's two Continental regiments would be supplied with one blanket, a hunting shirt, a pair of splatter dashers, and garters, being of opinion that the items were "absolutely necessary" and "was [*sic*] intended by the late Provincial Congress." (Recruiting efforts were under way as the council met.) The council also authorized that a second adjutant be authorized in each of the six military districts for the minutemen regiments, since it was "impossible for one person to attend the several Counties in some of the districts."

Although the provincial congress had adjourned only about five and a half weeks previously, the council members had already concluded that it might be "impracticable" to complete the minutemen regiments in some of the districts. The council decided that even though some regiments might not attain full strength (500 men, rank and file), the field officers and captains of such regiments should assemble those troops they had recruited and "proceed to training in the manner" directed by the provincial congress. The council appealed to the counties' and towns' committees of safety to "exert their utmost influence to forward and hasten the minute service," in order that the several regiments be completed "with all possible dispatch." Further, the council directed the captains of the companies in the First and Second North Carolina Regiments to report to the committees of safety in the towns and counties in which the companies were stationed (Edenton, New Bern, Salisbury, and Wilmington) the numbers of their recruits who were unarmed. The committees were directed to borrow guns from the populace and to supply the weapons to the unarmed soldiers. The owners of the guns were to receive compensation for the use of their arms by the colony's army. The council adjourned on October 22.[31]

On November 5 Samuel Johnston, anticipating that the province's two Continental regiments would eventually be taken into Continental service, wrote to Caswell, Hewes, and Hooper that the province was desperately in need of arms and ammunition for those units. When Johnston's letters arrived in Philadelphia is unknown, but on November 24 the Continental Congress appointed a committee to consider the condition of North Carolina. The committee's report, dated November 27, led Congress on the following day to adopt a series of resolutions through which the two North Carolina regiments were incorporated into the Continental army, and other provisions and suggestions were adopted for defense of the province.[32]

Bertie County leaders initiated efforts to raise its two companies of minutemen and arm the members. No muster rolls or pay rolls exist for the county's militia or minutemen companies; therefore, the full extent of military activities and efforts carried out within the county is not ascertainable. Furthermore, without such rolls, it is impossible to identify all of the officers and men in the county's militia and minute service units. Nevertheless, fragmentary information provides evidence that the county's residents were moved to respond to the provincial congress's call to arms. Charles W. Jacocks paid bounties for two unidentified minutemen. John Rhodes entered the service at Windsor on an undisclosed date as a "minute militia man." Elisha Rhodes provided five guns and a bayonet for use by the colony's military, for which he too was reimbursed in December 1775. Both men were members of a Bertie County minutemen company that would march against the Tories in southeastern North Carolina in February 1776. Lt. Col. Thomas Pugh was paid for attending forty-three musters as an adjutant. The evidence is insufficient to ascertain whether Pugh functioned solely as the Bertie County adjutant or possibly more broadly as an adjutant for the Edenton District's minutemen regiment.[33]

At this early stage of the Revolutionary movement, the military-age men of Bertie County obviously preferred to render their services to the county's militia and minutemen companies rather than enlisting in the province's two Continental regiments. In September 1775 the provincial congress appointed two county residents—John Oliver and Whitmill Pugh—as subordinate officers in the Second North Carolina Regiment; Pugh resigned his appointment within a few weeks. A contingent of the Continental force was stationed at Edenton, immediately across the Chowan River from Bertie County. In early December Col. Robert Howe assembled his Second North Carolina Continentals at Edenton, preparatory to marching to the aid of Virginia. About December 8 or 9 Howe's regiment departed Edenton for Great Bridge, Virginia, to reinforce Virginia militia units that were engaging British regulars. Howe's command arrived at Great Bridge on December 11 and immediately pushed forward and compelled the British to evacuate Norfolk. Apparently no Bertie County men were moved to travel to Edenton and enlist as volunteers in Howe's command.[34]

As efforts to organize military units and to prepare the men for the rigors of wartime sacrifices were under way, tensions and suspicions of patriotic convictions increased markedly among the inhabitants of the colony, including those in the Albemarle Sound region. Indeed, not every resident supported rebellious measures and military action against Great Britain. In certain instances the tensions and suspicions manifested into violence and uncivil treatment of members of the community. Cullen Pollock, the grandson of former governor Thomas Pollock and a wealthy and influential member of Bertie County's upper societal order, fell victim to the heavy-handed tactics of Chowan County officials and military officers. Pollock, a former commissioner for the town of Windsor, had substantial landholdings in Bertie County and maintained residences in Bertie County at Bal Gra (near the mouth of Salmon Creek) and immediately across the Chowan River in Edenton. About early to mid-November, Pollock and his wife Ann had traveled to Philadelphia and met with Joseph Hewes. During their return trip to North Carolina, the Pollocks stopped in Suffolk, Virginia, where they spent two nights before continuing their journey to Edenton. During their respite in the Virginia town, they stayed at the residence of a Mr. Donaldson, where they engaged in "General . . . conversation" with the homeowner and others who were present. During the interaction Pollock reportedly commented that he had heard a "gentleman" in Annapolis tell a Maryland militia officer that the gentleman's brother in London, England, had jocularly written in a letter that he thought the issue of confrontation "might be easily settled by hanging a half a Dousen [dozen] on each side of the Question [American and British]." A North Carolina militia officer who was present overheard Pollock's comments but construed them in a drastically distorted manner and reportedly attributed the essence of the comments directly to Pollock. The officer purportedly informed Wells Cooper, apparently a man of influence in the Suffolk area, that Pollock had said that "they must all be hanged"—apparently an inferred reference to the American revolutionaries.

During the ensuing day the Pollocks departed Suffolk to continue the trek to their Edenton residence. Wells Cooper was on the prowl for Cullen Pollock in Suffolk on that day, but the Pollocks departed before Cooper could catch up with them. Cooper allegedly boasted that he "would have blown out Mr. P's brains" had Pollock not departed Suffolk. Cooper sent a notice to the Edenton District Committee of Safety imploring the committee to have Pollock detained. Within a few days Boyd Blackburn of Chowan County caught up with Pollock in Edenton and advised him that he was not to leave the town and was to appear before the local committee of safety. Pollock, obviously infuriated at the dictatorial decree from Blackburn (acting on behalf of the committee), reportedly replied that he "had no Intention of leaving the Town" but would go where he pleased and would not "wait on" the committee. Within short order a "body" of about 150 armed soldiers appeared to detain Pollock. He resisted but was overwhelmed by the troops and taken into custody. In the fray Mrs. Pollock attempted to come to her husband's aid but was "pulled off" by the soldiers, expulsed into the street, and allegedly treated in a "savage manner."

The soldiers placed Pollock in the Edenton jail, where he was detained for two days and one night before he was brought before the committee of safety. On November 21, 1775, the committee interrogated Pollock, who signed an "association" document under the pressure of "a malicious few" individuals. Pollock promised to "conduct himself on all occasions . . . as a friend to the liberties of America." The committee of safety, satisfied with Pollock's responses to its questions regarding his loyalty and commitment to the American cause for liberty, directed that its findings be published in order to prevent any "injury" to Pollock's reputation. (The public document was published in the New Bern *North Carolina Gazette* on December 22, 1775.)

Pollock, upon being released from custody, retired to his residence. But his ordeal was not over: the night of his release, armed soldiers under the command of Lt. Clement Hall of the Second North Carolina Regiment appeared at Pollock's home. About two o'clock in the morning, Hall announced his presence outside the house and demanded to see Pollock. The soldiers proceeded to chop down the door to the house with axes and threatened Mrs. Pollock with their "guns pointed" at her face. Hall repeatedly demanded that Pollock be brought out of the house, which was surrounded by upward of two hundred soldiers. Pollock, unarmed since his wife had transferred all of his personal arms to a friend in town, surrendered.

The soldiers took Pollock to the courthouse grounds, where they threatened to "tar and feather" him in the midst of "hundreds" of people. Mrs. Pollock, who in the cold of the night had rushed to the scene in nightclothes, anxiously screamed at the people who seemed ready to make her husband "a sacrifice." Townspeople and soldiers constituted "the mob," which broke open some cellars and a storehouse in a frenzied search for liquor but found none. Eventually the "mob" quieted down and dispersed. Cullen Pollock was unharmed, even though he relinquished "a sum of money" to some members of the crowd. On December 23 Mrs. Pollock wrote to Joseph Hewes: "I am sure you never thought Soldiers [would be] necessary in this part of North Carolina[,] nor cou'd you have thought they were to be paid to ruin Individuals or disturb the peace of society." Mrs. Pollock informed Hewes that William Gray, the highly influential resident of Windsor and member of the Edenton District Committee of Safety, had declared that Lieutenant Hall and some others "shou'd be made examples of," but apparently Edenton officials took no such action. Evidently Pollock quietly put the unfortunate chain of events behind him, but most surely he never forgot how he was so disgracefully treated by his revolutionary neighbors solely over an incautious, innocent remark at an acquaintance's Virginia residence.[35]

As the year 1776 opened, a dark shadow of war hung over North Carolina. A substantial number of persons in the province who were loyal to King George III took up arms against the Whig Patriots. Gov. Josiah Martin, from his exile aboard a British warship in the Cape Fear River, had been busy planning his move against those citizens who were actively opposing the British.

Martin intended to organize as many as 9,000 Tories, Regulators, and Highland Scots to crush the "Rebels and Traitors" (Whigs). Martin's Loyalist army, coupled with British army and navy forces, was to initiate its move about the middle of February in the southeastern sector of the colony. The British viewed North Carolina as militarily the weakest colony in America, except for Georgia.[36] Martin surely exuded confidence as his plans began to materialize.

North Carolina's Patriot leaders assembled a confronting force comprised of more than 1,100 minutemen and Col. James Moore's First North Carolina Regiment, the whole under the overall command of Moore. The minutemen contingent was raised primarily in Craven, Dobbs, Johnston, and Pitt counties and was commanded by Cols. Richard Caswell and Alexander Lillington. A supporting force composed of minutemen from Bertie and Martin counties was organized to march to the Duplin-Sampson county area under the command of Col. William Williams of Martin County. The number of troops in Williams's command is not evident from available records, but the Bertie County component—a company under the command of Capt. Charles Worth Jacocks—totaled forty-six members, including Jacocks.[37]

Bertie County in general, and Windsor in particular, was the scene of busied activity in mid-February as officials hurried to ready Jacocks's minutemen to march. The troops, residing throughout Bertie County, had to be notified to assemble in Windsor and be ready to march in short order. William Knott provided a horse to an unidentified rider so that he could "warn in the men" for the forthcoming expedition against the "insurgents." Local residents provided cooked meals and baked goods to the minutemen. Jacocks, striving to outfit his company and prepare his men for the march, oversaw the collection of provisions, supplies, commodities, equipment, and haul animals. The residents responded to his and other officials' calls by furnishing desperately needed assorted items. The items gathered reflected the needs of a group of young men who were about to march off to war. The impressive list included more than 20 bushels of wheat and 3 bushels of corn (some ground at county gristmills and baked into bread); 3 barrels of pork; 30 hams; 2 quarters of beef; 120 pounds of bacon; and fat for cooking. Thirty-two firearms were obtained, some of which were cleaned and readied for use by local resident William Kelly. Gunpowder and lead were gathered, along with a single bayonet. Windsor merchant Thomas Ballard made 27 leather cartouche [cartridge] boxes for the troops. Almost a dozen kettles and assorted tin pans, along with rope, nails, saddle tacks, sewing needles (used as firearms nipple picks), and blankets were placed in horse-drawn carts for the expedition. Ballard also furnished forty yards of osnaburg (coarse cotton cloth) for a tent. Fifteen gallons of rum, a

TABLE 2

Compiled Roster of Capt. Charles Worth Jacocks's
Bertie County Company of Minutemen, February 1776

Anderson, James, private

Bardle, Henry, private

Bates, James, private

Billups, Richard, private

Brown, Arthur, private

Bryant, John, private

Cale, John, private

Cherry, James, private

Cherry, Solomon [Jr.], private

Collins, David, private

Collins, John, private

Fellow, William, private

Flood, John, private

Fort, Elias, private

Harrell, Adam, private

Howard, Solomon, private

Hubbard, Warburton, private

Hurst, William, private

Jacocks, Charles Worth, captain

Kelly, William, private

Knott, William, sergeant

Leggett, John, private

Lewis, Samuel, private

Liscombe, Wilson, private

Lowe, William, private

Murray, William, private

Oden, Robert, private

Oliver, Andrew, private

Perkins, William, private

Pollock, Jacob, lieutenant

Redditt, Job, corporal

Redditt, Samuel, private

Rhodes, Elisha, sergeant

Rhodes, James, private

Rhodes, John, private

Rhodes, Jonathan, private

Simmons, James, drummer

Simmons, Mallekiah, private

Turner, Amos, private

Urqhuart, Alexander, private

Walton, Timothy, private

Watson, Thomas, corporal

Watson, William, private

Whitmell, Thomas Blount, ensign

Whitmell, Thomas West, private

Wynants, Wynant, private

SOURCE: Weynette Parks Haun, comp., *North Carolina Revolutionary Army Accounts, Secretary of State, Treasurer's & Comptroller's Papers*, Journal "A" (Public Accounts), 1775–1776 (Durham: the compiler, 1988).

preferred form of refreshment, were also purchased. And to transport it all, almost two dozen horses and more than a half-dozen drivers and carts were assembled. For about three days, Windsor was the center of an intense logistics operation. Jacocks's company marched away from town February 19 or 20.[38]

In the early morning of Tuesday, February 27, the North Carolina Patriots and Martin's Loyalists (comprised of about 1,600 Highland Scots with no British regulars) fell upon each other in close-quarters combat at Moores Creek Bridge, eighteen miles from Wilmington. In a brief, decisive battle, Moore's forces overwhelmed the Loyalists. The carnage was horrendous: dozens of Loyalists were killed, and an estimated 850 were taken prisoner in the battle, which lasted mere minutes. Miraculously, the Whig forces lost only one man killed and one wounded. The North Carolina Patriots had achieved a "splendid victory," raising Whig morale and furthering the Revolutionary cause in the province. Colonel Williams's Bertie-Martin contingent was not involved in the battle, having arrived on the scene after the affair had concluded.[39]

John Rhodes, a member of Captain Jacocks's Bertie County minutemen, later recalled: "[I] entered the service of the United States as a minute militia man in the year 1776. I was under the command of Captain Charles Jacocks. [W]e marched from Windsor in Bertie County through the adjoining Counties to Cross Creek where an action had taken place between the Whigs and Tories before we reached said place & the Tories were defeated by the Whigs under Colonel Richard Caswell. . . . [W]e were ordered home and discharged."[40]

On Wednesday, the twenty-eighth, the North Carolina Provincial Council convened at New Bern. News of the victory at Moores Creek Bridge soon reached the council members. On Friday, March 2, the council ordered Colonel Williams to return with the Bertie and Martin County troops under his command to their homes. The council directed Williams to turn over any ammunition in his possession to Colonel Moore. The council, "in the warmest Terms," rendered its thanks to "the Gentlemen Officers and Soldiers" from the two counties "for their readiness and spirited Conduct in marching against the enemies of their Country." While Williams's troops had not been involved in the Battle of Moores Creek Bridge, several of them later recalled that they performed their patriotic duty by marching "against the Tories." Their expedition lasted about three weeks. On May 1, 1776, the province's committee of claims approved a payment of more than £291 to Captain Jacocks "for Services of his Company."[41]

On Thursday, April 4, the Fourth Provincial Congress convened at Halifax, and fifty-eight delegates (of the 135 delegates elected province-wide) arrived and took their seats. (Another forty-plus delegates joined the session before it adjourned almost six weeks later.) Three men from Bertie County—John Campbell, John Johnston, and Charles W. Jacocks—were elected to attend the congress. Campbell and Johnston were present when the session opened. Jacocks apparently had not traveled to Halifax, having vacated his seat, since he was an officer in the Bertie County "Minute Service." On April 10 the congress resolved that the "freeholders" of Bertie County meet at the courthouse in Windsor on Monday, April 15, and elect a delegate to sit and vote in the congress in the place of Jacocks. The Bertie voters nonetheless re-elected Jacocks, and he appeared and took his seat in the congress on Friday, the nineteenth.[42]

The members unanimously elected Samuel Johnston as president of the congress, a convention for which North Carolina's independence was the delegates' predominant and driving focus. On April 12 the members unanimously resolved that the province's delegates to the Continental Congress be empowered to concur with the delegates of the other colonies in declaring "independency" from Great Britain and forming foreign alliances. Those measures, known as the "Halifax Resolves," were the first official action by an American colony calling for independence. Other colonies soon followed North Carolina's lead.[43]

Implementing measures to prepare for a presumed British invasion consumed a great deal of the provincial congress's time and energy. Concurrently, the delegates took on the issue of devising a constitution for North Carolina. The members resolved that North Carolina reserve "the sole and exclusive right of forming a Constitution and laws" for the colony and appoint delegates from time to time to represent the colony in meetings (i.e., "congresses") with delegates of the other colonies. The delegates began deliberating a constitution; but after two weeks of pitched debate, they realized that the time had not yet come when the sitting provincial congress would take such a noteworthy step. The delegates agreed to revisit the topic at a later session.[44]

The provincial congress, in considering the command structure and arrangement of the province's militia, appointed a brigadier general for each of the military districts. Edward Vail (previously appointed colonel of the Edenton District minutemen) was appointed brigadier general for the subject district. The other appointments were Richard Caswell, New Bern District; John Ashe, Wilmington District; Thomas Person, Hillsborough District; Griffith Rutherford, Salisbury District; and Allen Jones, Halifax District. In addition, the congress appointed field officers of the militia in each of the counties. For Bertie County, the congress appointed Thomas Whitmell, colonel; Thomas

Pugh, lieutenant colonel; James Moore, first major; and Arthur Brown, second major. (The congress's action, in essence, reaffirmed the September 1775 appointments of those men.)[45]

The congress succeeded in revising the province's militia regulations. Principally, it decreed that all able-bodied men ages sixteen to sixty in each county were to be formed into one regiment. (The congress, at its discretion, could designate two or more regiments in a county, if necessary.) Field officers for each regiment would include a colonel (the regimental commander), a lieutenant colonel, and two majors. Each regiment was to be comprised of companies of at least fifty rank-and-file members. The province's overall militia forces were divided into six brigades—one brigade for each military district under the command of a brigadier general. To facilitate the timely raising and organizing of detachments of troops to be called into service, the members of every company were to be segregated into five divisions. One division was to be comprised of the "more aged and infirm men." The other four divisions were to draw lots for the first, second, third, and fourth turns to go into service. The commanding officer of every regiment was required to hold a general muster of his troops whenever ordered by the brigadier general of his district, but not more than two such gatherings annually. Each captain was required to muster and train his company, divided into divisions, once each month (unless directed to muster more often by the regiment's commanding officer). The congress further resolved that each militiaman be furnished with a good gun, bayonet, cartouche box, shot bag, powder horn, and cutlass or tomahawk. Those men whose personal means rendered them unable to afford the required arms and accouterments were to be provided the items at public expense. The congress also declared that militia units (brigade, regiment, company, or division) were to be commanded only by militia officers, except when such units were ordered by the province's civilian authorities to join Continental troops. In such instances, Continental officers of the same rank were deemed "superior denomination" and were to assume command over the joint Continental and militia forces.[46]

The provincial congress also addressed a number of other actions important to the province. It ordered £500,000 in paper bills of credit to be printed for the purpose of defraying the expenses of armaments, bounties, and other wartime contingencies that would be incurred within the colony while the congress was in recess. The congress also dissolved the provincial council and replaced it with the council of safety, which was "vested with full power and authority to do and execute all acts and things necessary for the defence and protection of the people of this Colony." The council was not, however, authorized to alter,

The provincial congress resolved that each militiaman be furnished with a good gun, bayonet, cartouche box, shot bag, powder horn, and cutlass or tomahawk. Image of these Revolutionary War-era artifacts is provided courtesy of the N.C. Museum of History.

suspend, or abrogate any resolution of any of the four provincial congresses or to (1) emit any bills of credit; (2) levy any taxes on the people; (3) impose any duties or imposts on goods or merchandise to be imported or exported; (4) give orders to draw on the Continental treasury; (5) erect any office or offices, courts, or jurisdictions; or (6) try, adjudge, or condemn any person or persons for any offence civil or criminal, except where expressly permitted by resolve of the congress. Furthermore, the congress dissolved the committees of safety in the six military districts, preferring that all matters previously within the purview of the subject committees be taken under the cognizance of the council of safety. The congress appointed the following men to be council members: Willie Jones, Halifax District, appointed "for the Congress"; James Coor and John Simpson, New Bern District; Thomas Jones and Whitmel Hill, Edenton District; Thomas Eaton and Joseph John Williams, Halifax District; Cornelius Harnett and Samuel Ashe, Wilmington District; Thomas Person and John Rand, Hillsborough District; and Hezekiah Alexander and William Sharpe, Salisbury District.[47]

The provincial congress, while celebrating Col. James Moore's victory at Moores Creek Bridge and thanking Col. Robert Howe for his service in Virginia in late December-early January, was faced with the threat of a British invasion of North Carolina. A formidable British force under the command of Gen. Charles Cornwallis and convoyed by the naval fleet of Adm. Sir Peter Parker had sailed from Ireland in February and was destined for the Cape Fear River. A force from New York, variously estimated at between 400 and 700 troops under the command of Gen. Sir Henry Clinton, had arrived off Cape Fear on March 12 and was awaiting the arrival of the forces from Ireland. Each day, Clinton menacingly exercised his troops by landing them on small Battery Island under the protection of naval warships' guns. The first ships of Parker's fleet sailed into view off the southeastern North Carolina coast on April 18.[48]

James Moore (now a brigadier general), stationed at Wilmington with his First North Carolina Regiment and some militia, wrote to the provincial congress and requested reinforcements of militia. In response, the congress on May 3 ordered 1,500 militiamen to be immediately drafted from four districts—Edenton, Halifax, New Bern, and Wilmington—and marched as quickly as possible to Wilmington. The militia draftees were to be formed into twenty-seven companies—six from the Wilmington District and seven each from the New Bern, Halifax, and Edenton districts. Col. Thomas Whitmell was to furnish one company of fifty troops from the Bertie County militia. Each of six other counties in the Edenton District was to furnish a company: Martin (50 men), Tyrrell (50), Hertford (50), Chowan (50), Perquimans (50), and Pasquotank (75).[49]

The provincial congress further ordered that the 1,500-man militia force be divided into two regiments. Col. Thomas Brown (Bladen County) was ordered to command the regiment comprised of companies from the Wilmington and New Bern districts. Col. Peter Dauge (also known as Peter Dozier, Pasquotank County) was placed in command of the regiment composed of troops from the Edenton and Halifax districts. The brigadier generals of the Halifax, Edenton (Edward Vail), New Bern, and Wilmington districts were directed to issue orders immediately to the commanders of the respective regiments within their districts to draft, organize, and march the militia detachments to Wilmington "with all possible expedition." Brig. Gen. John Ashe was to take command of the reinforcements upon their arrival in his district (Wilmington). The congress resolved that the drafted militiamen would not be obliged to serve longer than three months.[50]

In addition to militia reinforcements, the congress ordered that various articles of war be sent promptly to Wilmington. It ordered "2000 w[eigh]t of gunpowder [to] be immediately dispatched" from Halifax to General Moore. It also directed that provisions and ammunition be sent, and ordered the newly appointed colonels of the several regiments to have their recruiting officers "march their recruits as fast as they shall inlist . . . properly armed" to join Moore. Ten pieces of artillery (belonging to South Carolina) at New Bern, along with any other pieces found in the town, were to be immediately transferred to Moore. Charles W. Jacocks, the recently appointed commissary for the Edenton District, was ordered to provide arms, camp kettles, and equipage to Col. Thomas Polk's Fourth North Carolina Regiment. Jacocks was responsible for obtaining a sufficient quantity of provisions to supply the seven companies from the Edenton District. Jacocks was authorized to purchase provisions from Nathaniel Rochester, the province's deputy commissary general. He also acquired goods and commodities from Bertie County citizens. The congress advanced the sum of £200 to Jacocks upon receiving his security bond.[51]

Command of the Bertie County company fell to Capt. Andrew Oliver. Oliver's unit was comprised of 55 privates, 2 noncommissioned officers, a musician, and 3 officers (including Oliver)—a total of 61 men. The date on which Colonel Dauge's regiment, including Oliver's company, arrived in Wilmington is not evident from available records, but the force likely arrived after the middle of May. As General Moore consolidated his forces and augmented his defenses, British general Clinton concluded that North Carolina was not worth the effort and cost of an assault. The British naval vessels transporting the accompanying army forces sailed out of the Cape Fear River on May 31, 1776 (the day that Governor Martin fled from New Bern and sought refuge in Fort Johnston, near Wilmington), and headed southward toward Charleston, South Carolina—a more strategic objective. Despite the exodus of the British military from the Cape Fear–Wilmington sector, General Moore maintained his defensive vigil with the joint militia-regular army force.[52]

With British forces arriving on North Carolina soil and in its maritime regions, military preparations obviously consumed a great deal of the provincial congress's agenda. The body resolved that two army regiments, over and above those directed to be raised by the Continental Congress, be raised in the province. By mid-April 1776 the Continental Congress had authorized North Carolina to raise four, and optionally five, regiments for the Continental establishment. On April 17 the North Carolina Provincial Congress appointed the field and company officers for the Third, Fourth, Fifth, and Sixth Regiments. The colonels and lieutenant colonels were:

Third Regiment: Jethro Sumner (Bute County), colonel
                     William Alston (Bute County), lieutenant colonel
Fourth Regiment: Thomas Polk (Mecklenburg County), colonel
                     James Thackston (Cumberland County), lieutenant colonel
Fifth Regiment: Edward Buncombe (Tyrrell County), colonel
                     Henry Irwin (Edgecombe County), lieutenant colonel
Sixth Regiment: Alexander Lillington (New Hanover County), colonel
                     William Taylor (Duplin County), lieutenant colonel

The congress appointed six Bertie County residents as officers for the regiments: John Pugh Williams, captain; Thomas Whitmell Pugh, first lieutenant; Jacob Pollock, first lieutenant; Thomas Blount Whitmell, second lieutenant; Elisha Rhodes, ensign; and William Knott, ensign. Fourteen other men from counties within the Edenton District received officer appointments.[53] Additionally, the congress appointed Francis Nash colonel and Thomas Clark (Bladen County) lieutenant colonel of the First Regiment, James Moore having been appointed to the rank of brigadier general by the Continental Congress. Further, the congress appointed (i.e., promoted) Alexander Martin to colonel of the Second North Carolina Regiment, Col. Robert Howe having been appointed brigadier general in the Continental establishment on March 1, 1776. John Patten (Beaufort County) was promoted from major to lieutenant colonel of the unit.[54]

In order to facilitate recruiting men for the Continental regiments, the congress issued "instructions and orders for the recruiting officers." The instructions/orders stipulated that recruiting officers enlist only able-bodied men at least five feet four inches tall who were fit for service and capable of marching well. Recruits who were "well practiced in the use of fire arms" were preferred. Recruits were to be committed to "American liberties" and possess "regard to moral character, particularly sobriety." The officers were to "exert themselves" to complete their companies, but the colonels or other appropriate field officers of their respectful regiments could reject any men whom they determined to be unfit for service. Each recruit was to take an enlistment oath and receive a forty-shilling enlistment bounty. All recruits were to be enlisted for the term of two years and six months but could be dismissed sooner in case the Continental Congress judged such dismissals necessary.[55]

The provincial congress appointed two "commissioners" from each county to receive, procure, and purchase firearms for the troops. Zedekiah Stone and Jonathan Jacocks were appointed commissioners for Bertie County.

The congress stipulated that the colony's arms commissioners take possession of all arms, swords, dirks, pistols, and other implements of war that had been confiscated from Tories. All firearms purchased were to be fit for immediate use by the troops or were to be readily repairable. All arms in need of repair were to be provided to competent gunsmiths, who were to expedite repairing the weapons and returning them to the commissioners. The congress advanced £300 to the commissioners of each county so that they could expeditiously set about their duties. The commissioners were to provide arms to the colonels of the North Carolina Continental regiments for distribution to recruits. Surplus arms were to be turned over to Nathaniel Rochester (Hillsborough), deputy commissary general. Before the end of the year, Stone and Jacocks had acquired firearms costing more than £299, having expended the sum earlier provided to them by the provincial congress. The congress appointed Charles W. Jacocks as commissary for the Edenton District militia. By the time Jacocks received the appointment, he had already acquired twenty-one barrels of gunpowder and five pounds of lead for musket projectiles.[56]

The provincial congress adjourned on May 14, completing a challenging but productive session. As a result of that body's actions, North Carolina stood at the forefront of the American colonies advocating independence.[57] A spirit of independence pervaded the province.

During the spring and early summer of 1776, a number of men from across Bertie County were moved to serve in North Carolina's Continental Line regiments and journeyed to the fledgling county seat of Windsor, where they volunteered for service. While the volunteers were enlisted into several regiments, they predominantly joined the Fourth and Fifth Regiments—units to which the state provincial congress had assigned several Bertie County residents as officers. The congress appointed John Pugh Williams to the rank of captain and placed him in command of a company of the Fifth North Carolina Regiment. Fellow county residents Thomas Whitmell Pugh and Elisha Rhodes were appointed the same day as subordinate officers and placed under Williams's command. Company commanders were required to recruit men for their companies and fill their ranks. Accordingly, from mid-April through about mid-May, Williams and his Bertie County officers set about recruiting, coaxing, and persuading their fellow county residents to enlist in their company. About a dozen men responded. Zachariah Carter enlisted with Captain Pugh, initially rendezvousing at "Col. Pugh's Tavern in Bertie County." Pugh, along with other enlistees, was marched to Windsor, where they took the state oath of allegiance before departing for Edenton.[58]

Similarly, the provincial congress appointed three other Bertie County residents—William Knott, Jacob Pollock, and Thomas Blount Whitmell—as subordinate officers and assigned them to the Fourth North Carolina Regiment. As Captain Williams and his subordinate officers were recruiting and enlisting county men for the Fifth North Carolina, so were Knott, Pollock, and Whitmell. During the period between mid-April and mid-May, a number of Bertie County men signed up to serve in the Fourth North Carolina Regiment.

A few county residents enlisted during the spring of 1776 to serve in the First and Third North Carolina Regiments. Although the colony's provincial congress appointed no Bertie County residents as officers in those regiments, officers for the units apparently visited Bertie County for recruiting purposes. The men who enlisted in the First Regiment joined for three-year terms of service, while those who enlisted in the Third, Fourth, and Fifth Regiments predominantly signed up for two and one-half years of service (the term stipulated by the provincial congress on April 27, 1776).[59]

By May 15 the flurry of recruiting activities abruptly subsided in Windsor as the officers and their recruits departed the town. Obviously, no Continental army recruiters were placed in the town, and not until almost the end of the year would another county man enlist in the army. William White enlisted in the Seventh North Carolina Regiment on December 10.[60] Bertie County's white, male, military-age population (ages sixteen to sixty years) were, by law, members of the county's militia (with certain persons excepted) and thus were subject to being called into service at the discretion of the province. The county's military-age men, as members of the militia, were committed to military service, usually at the time of invasion, insurrection, or crises and generally for short durations. Such contingent military service likely influenced many men to forgo enlisting for significantly longer terms in the regular army.

The recently appointed Bertie County officers and their enlistees joined other officers and recruits of the North Carolina Continental Line regiments at Edenton, from which they immediately marched to Wilmington. The majority of the province's soldiers were ultimately destined for Charleston, South Carolina, a target of British military forces. British naval and army forces had besieged the city in June, and North Carolina's First, Second, Third, and Fourth Regiments—all of which were about half strength, with "green" recruits—had been rushed to the port city to bolster its defenses.[61]

Richard Caswell (1729–1789), William Hooper (1742–1790), Joseph Hewes (1730–1779), and John Penn (1740–1788) variously represented North Carolina in the Continental Congress from 1774 through 1780. Caswell (1774–1775), Hewes (1774–1776,

On June 28 British naval forces attacked Sullivan's Island, on the outskirts of Charleston. Adm. Sir Peter Parker, Gen. Henry Clinton, and Gen. Charles Cornwallis, commanders of the British military forces, intended to take the island and utilize it as an operating base to subdue and capture Charleston harbor and the city. Nine British warships mounting nearly 270 cannon pounded American positions on Sullivan's Island. Clinton and Cornwallis's ground forces, utilizing small boats, were to attack Col. William Moultrie's garrison from the rear, but treacherous tides and turbid waters, coupled with American infantry, prevented the British ground forces from landing. Colonel Moultrie, controlling only thirty-one cannon in an uncompleted sand fort, ordered his men to not waste ammunition and powder. At one point Moultrie's cannoneers ceased firing altogether in order to reserve powder for muskets that would surely be needed against a land attack. Approximately four hundred Continental soldiers thoroughly repulsed the numerically superior British forces in a ten-hour confrontation. The British military's first test in southern waters failed miserably.[62]

John Butler of Bertie County as a recently enlisted private in the Fourth North Carolina Regiment later stated that he was present at Charleston during

1779), Hooper (1774–1777), and Penn (1775–1780) were active in preparing North Carolina to confront Great Britain militarily. Hewes, Hooper, and Penn were signers of the Declaration of Independence. Caswell served as a general in North Carolina's militia and as the state's first and fifth governor. Images provided courtesy of the State Archives.

the action at Sullivan's Island.[63] Most assuredly, his fellow county recruits who enlisted in the North Carolina regiments in Bertie County in April and May were likewise present.

On June 5—five days after British forces departed the Wilmington-Cape Fear River area—the North Carolina Council of Safety convened in Wilmington. For seven weeks the council, under the presidency of Cornelius Harnett, daily handled the affairs for the province. The council met in Wilmington through Saturday, June 15, before relocating to Dobbs County. The council principally appointed officers to North Carolina's army regiments and militia units and authorized payments to various persons for sundry expenses incurred (or to be incurred) on behalf of the province. On June 28 the council authorized either of the two provincial treasurers (Samuel Johnston, Northern District, and Richard Caswell, Southern District) to pay £500 to Charles W. Jacocks to enable him to procure provisions for the Edenton District troops on duty at Wilmington.[64]

On Thursday, July 4, 1776, as Capt. Andrew Oliver's Bertie County militiamen and other North Carolinians maintained their vigil at Wilmington, more than 500 miles to the north in Philadelphia, delegates to the Continental Congress signed the Declaration of Independence. Each of North Carolina's delegates—Joseph Hewes, William Hooper, and John Penn—signed the cornerstone document.[65] North Carolina's push for a united colonial declaration as espoused in the "Halifax Resolves" had come to realization.

Peter Dauge's militia regiment was still stationed at Wilmington on July 31 when Captain Oliver's company reported thirty-eight privates fit for duty. Seventeen men were absent from the ranks—fourteen were reported sick, and three were on furlough.[66] By early August it was clear to the province's council of safety that the threat of an imminent British invasion of North Carolina had passed. The British forces that had initially sailed into the Cape Fear basin had departed and reassembled in Charleston harbor, where they besieged and attacked the port city. On August 8 the council of safety wrote to Gen. John Ashe, ordering him to dismiss the militia brigade under his command. Ashe received the order during the evening of August 12. Early the following morning he dismissed the militiamen, including Oliver's Bertie County contingent, and issued "Marching Orders" for the citizen soldiers to return home.[67]

On October 15 Bertie County voters elected William Gray, Noah Hinton, John Johnston, Thomas Pugh, and Zedekiah Stone to represent their community at the forthcoming Fifth Provincial Congress. That body convened at Halifax on Tuesday, November 12. Seventy-nine delegates (of 169 who were elected) were present when the congress assembled. Gray, Hinton, and Stone were present from Bertie County. Johnston appeared on November 20. Apparently Thomas Pugh (lieutenant colonel of the Bertie County militia) did not attend the congress. Eventually nearly every elected delegate appeared and unanimously chose Richard Caswell (Dobbs County) as president of the body.[68]

The congress agreed to and published the North Carolina Constitution on December 18, 1776. The body did not submit the document to a vote of approval by the people but issued an accompanying Declaration of Rights (December 17, 1776). The constitution established North Carolina's framework of government. It affirmed the separation of power among the three branches (legislative, executive, and judicial) of government. The document shifted political power from the governor (who had total governmental control under royal rule) to the General Assembly. Under the new constitution, the governor would be elected and removed by the assembly and react to its direction in managing the state's affairs. The document also provided for a council of state to assist and guide the governor. The General Assembly, comprised of two houses—a senate and a house of commons—held the true power. Each county would have one senator and two commoners. Free men could vote for commoners, but only those owning at least fifty acres of land could vote for senators. To serve in the senate, an individual was required to own 300 acres of land in the county; a member of the house of commons was obliged to own 100 acres. The constitution did not provide for a system of local government. The congress directed that copies of the constitution and bill of rights, signed by the president and secretary, be printed and immediately distributed to each county in the state.[69]

In late November the congress authorized three additional regiments for the North Carolina Continental Line. The Continental Congress previously had authorized the regiments in September 1776. The provincial congress appointed James Hogun (Halifax County) colonel and Robert Mebane (Orange County) lieutenant colonel of the Seventh Regiment; James Armstrong (Pitt County) colonel and James Ingram (Northampton County) lieutenant colonel of the Eighth Regiment; and John Williams (Craven County) colonel and John Luttrell (Chatham County) lieutenant colonel of the Ninth Regiment. Additionally, the congress appointed two Bertie County men to company officerships—John McGlaughon, captain, and Thomas Watson, first lieutenant. McGlaughon assumed command of a company in the Seventh North Carolina Regiment, while Watson served as McGlaughon's subordinate officer.[70]

In business directly affecting residents of Bertie County, the Fifth Provincial Congress on December 4 appointed Zedekiah Stone to be a commissioner to purchase firearms for the state's troops. (That action was actually a reaffirmation of Stone, inasmuch as the Fourth Provincial Congress had previously appointed him an arms commissioner for Bertie County in April 1776.) The congress directed either of the state treasurers to provide Stone with £140 to enable him to purchase firearms. A few days later Jonathan Jacocks appeared before the committee of accounts. Jacocks, executor for his deceased brother's (Charles W. Jacocks) estate, presented a number of financial accounts (claims) related to expenses incurred by his brother in providing rations to members of the Edenton District militia. Jacocks produced vouchers totaling more than £1,008. The committee determined that there was a charge for the use of "two provision carts for each company [of minutemen], amounting to £503" that was not listed in "the deceased man's book." Charles had apparently died without hiring wagon masters and before "his accounts could be finished." Therefore, the committee concluded that it was impossible for Jonathan Jacocks to produce the vouchers required by law. The committee recommended to the congress that the charge for the carts be approved, along with the properly vouchered claims. The congress concurred. In total, Jonathan Jacocks was paid more than £1,575 as his deceased brother's representative for rations, provisions, and the hire of carts.[71]

The congress appointed twenty-one Bertie County men as justices of the peace. They were: William Benson, James Bryan, William Bryan, James Campbell, John Campbell, Peter Clifton, Abner Eason, John Freeman, William Ghoby, William Gray, Humphrey Hardy, Jonathan Jacocks, George Lockhart, Reuben Norfleet, Andrew Oliver, Thomas Pugh, William Pugh, Thomas Rhodes, George Ryan, Simon Turner, and Thomas Ward. These men, as a collective group, would in essence serve as the local county government under the provisions of the state constitution.[72]

The congress appointed Richard Caswell as governor and Thomas Burke, William Hooper, and Joseph Hewes as delegates to the "Congress of the United States of America." It also set March 10, 1777, for county elections for senators and representatives to the North Carolina General Assembly. The congress adjourned two days before Christmas.[73]

As 1776 came to an end, North Carolina stood as a declared independent state in the loose union of thirteen American states. The journey down the path to confirmed statehood and absolute independence from Great Britain had only commenced, however. Years of conflict, turmoil, and sacrifice were still to be endured by its residents, including those of Bertie County, before affirmed independence and sovereignty would be achieved from the auspices of the British throne and government.

Notes

1. William L. Saunders, ed., *The Colonial Records of North Carolina*, 10 vols. (Raleigh: State of North Carolina, 1886–1890), 10:11–12; William S. Powell, *North Carolina: A History* (Chapel Hill and London: University of North Carolina Press, 1977), 61; Joseph Hewes to Samuel Johnston, May 11, 23, 1775, Paul H. Smith and Ronald M. Gephart, eds., *Letters of Delegates to Congress, 1774–1789*, 26 vols. (Washington, D.C.: Library of Congress, 1976–2000), 1:342–343, 396–397. Samuel Johnston of Chowan County—a lawyer, assemblyman, governor, and delegate to the Continental Congress (1780–1782)—was one of the most influential leaders in the North Carolina Revolutionary movement.

2. In 1775 North Carolina's militia was generally organized on a regimental basis at the county level. North Carolina law (enacted during royal rule) stipulated that each captain of a company was required to muster his command once every six months, and the colonel of each regiment was required to hold a general muster annually at the courthouse of his county. The law further mandated that all freemen and servants within the province between

the ages of sixteen and sixty be members of the militia, except that certain categories of individuals (such as royal officials, members of the assembly, ministers, justices, physicians, and surgeons) were exempted. Militiamen were responsible for furnishing their arms, ammunition, and accouterments. The governor (or a designated commander-in-chief in the absence of the governor) was authorized to call into service the province's militia. Walter Clark, ed., *The State Records of North Carolina*, 16 vols. (11–26) (Raleigh: State of North Carolina, 1895–1906), 23:940–945.

3. Jeffrey J. Crow, *A Chronicle of North Carolina during the American Revolution, 1763–1789* (Raleigh: Division of Archives and History, Department of Cultural Resources, 1975), 21.
Because of the paucity of muster rolls, pay rolls, and returns for North Carolina's militia units, the author was unable to comprehensively identify all "influential men" who were officers in the province's militia and who opposed Gov. Josiah Martin's action during the prewar crisis. Nonetheless, the author was able to identify a number of members of the province's prewar legislative assemblies of the early 1770s who were also officers in the province's militia prior to 1775. These men were: Samuel Jarvis, John Woodhouse, Samuel Smith, Joel Lane, Solomon Perkins, Michael Rogers, Tignal Jones, Nathan Joyner, and George Wynns. The author is confident that additional men similarly served both in assemblies and as militia officers. Furthermore, the author identified more than three dozen members of the province's prewar assemblies who were subsequently appointed militia officers by the provincial congress. It is the author's opinion that the men who served in North Carolina's legislative assemblies under royal rule and later served as militia officers under the revolutionary government would have been at odds with Governor Martin during the crisis leading up to the outbreak of hostilities in North Carolina.

4. On May 18 the Continental Congress resolved that there was "indubitable evidence that a design is formed by the British Ministry of making a cruel invasion from the province of Quebec, upon these colonies [New York, New Hampshire, Massachusetts, and Connecticut], for the purpose of destroying our lives and liberties, and some steps have actually been taken to carry the said design into execution." Worthington Chauncey Ford, ed., *Journals of the Continental Congress*, 34 vols. (Washington, D.C.: Government Printing Office, 1904–1937), 2:55–60, 65, 74–75, 85, 91–92.

5. Saunders, *Colonial Records*, 10:20–23.

6. Ford, *Journals of the Continental Congress*, 2:106–107.

7. Alan D. Watson, "The Committees of Safety and the Coming of the American Revolution in North Carolina, 1774–1776," *North Carolina Historical Review* 73 (April 1996): 148.

8. Saunders, *Colonial Records*, 4:224, 1181; 5:232, 10:205. Col. Thomas Whitmell, a respected member of Bertie County's political and societal order, epitomized the stature commensurate with his position as the top officer in the county's "gentlemen's service" (militia officerships).

9. Watson, "Committees of Safety," 148. The author concluded that despite the lack of extant muster and/or pay rolls, it is obvious that the Bertie County militia companies mustered

during the spring of 1775; otherwise, county officials likely would not have had a definitive basis for concluding that the militiamen were short of gunpowder.

10. Crow, *A Chronicle of North Carolina*, 23; Powell, *North Carolina*, 62. John Ashe and Cornelius Harnett resided in New Hanover County; Robert Howe, in Brunswick County. See Saunders, *Colonial Records*, 9:1178–1179.

11. Saunders, *Colonial Records*, 10:88; Powell, *North Carolina*, 62.

12. Saunders, *Colonial Records*, 10:164–167. The author uncovered no election return or other documentation to confirm the date and the specific results of the voting for Bertie County's delegates to the provincial congress. However, based on information from the cited source, the author concluded that such an election was held consistent with Samuel Johnston's request of July 10.

13. Saunders, *Colonial Records*, 10:164–170; Ford, *Journals of the Continental Congress*, 1:75–80.

14. Saunders, *Colonial Records*, 10:170–174.

15. Saunders, *Colonial Records*, 10:174–175, 186.

16. Saunders, *Colonial Records*, 10:164–165, 186–188, 287; Ford, *Journals of the Continental Congress*, 2:107. The provincial council accepted Whitmill Pugh's resignation as an ensign in Capt. Michael Payne's company of the Second North Carolina Regiment on October 20, 1775.

17. Saunders, *Colonial Records*, 10:196–197, 207.

18. Saunders, *Colonial Records*, 10:199, 207.

19. Saunders, *Colonial Records*, 10:196–198.

20. Saunders, *Colonial Records*, 10:198.

21. Saunders, *Colonial Records*, 10:199–200. The designations "regiment" and "battalion" were used interchangeably by North Carolina and Continental Congress leaders. Following historian Hugh F. Rankin's practice in *The North Carolina Continentals*, the author has employed the designation "regiment" throughout, except for quotations. See Hugh F. Rankin, *The North Carolina Continentals* (Chapel Hill: University of North Carolina Press, 1971), xiv.

22. Saunders, *Colonial Records*, 10:200.

23. Saunders, *Colonial Records*, 10:204–205.

24. Saunders, *Colonial Records*, 10:208–210.

25. Saunders, *Colonial Records*, 10:214.

26. Whitmel Hill was born in Bertie County, where he resided until about late 1774 or early 1775. Bertie County deed (M-206), dated November 1774, indicates that he and his wife were residents of Bertie County when they sold land to Josiah Williams. This document is

the last one to show Hill's residence as Bertie County. Bertie County deed (M-516), dated April 1775, notes his residence as Halifax County. An October 1777 deed (M-475) indicates that Hill was residing in Martin County. Hill was a Martin County delegate at the Third Provincial Congress, but he continued to have dealings and own property in Bertie County even after changing his residence to Martin. For example, in February 1780, Bertie County justices authorized Hill to construct a "Publick Grist Mill" across "Flagg Run where he ownes both sides." During that same session the justices authorized him "to keep two swinging gates a Cross the Road that Leads from his Ferry through the Uneroy Marshes." Cited deeds, Bertie County Register of Deeds Office, Windsor (hereafter cited as Bertie County deed(s), with book and page of subject document); Saunders, *Colonial Records*, 10:165; Weynette Parks Haun, comp., *Bertie County, North Carolina, Court Minutes, 1772–1780, Book IV* (Durham: the compiler, 1979), 113.

27. Saunders, *Colonial Records*, 10:208, 212, 214–215.

28. Saunders, *Colonial Records*, 10:215.

29. Saunders, *Colonial Records*, 10:213. The author found no minutes or other official records for a Bertie County committee of safety.

30. Saunders, *Colonial* Records, 10:220; Powell, *North Carolina*, 62.

31. Saunders, *Colonial* Records, 10:283, 286–287, 292, 294.

32. Samuel Johnston to Richard Caswell, Joseph Hewes, and William Hooper, November 5, 1775, Smith and Gephart, *Letters of Delegates*, 2:393–394; Ford, *Journals of the Continental Congress*, 3:387–388. In addition to directing that the two North Carolina regiments be incorporated into the Continental army, the Continental Congress instructed North Carolina officials to contact their counterparts in Pennsylvania and South Carolina to seek "so much gun powder" as those two provinces could spare and provide it to North Carolina; directed the North Carolina Provincial Congress (or "committee of safety" [provincial council]) to employ immediately all of the gunsmiths in the colony to manufacture muskets and bayonets; and recommended that the North Carolina Provincial Congress (or "committee of safety" [provincial council]) substitute militia units for minuteman units, should the minutemen prove to be an inadequate "method" for defending the colony.

33. Weynette Parks Haun, comp., *North Carolina Revolutionary Army Accounts, Secretary of State, Treasurer's & Comptroller's Papers, Journal "A" (Public Accounts), 1775–1776* (Durham: the compiler, 1988), 58 (hereafter cited as Haun, *Army Accounts, Journal A*); Weynette Parks Haun, comp., *North Carolina Revolutionary Army Accounts, Accounts of the United States with North Carolina [Treasurer, State], Book C, [Part XIV]* (Durham: the compiler, 1999), 1877.

34. Colonel Howe's command entered Norfolk on December 14. On New Year's Day 1776, British naval artillery began bombarding Norfolk. The British landed troops, who set fire to the town, totally destroying it. The destruction of Norfolk served no military purpose, but the act inflamed Virginians and North Carolinians and hastened the development of a sentiment for independence. R. D. W. Connor, *History of North Carolina: The Colonial and Revolutionary Periods (1584–1783)* (Chicago and New York: Lewis Publishing Company,

1919), 383–384. Muster rolls for North Carolina's Continental Line regiments are meager. The author thoroughly reviewed available records and documents (letters, pension files, and battle reports/accounts) with a view toward documenting any Bertie County inhabitants who may have joined Colonel Howe's command. He identified none. While it appears that no Bertie County men were members of the subject regiment in early December 1775, the author cannot conclude such with absolute certainty because of the paucity of official records. Information derived from pension files for a number of non-Bertie County members of Howe's regiment provides documentation of the assembling of the regiment at Edenton in early December 1775. Edmond Love, declaration dated May 3, 1833, Revolutionary War pension file for Edmond Love (S4563); Caleb Mason, declaration dated February 8, 1821, pension file for Caleb Mason (S1917); James Skipper, declaration dated September 16, 1834, pension file for James Skipper (R9639); and Augustin Wilson, declaration dated July 22, 1832, pension file for Augustin Wilson (S7920). The foregoing pension files are found in Revolutionary War Pension and Bounty Land Warrant Files, 1800–1900, (microfilm, M804), Record Group 15, National Archives, Washington, D.C. (hereafter cited as Revolutionary War pension files); Saunders, *Colonial Records*, 10:188, 287.

Regarding the Bertie men's apparent preference for militia service over serving in the army, Col. Alexander Martin of the Second North Carolina Regiment later declared that "it is vain to attempt inlisting Volunteers in any part of . . . [North Carolina] when the Militia have gained such preference to the regular Service." Alexander Martin to Richard Caswell, April 20, 1777, Richard Caswell, Governors Papers, State Archives.

35. Saunders, *Colonial Records*, 10:1027–1032; *North Carolina Gazette* (New Bern), December 22, 1775; Watson, "Committees of Safety," 145–147; Cullen Pollock, a commissioner for the town of Windsor (and a grantor of deeds for acquisition of lots in the town), L-163 (December 29, 1768), L-179 (two deeds dated October 6, 1768), M-24 (June 27, 1769), and M-167 (December 9, 1768); Clark, *State Records*, 23:755. Clement Hall was appointed a lieutenant in the Second North Carolina Regiment on September 1, 1775. See Saunders, *Colonial Records*, 10:187.

In addition to Lieutenant Hall, Ann Pollock named a number of other officers of the Second North Carolina Regiment (which, at the time, was staging in Edenton in preparation to marching to southeastern Virginia) who were directly involved with the treatment inflicted upon Cullen Pollock. The officers, all residents of the Albemarle Sound region, were: Michael Payne, captain; Edward "Ned" Vail Jr., lieutenant (and son of Brig. Gen. Edward Vail of the Edenton District militia); Henry I. Toole, captain; and Joseph Worth, lieutenant-to-be. According to Mrs. Pollock, the soldiers acted under "express" orders of prominent Edenton citizen Thomas Benbury, lieutenant colonel of the Edenton District militia, member of the committee of safety, delegate to all five provincial congresses, and future Chowan County justice of the peace.

36. Powell, *North Carolina*, 62–63; Crow, *A Chronicle of North Carolina*, 26; Rankin, *North Carolina Continentals*, 29. Rankin's chapter 2, "The Moore's Creek Bridge Campaign," provides a detailed account of the Battle of Moores Creek Bridge, February 27, 1776, and the events that led up to that confrontation.

37. Powell, *North Carolina*, 63; Crow, *A Chronicle of North Carolina*, 27; Rankin, *North Carolina Continentals*, 38; Saunders, *Colonial Records*, 10:472; Haun, *Army Accounts, Journal A*, 58–61. The author used Ms. Haun's work to compile a roster of Captain Jacocks's company.

38. Haun, *Army Accounts, Journal A*, 58–61. The author estimated the three-day preparation time for Jacocks's company; the officers were paid for twenty-one days' service, whereas the privates were generally paid for eighteen days. The author assumed that the officers were getting the company and materials organized for a period of time (three days) equal to the difference between their service times and those of their men. The author calculated the likely date that the company departed Windsor based on information from (1) Haun's document, (2) Saunders, *Colonial Records*, (3) the distance from Windsor to the Sampson-Duplin County region, and (4) an approximate daily marching distance of thirty miles. Available records do not disclose the dates that the Bertie County troops marched from, or returned to, Windsor.

39. Powell, *North Carolina*, 63; Crow, *A Chronicle of North Carolina*, 27; Rankin, *North Carolina Continentals*, 48–49.

40. John Rhodes, declaration dated November 23, 1832, Revolutionary War pension file for John Rhodes (S4084). Christopher Snail volunteered for the Martin County company and, like Rhodes, later recalled that his company "was marched to a place called Cross Creek, to the relief of Colonel Caswell." Christopher Snail, declaration dated October 1, 1832, Revolutionary War pension file for Christopher Snail (S31383).

41. Saunders, *Colonial Records*, 10:472–473; Weynette Parks Haun, comp., *North Carolina Revolutionary Army Accounts [Treasurer's and Comptroller's Papers], Volume XI, [Part X]*, (Durham: the compiler, 1999), 1250 (hereafter cited as Haun, *Army Accounts, Volume XI*); Weynette Parks Haun, comp., *North Carolina Revolutionary Army Accounts [Treasurer, State], Book B [Part XIII]* (Durham: the compiler, 1999), 1727 (hereafter cited as Haun, *Army Accounts, Book B, Part XIII*); William Jones, declaration dated September 12, 1832, Revolutionary War pension file for William Jones (S8765); Henry Lee, declaration dated October 12, 1832, Revolutionary War pension file for Henry Lee (S8833); Alexander Wheatley, declaration dated August 28, 1832, Revolutionary War pension file for Alexander Wheatley (W102). Jones, Lee, and Wheatley were members of the Martin County militia. Jones stated that Colonel Williams's command marched to Duplin County, where "news arrived that the Tories were defeated at Moore's Creek Bridge." No muster rolls exist to document the identities of the men from Bertie and Martin counties who participated in the expedition. The North Carolina Provincial Congress established the Committee of Claims on April 7, 1776, "to settle and allow military and naval accounts." John Campbell of Bertie County was a member of the committee. Saunders, *Colonial Records*, 10:504.

42. Saunders, *Colonial Records*, 10:499–502, 508, 527.

43. Saunders, *Colonial Records*, 10:502, 512; Crow, *A Chronicle of North Carolina*, 28.

44. Powell, *North Carolina*, 65.

45. Saunders, *Colonial Records*, 10:530.

46. Saunders, *Colonial Records*, 10:560–563.

47. Saunders, *Colonial Records*, 10:572–573, 580–582.

48. Saunders, *Colonial Records*, 10:513, 544, 556; Rankin, *North Carolina Continentals*, 58–60.

49. Saunders, *Colonial Records*, 10:545, 558. The Continental Congress appointed James Moore to the rank of brigadier general in the Continental army on March 1, 1776. See Ford, *Journals of the Continental Congress*, 4:181.

50. Saunders, *Colonial Records*, 10:558–559, 564, 577.

51. Saunders, *Colonial Records*, 10:543, 554–556, 587.

52. Saunders, *Colonial Records*, 10:680; Rankin, *North Carolina Continentals*, 61; Crow, *A Chronicle of North Carolina*, 30.

53. Saunders, *Colonial Records*, 10:517.

54. Saunders, *Colonial Records*, 10:506, 508–509, 520.
On June 26, 1775, the Continental Congress recommended that in case the North Carolina Provincial Congress thought it "absolutely necessary" for the support of the American Association and the safety of the colony to raise a military force not exceeding one thousand men, then the Continental Congress would consider the force as an American army and provide for the troops' pay. A force of one thousand men, rank and file, was equivalent to two regiments during the eighteenth century. The North Carolina Provincial Congress authorized the First and Second Regiments North Carolina Continental Line on September 1, 1775. On November 6, 1775, the Continental Congress paid $3,750 to North Carolina, the funds representing "part of the expense incurred" by the province in raising the thousand-man force (First and Second North Carolina Regiments). The funds were paid to North Carolina's delegates to the Continental Congress (William Hooper, Joseph Hewes, and John Penn). On November 28, 1775, the Continental Congress resolved that the two regiments "which the Congress directed to be raised in the province of North Carolina, be increased to the continental establishment." The body further directed that the two regiments be "kept in pay at the expence of the United Colonies for one year from this time, or until the further order of Congress." On January 16, 1776, the Continental Congress resolved that another regiment (the Third) be raised in North Carolina. On March 26, 1776, the Continental Congress resolved that if the North Carolina legislators judged it necessary for the common safety to raise one or two more regiments (the Fourth and Fifth), those units would be "taken into pay of the continent[al establishment] once they were armed, mustered, and fit for service." On April 13, 1776, the provincial congress authorized the Sixth Regiment North Carolina. Since there had been no specific authorization from the Continental Congress to raise a sixth regiment, that unit, once organized, was considered a provincial unit. Ford, *Journals of the Continental Congress*, 2:107, 3:330, 387, 4:59, 237; Saunders, *Colonial Records*, 10:186–187, 513.

55. Saunders, *Colonial Records*, 10:520, 528–529, 543–544.

56. Saunders, *Colonial Records*, 10:166, 524–526, 575, 587, 937; Weynette Parks Haun, comp., *North Carolina Revolutionary Army Accounts, Secretary of State Treasurer's & Comptroller's Papers, Vol. III, Vol. IV, Part III* (Durham: the compiler, 1991), 399–400 (hereafter cited as Haun, *Army Accounts, Part III*); Haun*, Army Accounts, Volume XI*, 1260; Haun, *Army Accounts, Book B, Part XIII*, 1736.

57. Saunders, *Colonial Records*, 10:499, 590; Crow, *A Chronicle of North Carolina*, 28.

58. Betty J. Camin, "Revolutionary War Pension Applications at the NC Archives," *North Carolina Genealogical Society Journal* 11 (August 1985): 170–172.

59. Saunders, *Colonial Records*, 10:543. The author calculated the number of Bertie County residents who enlisted in the First, Third, Fourth, and Fifth North Carolina Regiments in the spring of 1776 from information he compiled for the putative roster of Continental Line troops. The men who enlisted in the subject regiments are identified in the cited roster. See Appendix 1.

60. Clark, *State Records*, 16:1185; William White, declaration dated May 14, 1822, Revolutionary War pension file for William White (S42071); Bertie County Miscellaneous Records, Revolutionary War Papers, C.R.010.928.12, State Archives.

61. William Farmer, who enlisted under Capt. John Pugh Williams in Bertie County, later stated that he joined his regiment at Edenton before marching to Wilmington. Zachariah Carter stated "he took the State oath [at Windsor] . . . from thence he marched [to] Edenton." Rankin noted that the North Carolina Continentals were "raised in haste to repulse a possible invasion" of South Carolina. William Farmer, declaration dated August 25, 1818, Revolutionary War pension file of William Farmer (S35919); Rankin, *North Carolina Continentals*, 69; Camin, "Pension Applications," 171.

62. Robert K. Wright Jr., *The Continental Army* (Washington, D.C.: Center of Military History, United States Army, 1963), 75; Rankin, *North Carolina Continentals*, 74–75.

63. John Butler, declaration dated November 17, 1820, Revolutionary War pension file for John Butler (S41463).

64. Saunders, *Colonial Records*, 10:618–647.

65. Ford, *Journals of the Continental Congress*, 5:510–515.

66. Saunders, *Colonial Records*, 10:680. In August 1833 William Freeman, a former resident of Bertie County, stated that in 1776 he served for three months in the militia under the command of Capt. Andrew Oliver at Wilmington. William Freeman, declaration dated August 20, 1833, Revolutionary War pension file for William Freeman (W10042).

67. Saunders, *Colonial Records*, 10:743–744.

68. Saunders, *Colonial Records*, 10:520, 913, 915–916, 927.

69. Saunders, *Colonial Records*, 10:961, 1003–1013; Powell, *North Carolina*, 67; Crow, *A Chronicle of North Carolina*, 32–33.

70. Saunders, *Colonial Records*, 10:941–942, 944, 948. The author uncovered no citations or military records for Watson other than the source cited in this note. McGlaughon's name is also variously noted in records as "Glaughon."

On September 16, 1776, the Continental Congress authorized the thirteen states to enlist eighty-eight regiments for the Continental Line. North Carolina's "quota" was nine regiments, three more than had previously been authorized. Ford, *Journals of the Continental Congress*, 5:762.

71. Saunders, *Colonial Records*, 10:524, 952, 968, 989; Haun, *Army Accounts, Part III*, 399; Haun, *Army Accounts, Volume XI*, 1261; Haun, *Army Accounts, Book B, Part XIII*, 1736.

72. Saunders, *Colonial Records,* 10:992–993.

73. Saunders, *Colonial Records*, 10:977, 989, 1001, 1003.

"STAND UP FOR THE KING"

The American colonies' (subsequently states') war for independence was not only a conflict of rebellion against British authorities and rule but at certain levels and within certain locales it was also a civil struggle between various factions within the colonies. Civil turmoil between Whigs and Tories existed throughout the thirteen colonies, including North Carolina. While Brig. Gen. James Moore's crushing defeat of Gov. Josiah Martin's Loyalist forces at Moores Creek Bridge in February 1776 subdued overt Tory activity and momentum in North Carolina, by the spring of 1777 a faction was showing signs of resurgence and renewed activity in the state's northeastern region. The resurgence and reinvigorated activism occurred almost simultaneously with the implementation of the new government under the state constitution. Gov. Richard Caswell wielded little power under the constitution.[1] Nonetheless, he and the new state government would be tested in the coming months as insurrection against the rebellion was brewing within the state.

Following the campaign against Martin's Tories, the Fourth Provincial Congress in May 1776 instituted measures intended to intimidate and further subdue the Loyalists. On May 13 the congress resolved that any inhabitant of North Carolina who thereafter took up arms against America, or who gave intelligence or aid to the "open enemies" of the province, was to be convicted of the facts by a vote of the provincial congress or other appropriate judicial power. An individual so convicted was to "forfeit all his goods and chattels, lands and tenements, to the people of the . . . Colony." The congress, or other representative entity of the provincial government, would thereupon dispose of the property. Moreover, the individual would be confined as a prisoner of war unless "mitigated or pardoned by the [provincial] Congress, or other general representation."[2]

In North Carolina, substantial numbers of Loyalists staunchly supported and defended the Crown. As with most rebellions, support for the Revolution was not unanimous or uniform across North Carolina or within distinct regions. The Loyalists were not a homogeneous group, as their ranks were comprised of people from all social and economic groups—farmers, merchants, shopkeepers, officeholders, and professional people. Similarly, they held differing persuasions and reasons for supporting King George III. While there were many conflicting reports about the number, wealth, activity, and influence of the disaffected persons, such reports were sufficiently convincing to cause George III and his informants (including Gov. Josiah Martin) to believe optimistically that North Carolina was "filled" with Loyalists.[3]

Bertie County, politically dominated by Whigs, had supported North Carolina's cause and moves for independence. The county's delegates to the provincial congresses had served on a number of key committees, and the delegates had voted in the affirmative on critical resolutions and measures. Nevertheless, within the county there were persons who did not approve of the Whig actions and did not support the war against Great Britain. The number of persons who supported King George III is obviously not known. According to one eminent North Carolina historian, "while Bertie contributed to the successful patriot cause, evidence suggests that many in the county were reluctant to break with England. The county did not seem to be a vigorous participant in the early proceedings that led to the revolution."[4]

One of the first inhabitants of Bertie County publicly to espouse support for the Crown was Rev. Francis Johnston, rector of Society Parish in the county. In January 1768 he and fellow clergyman Henry Burgess had departed North Carolina for England to receive "Holy orders." In 1770 Rev. Francis Johnston returned to the colony and located in Bertie County, where he succeeded Rev. Thomas Floyd as rector of Society Parish. Johnston, as a man of the Church of England, opposed the American colonies' move for independence from Great Britain. His stance drew the ire of North Carolina's three delegates to the 1775 session of the Continental Congress. On June 19, 1775, the delegates—Richard Caswell, Joseph Hewes, and William Hooper—penned a letter to the colony's committees of safety in which they ostracized Johnston. According to the three men, "Johnston [was] a pensioned tool of the ministry." The delegates declared that Johnston spoke "the intentions of [an] administration in a language too plain to leave any thing to doubt." According to the three, Johnston's writing asserted that "The slaves should be set free, an act which the lovers of liberty must surely commend, if they are furnished with arms for defence and utensils for husbandry, and settled in some simple form of government within the country, they may be more honest and grateful than their masters." Freeing and arming slaves on behalf of the British government represented a reprehensible proposition to the congressional delegates and the Whigs. Caswell, Hewes, and Hooper termed Johnston a "prostituted court-favorite."[5]

By the spring of 1777, a conspiratorial movement against the Whigs in the initial guise of loyalty to the Anglican Church was under way in Bertie and other counties of the Albemarle Sound–Roanoke River region. The fundamental agenda of the conspiracy, opposition to introduction of the Roman Catholic religion, may have originated in Virginia. By March 1777 John Llewelyn of Martin County had become the self-proclaimed champion of the plot in northeastern North Carolina and was espousing anti-Whig rhetoric to his friends. Llewelyn, a planter of substantial means, had been appointed a justice for Martin County by the provincial congress in December 1776. Obviously, the congressional delegates did not doubt that Llewelyn supported their rebel cause; otherwise, they surely would not have granted him a judicial appointment under the auspices of the new state government and constitution.[6]

In late March Llewelyn attended a muster of the Tyrrell County militia at Plymouth. (Plymouth is presently the county seat of Washington County; in 1777 the town and the surrounding area formed the western portion of Tyrrell County.) Llewelyn departed the muster in the company of fellow Martin County residents James Rawlins and John Carter. As the three men traveled toward their homes, Llewelyn mentioned that "the Country was Like[ly] to become subject to popery." He then commented that there was "a Necessity of Indeavoring to seek relief" (from the purported introduction of Roman Catholicism) and that he thought the proper means of such relief was a written instrument or oath to which people might agree (to support the Anglican religion and oppose the Roman religion). A few days thereafter, Llewelyn and his son William visited Rawlins at his home, where the elder Llewelyn reportedly "declared the form [a religious constitution for the developing conspiracy] . . . contained much writing." Llewelyn requested Rawlins to write (draft) an oath, to which Rawlins refused. Even so, Rawlins agreed to assist Llewelyn "in Hope of a Reward."[7] The embryonic roots of the conspiracy and a secret subversive society had sprouted.

The fundamental agenda of the Llewelyn conspiracy was opposition to the Roman Catholic religion. This line engraving shows four bishops crossing hands over the Quebec Bill, which allowed French Canadians the freedom to practice Catholicism. Whigs and Tories both preyed on anti-Catholic fears during the Revolution. Image from the *London Magazine* (July 1774), p. 312.

As early as 1715 the North Carolina colonial legislature had recognized the Anglican Church as the only established sect to have public encouragement. Because of the rural nature of North Carolina's population, Anglican churches and ministers were rare; but when the Revolution erupted, those Anglican clergy in the colony (such as Rev. Francis Johnston) tended to remain loyal to the Crown or neutral. Some Anglicans even departed North Carolina and relocated to Canada after the war began. The Revolution endangered the Anglican Church, and many members who held strong ties to the institution also felt deep loyalty to the Crown and Parliament. Thus, the political-religious environment in Bertie and other Whig-controlled counties (including Edgecombe, Hyde, Martin, and Tyrrell) was set as the Whigs plunged North Carolina into the war. Then, about late 1776, rumors circulated that more than a dozen members of the Fifth Provincial Congress wanted to introduce the "Romish religion," in which people "worship Images." To John Llewelyn, a devout Anglican, it was imperative that all good members of his religion stand to uphold their Protestant faith and halt "Popery." One of the rumored supporters of the introduction of the Catholic religion was Whitmel Hill, a fellow Martin County justice and delegate to the provincial congress (and also a former resident of Bertie County).[8]

Article XXXIV of the state constitution likely inflamed Llewelyn and other Anglicans, in that it disestablished the Anglican Church as the singularly preferred religion in the state. The article provided that "there shall be no Establishment of any one religious Church or Denomination in this State in Preference to any other." It also stipulated that no person "on any pretence whatsoever, [shall] be compelled to attend any Place of worship contrary to his own Faith or Judgment, or be obliged to pay for the Purchase of any Glebe, or the building of any House of Worship, or for the maintenance of any Minister or Ministry, contrary to what he believes right, or has voluntarily and personally engaged to perform." Finally, the article provided that "all persons shall be at Liberty to exercise their own mode of Worship." The constitutional passage did not specifically refer to the Roman Catholic religion, but it did provide Llewelyn a basis for concluding that his beloved church would no longer be the preferred denomination in the state. Whitmel Hill had served on the congressional committee that drafted the constitution. Additionally, he had been a prominent member of a committee that had investigated Loyalist activities. Thus Llewelyn, whose beliefs and inclinations were contrary to Hill's positions, subsequently considered Hill an enemy.[9]

Llewelyn was the chieftain of the conspiracy. Within Martin County three men—James Sherrard, Daniel Leggett, and James Hayes—intimately involved themselves in the plot with Llewellyn. The men traveled about the Albemarle Sound-Roanoke River region seeking to enlist participants. Within short order a network of clandestine enclaves arose within counties situated in close proximity to Martin County. Eventually Llewelyn had subordinates in each county of the region who, as his lieutenants, were leaders of the conspiracy in their home counties and were termed "senior wardens" (based on Anglican terminology).[10]

Sometime in the spring of 1777, Llewellyn or one of his Martin County counterparts proposed the plot to Thomas Bogg, a Loyalist sea captain who resided in Bertie County but maintained Tyrrell County affiliations. According to William Skiles, also of Bertie, "Capt. Bogg approved the scheme highly to [James] Sherrard," one of Llewelyn's confidants. Even though Bogg reportedly approved of the scheme, he was also "rather fearful of its success."[11]

As Llewelyn and his cohorts were organizing the plot and beginning to indoctrinate members, the first session of the General Assembly under the new state constitution convened in New Bern on April 7. The body passed two statutes that the conspirators specifically deplored. First, it enacted a new state militia law that, among other stipulations, provided that "all persons within the ages of sixteen and fifty shall be liable to be drafted [for active military service], and every person so drafted, [was] obliged to serve or find an able bodied person" as a substitute. (The statute also continued in effect the provisions made by the provincial congress in May 1776 "for drafting the militia in . . . several counties in this State.") Second, the legislature enacted a statute that required all persons residing within North Carolina to "pay Allegiance to the State." The law mandated that residents subscribe to a specific oath of allegiance:

> I will bear faithful and true Allegiance to the State of North Carolina, and will to the utmost of my Power, support and maintain, and defend the independent Government thereof, against George the Third, King of Great Britain, and his Successors, and the Attempts of any other Person, Prince, Power, State, or Potentate, who by secret Arts, Treasons, Conspiracies, or by open Force, shall attempt to subvert the same, and will in every Respect conduct myself as a peaceful, orderly Subject; and that I will disclose and make known to the Governor, some Member of the Council of State, or some Justice of the Peace, all Treasons, Conspiracies, and Attempts, committed or intended against the State, which shall come to my Knowledge.

Those persons who refused to subscribe publicly to the oath were to depart North Carolina within sixty days of their refusals.[12]

The conspirators unanimously viewed the "oath of allegiance" mandated for all residents as absolutely appalling. They vehemently opposed it, swore singularly and severally that they would not recite it, and declared their support for other men who refused to submit to it. William Tyler of Martin County encouraged others to "oppose any power that shood ofeer [offer] the State oath." James Sherrard represented the oath to others "in a very dreadful light."[13]

Additionally, the law stipulated that certain activities undertaken by individuals to harm North Carolina (or the United States) were to be viewed as treason or misprision of treason. Specifically, the statute provided that any person who:

- attempted to convey intelligence to the enemies of the state or of the United States;
- publicly and deliberately spoke or wrote against the state's public defense;

- maliciously and advisedly endeavored to excite the people to resist the government of the state or persuade them to return to a dependence on the British Crown;
- knowingly spread false or dispiriting news;
- maliciously or advisedly terrified and discouraged the people from enlisting into the service of the state;
- stirred up or excited tumults, disorders, or insurrections in the state; or
- disposed the people to favor the enemy or oppose and endeavor to prevent the measures carried on in support of the freedom and independence of the United States

was liable to be "legally convicted" by the evidence of two or more creditable witnesses and "adjudged guilty" of misprision of treason. Those persons so convicted were subject to being imprisoned and forfeiting to the state one-half of their lands, tenements, goods, and chattels. Further, any person who formed, or was in any way concerned in forming any plot or conspiracy that betrayed the state, or the United States, was subject to being charged with treason.[14] Llewelyn's budding conspiracy clearly fell within the scope of activities targeted by the law.

Llewelyn's conspiratorial plot evolved and quickly became more complex as to its objectives. Its participants were to be sworn to secrecy, asked to commit to an oath, and communicate with other persons only after pre-established confirmations of the parties' participation were substantiated. The conspirators devised a constitution that contained various articles. First, the members were to "stand up" and protect the Anglican Church. Second, the members opposed militia drafts by the state and were committed to defend and protect all men who were drafted or "[im]pressed to go to War against there [sic] will." Third, the participants were to defend and protect distressed or oppressed persons (i.e., Loyalists) and those individuals "called Tories." Further, each member was to "provide himself" with a half pound of gunpowder and lead (for musket balls/projectiles).[15] Members of the society from Pitt and Martin counties were to take possession of the state's military magazine at Halifax and secure the arms and ammunition stockpiled there. Daniel Leggett had reputedly boasted that "about half of the 5th Regiment of Continental Forces raised in this state [North Carolina] were Friends to their Cause."[16] (Obviously, if Leggett made such a statement, he was totally exaggerating for effect, since (1) it would have been impossible to indoctrinate two hundred soldiers, and (2) so many soldiers, assembled together in a military organization, would very likely have been unable to maintain the code of secrecy meticulously implemented by the primary conspirators.)

Peleg Belote of Bertie County was viewed as a candidate for the society. In early June, Absalom Leggett (Martin County) talked with Belote concerning a "Report which was then prevalent among some People that there was a design to impose a new Religion on the People, and Compel them to worship Images." Both men expressed a "very strong disapprobation of such a design." Leggett then persuaded Belote to attend a forthcoming sermon in Martin County to be preached by James Sherrard. Belote agreed to attend and in a few days traveled to Sherrard's residence accompanied by Leggett and his son.

At the residence, James Rawlins approached Belote and inquired if he could keep a secret, to which Belote replied in the affirmative. Rawlins then produced a book (likely a prayer book) out of his pocket and gave it to Belote, who kissed it and promised "to keep secret what Rawlins" was about to tell him. Rawlins conveyed that a "good many" persons had concluded to support the Church of England. Rawlins again inquired if Belote could keep a secret, and, for the second time, he affirmed that he could and "again kissed the book in ratification of a promise of this kind." Rawlins told Belote that "Sherrard was the Man" and gave him a stick with three notches, which he was to show to Sherrard. Belote spent the night at Sherrard's residence, and the next morning the two men walked out to Sherrard's barn to keep from being overheard, as at that time a number of people were in the area to attend church service. Belote presented the notched stick to Sherrard, who retrieved a box "concealed in a private part of the barn." Sherrard extracted from the box a document that in essence called for the members of the society "to support the religion that had been used, to decide disputes among the subscribers through arbitration, and to oppose draughts . . . and protect Men being draughted from being obliged to serve." The men left the barn, and Sherrard raised one more item he had forgotten to mention to Belote—the latter should acquire a half pound of gunpowder and two pounds of lead.[17]

Absalom Leggett also targeted William Skiles of Bertie County as a potential member of the society. According to Skiles, he heard Leggett say that he would not serve as a soldier if he were drafted. Leggett reportedly further stated that "if any person draughted should consent to go in the Army, they [members of the society] should shoot him on the spot." Leggett administered the oath of secrecy to Skiles and conveyed to him the tenets of the society's constitution—support the Anglican religion, defend and protect drafted and distressed persons, and maintain the secrecy of it. He gave Skiles a small stick

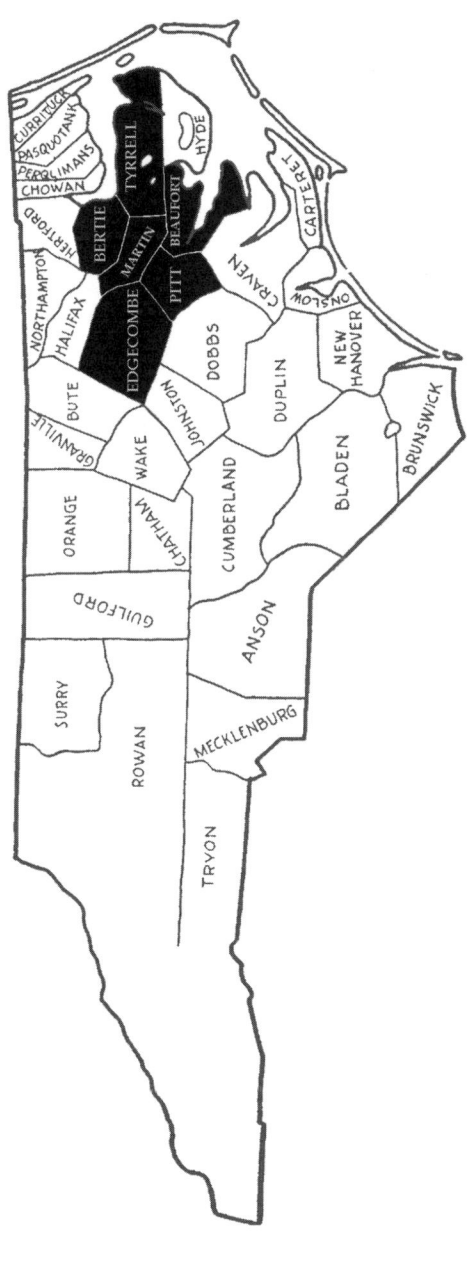

John Llewelyn, chieftain of a 1777 conspiracy against the nascent state of North Carolina, resided in Martin County. His diabolical scheme drew supporters in a number of counties in the state's northeastern region, including Beaufort, Bertie, Edgecombe, Pitt, and Tyrrell, as well as present-day Washington County. Map by L. Polk Denmark from David Leroy Corbitt, *The Formation of the North Carolina Counties, 1663–1943* (Raleigh: Division of Archives and History, 1987), 286.

with three notches, to be provided to another person who would inquire what the stick was for and then receive the sign of the society. Leggett also informed Skiles that members of the society were intending to seize several arms magazines.[18]

Other Bertie County men were approached to join the "club." Absalom Leggett contacted Michael Ward, swore him to secrecy, and gave him some signs so that he could recognize the "Brethren" of the society. Ward was to appear before Daniel Leggett for further instructions. "Some time" passed before Ward and John Garrett (Tyrrell County) visited Peleg Belote at his residence, at which Daniel Leggett again swore Ward to secrecy. Ward was advised that "this Clubb . . . was to stand up for the King," oppose drafts, and protect all deserters.[19] Absalom Leggett also approached John Allen, whereas John Garrett approached Samuel Hyman. And at least one other individual, William Burkett, upon learning of the society, took the initiative to join. Burkett visited Absalom Leggett "to enquire . . . how he might be initiated into a new Club."[20]

As the spring turned into summer, Llewellyn's secret society was growing and recruiting sympathetic persons. But Llewellyn was becoming even more radical, deluded, and, apparently, even a bit paranoid. The conspiracy had been conceived under Llewelyn's idealist goal of protecting and perpetuating the Anglican Church, but by June he was inserting his personally retributive aims, including murder, assassination, and civil chaos. Llewellyn told James Rawlins that if they "could destroy Whitmel Hill, Colonel [William] Williams, Thomas Hunter, Nathan Mayo, Colonel Salter and one Taylor, then the Country would soon be settled In Behalf of the King." Llewelyn also held grudges against the brothers Nathan and James Mayo, Whig leaders. Llewelyn was convinced that the brothers were watching him. Llewelyn had boasted to a number of his associates that if he could get ten men to join him, he would kill every one of them (Martin County Whig leaders). Llewelyn further felt that "it would be a good scheme to Git some Body to Diseffect the negroes." An uprising by slaves, in Llewelyn's view, "would draw the soldiers out of Halifax," enabling him and others to kidnap Gov. Richard Caswell and seize the magazine at that place. At the time when Llewelyn proposed the "scheme," Caswell was absent from Halifax, so it was dropped for the short term. Llewelyn, fully aware of how extreme the plan was and that not every member of the society would concur, threatened to kill anyone who divulged the plan. Llewelyn was now actively contemplating assassination and murder. Moreover, he considered journeying to New York to meet with Gen. Sir William Howe, commander of all British army forces in the American states, to elicit his support. Llewelyn and James Rawlins set out for New York sometime about the latter part of June, but only reached Scotland Neck (about forty-five miles) before they gave up on the trip—a less-than-enthusiastic effort to visit General Howe for men so adamantly avowed to their scheme of chaos.[21]

Tuesday, July 1, 1777, was a day of revelation in Windsor as Bertie County justices took sworn depositions from several residents of the county—John Brogden, William Brogden, and William Skiles. Bertie County Whig officials had placed all three men under "Sundrey Suspicions" regarding their involvement in the conspiracy. The men may have been ousted by an individual who lived near them. William Burkett, a poor illiterate citizen who resided in southern Bertie County within close proximity to the Roanoke River voluntarily informed Whig officials of the boding conspiracy. The plot was now unraveling quickly. On that same day, Daniel Leggett, one of Llewelyn's chief subordinates, was busy in Martin and Tyrrell counties seeking additional members for the society. Leggett visited with a number of men during the day, unaware that in Windsor the "game was up" for the society as its principal participants and their secrets and conspiratorial objectives had been divulged.[22]

On Friday, July 4 (the first anniversary of the signing of the Declaration of Independence), former Crown official William Brimage traveled from Bertie to Tyrrell County. Brimage, a prominent resident of Bertie, had presided over the vice admiralty court in 1769 and served as a prosecuting deputy attorney in New Bern in 1771. Residents of Bertie County had elected Brimage one of their delegates to attend the Third Provincial Congress in August 1775, but he had declined. More recently (January 1777), the North Carolina Council of State had appointed him a judge in the Edenton District court of oyer and terminer, but again he refused to act in any official capacity on behalf of the new state government.[23] Thus, on this day Brimage was specifically looking to meet with Daniel Leggett, the conspiracy's senior warden for Tyrrell County.

Brimage arrived at the farm of Thomas Harrison Jr. and inquired as to the whereabouts of Leggett. Soon Brimage found Leggett at the Harrison plantation house. The two men, along with Thomas Harrison Sr., walked away from the house and into the nearby woods, where they conversed regarding the plot. Brimage submitted to the oaths of secrecy and to oppose militia drafts. The three men then separated. Brimage walked back to the house to retrieve his horse, while Harrison and Leggett walked over to Harrison's son's wheat field. In short order Brimage rejoined the other two and met Samuel Black, also a key member of the conspiracy. The four men departed the edge of the wheat field and walked again into the woods, obviously to ensure privacy from other persons about the plantation. Once back in the concealment of the foliated, summertime woods, Leggett proposed to Brimage that he "act as Senior Warden for this Society in Bertie County." Brimage immediately consented, and Leggett swore him "into the said office." Brimage, in his conspiratorial position, was now responsible for "Gaining & Swearing in members in this Association & Conspiracy In the County of Bertie." He asked Leggett for a copy of the conspiracy's constitution, as well as a copy of the required oaths; he obviously needed the documents to enable him to fulfill his duties. Leggett did not have extra copies but promised to deliver them to Brimage the following day. The next morning Thomas Harrison Sr. (at Leggett's request) provided the documents to Samuel Black, who was responsible for transmitting them to Brimage.[24]

William Brimage's appointment as senior warden for Bertie County on July 4 is perplexing from a number of perspectives. Brimage, as a former prominent Crown official, was intensely loyal to King George III. His loyalty had been overtly substantiated, as he declined to attend the Third Provincial Congress (August–September 1775) and, noticeably, had not been involved in Whig activities in Bertie County for more than two years into the war. The Llewelyn conspiracy had been ongoing for at least four months, and Daniel Leggett's father, Absalom Leggett, had personally recruited Bertie County men into its folds. Surely Brimage had been made aware of the plot, or he would not have traveled across Albemarle Sound to Tyrrell County to seek out Daniel Leggett. Therefore, the question arises: did he personally seek to be appointed senior warden in Bertie County, or did Leggett first approach him? Moreover, by July 4 a number of persons had already been called before justices in Bertie, Martin, and Pitt counties and submitted sworn depositions regarding their involvement and knowledge of the conspiracy.

Logically, rumors would have quickly circulated among the populace regarding a topic as fiery as a conspiracy against the state. Had not Brimage become aware of the exposure of the conspiracy? If he had, then was his consent to serve as senior warden a personal act of intense loyalty to the throne, or of animosity toward the Whig leaders? And, obviously unbeknown to Brimage (as well as to Leggett, Black, and Harrison), on the day they gathered at Harrison's plantation, a number of conspirators were in Martin County court a few miles away, providing depositions to county justices.[25] Precisely at the time William Brimage was becoming actively involved with Llewelyn's conspiracy, the cabal was abruptly imploding. Brimage could not have selected a more inopportune time to join the plot than early July, unless he was of the

This deposition, made by David Taylor on June 4, 1777, alleged that Jas. Rollins informed Taylor of a "secret Scheme against the State, for that the Congress had given up the Country to the French to be governed by them, and the Popery would come into the Country." From Chowan County Miscellaneous Records, Chowan County Papers, XV, 1772–1777, State Archives.

opinion that the conspiracy was supported by a sufficient number of persons in the region to withstand the Whig scrutiny and retribution.

As Brimage and the other men were meeting in Tyrrell County, in Martin County, their leader, John Llewelyn, was already fully aware that his conspiracy had been discovered and would quickly disintegrate under the crushing hands of the state's Whig leadership. His violent intrigues would never be executed Within a few days after Llewelyn and Rawlins abandoned their excursion for New York, the men learned that the conspiracy had been discovered. Indeed, two associates—David Taylor and Joseph Taylor—had testified on June 4. And, later in the month, a conspirator was detained with incriminating papers in his pocket. It is unclear who apprised Llewelyn and Rawlins of the lost secrecy of the conspiracy—what surely to them was a revolting and distressing development. They may have continued to perpetuate the conspiracy until

July 4, when five members of their "club" were deposing statements before Martin County justices. In any event, Llewelyn, aware that the plan was no longer secret and that Whig officials would move quickly, persuaded Rawlins to flee and "not be taken by any means." Rawlins fled with his family from Martin County on July 5 and headed toward North Carolina's Outer Banks.[26] Precisely as Rawlins was fleeing, William Brimage was jumping into the plot!

Not every person Llewelyn or his lieutenants approached concurred with or supported the plot. While the conspirators obviously approached only those individuals whom they believed would share their philosophies and views, some solicited persons declined to join the society. As a result, a number of persons became aware of the plot but had not joined the society. Even though such persons had sworn to secrecy, logically they (or some of them) would have been inclined to divulge and discuss such a radical plot with others. Thomas Stubbs Sr. of Tyrrell County, having heard of the association, "used every persuasive means to dissuade Thomas Harrison from being concerned in the scheme."[27]

John Clifton, following a visit to Bertie County about the middle of May, was returning to his home in Anson County when he stopped to see William Tyler in Martin County to discuss "private business." During their discussion, Tyler offered to inform Clifton of the secret society. Clifton was "entirely ignorant" of the group and its agenda. John Staten escorted Clifton to meet with James Rawlins, who, after briefly talking with Clifton, informed him that he (Rawlins) would go find John Llewelyn and bring him to the gathering. Staten and Clifton waited at a schoolhouse about half a mile from Rawlins's residence. Soon Rawlins returned with Llewelyn and his son; all three men were armed. As with all "orientations" to prospective members, Llewelyn swore Clifton to secrecy, advised him of the society's constitution, suggested that he gather gunpowder and lead, and so on. Llewelyn desired that Clifton be a "Reader" (recruiter) for the conspiracy and provided him a "paper." Then, obviously to intimidate Clifton, Llewelyn and Rawlins in unison declared that "they would shoot any Man who divulged the secret."

John Clifton's brother Peter was a Bertie County justice, former sheriff, and delegate to the Fifth Provincial Congress. John may have initially been intrigued with the plot, but "soon after" he left Llewelyn and other men in Martin County, he purportedly began to have reservations about getting involved with the conspirators. He later stated that he disapproved of their purpose and "had a great desire to reveal it [the plot]." Nonetheless, he was fearful of doing so since he had taken an oath to secrecy. His honor (not to violate the oath he had taken) was at stake. Clifton stated that he burned the paper the day after the meeting and that he had not shown it to anyone. He later declared that he never attempted to influence any person to join the "Association." Nevertheless, on August 2, 1777, a Benjamin Morris stated on oath before Martin County justice John Griffin that about the middle of May John Clifton "Wanted him [Morris]" to join "an Arme [army] of men in be halph [behalf] of the King." Morris further swore that Clifton had stated that he [Clifton] would not "Let his too [two] Sons list [enlist] in the Regular Sarvis [service]." Morris concluded that Clifton had tried to "[en]list" him "Against the State."[28]

In Edgecombe County Lt. Col. Henry Irwin of the Fifth North Carolina Regiment, along with about twenty-five soldiers, stopped a group of about thirty men who were involved in the "wicked conspiracy" as they made an "attempt on" Tarboro. Irwin wrote to Governor Caswell on July 16 that "too many evil persons in this and the neighboring Counties" had joined the cabal. Even so, the colonel was hopeful that the affair had run its course, since a number of persons from the county had come to Tarboro and given depositions. He conveyed to the governor that he was "in hopes it [the conspiracy] may be stopped, as many had come and made [known] all the discovery they knew of."[29]

By the middle of July, public excitement surrounding the exposure of John Llewelyn's conspiracy was at a fever pitch as members were brought before Whig justices in a number of counties. During the first sixteen days of the month, at least twenty-four people (twenty-two men and two women) appeared before justices in Bertie (4), Martin (7), and Tyrrell (13) counties and gave sworn depositions. Men who previously had stood in fields, gourd patches, woodlots, and barns and devoutly swore the utmost secrecy to a plot against the new state government were now standing in front of justices appointed by that government and telling all they knew about the conspiracy. The prospect of losing their lands and other property, as well as spending time in North Carolina county jails or being exiled from the state, was not appealing to the seemingly repentant deponents. Looming charges of treason against the state and misprision of treason proved worrisome and highly troubling to the men. Nearly half of those who offered depositions through July 15 were illiterate—they could not read the conspiracy constitution and oath documents and "signed" their depositions with their "marks."[30]

On July 23—more than two months after meeting with Llewelyn and the others—John Clifton could no longer keep the secret. He left Anson County and traveled to see his brother Peter in Bertie County and conveyed his knowledge of the society to his sibling. The following day John and Peter met with Thomas Pugh, Bertie County justice and lieutenant colonel of the county's militia, and John submitted a statement "on oath."[31] By that time, the "Llewelyn conspiracy" had become public knowledge as justices in a number of counties, including Bertie, had already hauled in various members of the society and taken sworn depositions. The fact that the conspiracy had been widely exposed may have influenced John to break his vow of secrecy and testify. There were no secrets to be maintained any longer. John Clifton very likely became worrisomely concerned that he would be implicated as a willing participant in the plot, having personally met with Llewelyn and accepted documentation from the chieftain.

William Brimage decided sometime in July to flee from Bertie County. Surely state and county Whig leaders had to be on the verge of apprehending him, as his involvement in the conspiracy, although brief in duration, was now known. And just as surely, he must have concluded that the Whig leaders would vehemently and publicly ostracize him, a former Crown official caught up in a subversive plot against the new North Carolina government. Indeed, his refusal to perform the functions of judge on behalf of the "New State" government had earned for him "the heavy resentment" of Whig officials. Brimage secretly departed Bertie County, most likely between July 15 and 25.[32]

By July 27 Gov. Richard Caswell had received copies of affidavits from the Edenton justices respecting William Brimage's involvement in the Llewelyn conspiracy. Caswell concluded that it appeared to him "beyond a doubt that he [Brimage] has been one of the powers of their diabolical plan." Brimage was "charged with being in the late conspiracy against the State, and concerned in certain treasonable practices." On the twenty-seventh, Caswell wrote to Maj. David Barrow of the Craven County militia and requested him to obtain orders from Col. William Bryan (of the Craven militia) to dispatch a party of militiamen to "immediately . . . apprehend & bring Mr. Brimage back to Newbern." Caswell recommended that the militia obtain an arrest warrant from a Craven County justice. Caswell badly wanted Brimage arrested, writing: "When he [Brimage] is taken, I will furnish testimony, which, I apprehend, will be sufficient for detaining him in close gaol till his trial. Secrecy is necessary in the present case. A word to the wise is enough."[33]

Simultaneously, Caswell wrote to Robert Smith, a Chowan County justice in Edenton. He directed Smith and Thomas Benbury, a fellow justice, to "assure yourselves that every step . . . shall be taken to secure Mr. Brimage."[34] A region-wide manhunt was instituted in eastern North Carolina.

Major Barrow replied to Caswell on the twenty-eighth that he had already dispatched an officer, Lt. Shadrach Fulcher, with a party of men to find Brimage and "not to return without him, provided he has not left the State." Barrow had also obtained an arrest warrant from Justice James Davis of Craven County. Barrow was under the impression that the Craven County authorities had set in motion the apprehension of Brimage "some days" prior, but upon his inquiry found that it was "neglected."[35]

By the time the manhunt commenced, Brimage had made his way to Ocracoke, or was in close proximity to the little village. He was traveling with another man, who alleged that his name was "Campbell" and who claimed to be a "lieutenant" of a man-of-war. Brimage and the "lieutenant" were endeavoring to reach Virginia, where British forces were present and they could board a British ship. Upon reaching Ocracoke, Brimage encountered John Smith, a Bertie County blacksmith. Smith joined in with Brimage and the "lieutenant."[36]

In the early morning of Monday, July 28, Brimage, Smith, and "Lieutenant Campbell" appeared at the Austin family's residence in or near Ocracoke. The trio was seeking transportation to Roanoke Island. After negotiating with Mr. Austin and his sons (Cornelius and Daniel) regarding the amount to be paid for the transportation (by boat), the three men and the two Austin sons set sail northward toward Roanoke Island. As they were sailing, Brimage and the "lieutenant" conferred and then informed the Austin brothers they wanted to go to New Inlet, not Roanoke Island. John Smith declared that he wanted to continue on to Roanoke Island, but "Campbell" and Brimage "insisted." The Austins changed course and sailed "peaceably and quietly" to the inlet, where they landed "on the beach" and all disembarked. Brimage asked "Campbell" to walk with him down the beach as the latter untied a handkerchief and revealed two pistols. Daniel Austin, alarmed by the sudden show of arms by the "lieutenant," asked if he (the lieutenant) "intended to hurt him." The "lieutenant" replied only that he "must have his boat for he must make his Escape."

Daniel Austin alerted his brother that "they were prisoners" and "begged" the "lieutenant" not to take his life. Brimage and Smith (also surprised at the revelation of weapons) attempted to assure the brothers that they "should not be hurt." Cornelius considered jumping and disarming the "lieutenant." He inquired of Smith, "Will you stand by me if I attempt to take the Lieutenant[?]" Without waiting for affirmation, Cornelius impulsively started at the "lieutenant" for "a step or two." Smith stopped him, begging him to "not do any thing of that kind" as "the Lieutenant was a blooded minded Fellow," and Smith "was afraid he would kill some of them." Upon Smith's intervention,

Cornelius desisted and privately acknowledged that he and his brother were, unfortunately, prisoners.

John Smith, the Bertie County blacksmith, realized that he had gotten himself into a precarious situation. He turned to Daniel Austin and "begged" that in case the "lieutenant" and Brimage took the boat, he (Smith) desired to stay with the Austin brothers and "go home" with them. Daniel concurred. The five men soon reembarked on the vessel and sailed to a nearby island to "ballast the boat." Once on the island, Brimage, Smith, and the "lieutenant" persuaded the Austins to sail them to Currituck. If the Austins complied, then they were to have their boat back, and Brimage and his cohorts would give them (the Austins) all the money they had with them. The Austin brothers, having no leverage in the tense situation, "agreed to go," and they all "set off."

As the five men were again sailing in the sound, both Brimage and Smith apparently became remorseful for the treatment to which the Austins were being subjected. Brimage and Smith told the brothers that "they had done no harm, but being suspected tories, had come away [from Bertie County], as they would not take the oath [of allegiance to the state of North Carolina]." As fortune would have it, a summer thunderstorm was brewing to the west of the sound, and the men sought safety on shore at a place called Dolbey's Point. Brimage was afraid that he would be spotted on the beach and, despite the approaching storm, forced all the men to get back in the boat and "set sail." The party was able to proceed only "a small distance," however, before the "very Dismal" weather forced them to go to shore again. All got out of the boat and went a distance from it and sat down under a tree to wait out the storm. Daniel Austin concluded that his brother and he needed to get away from Brimage and his two partners. After sitting for some time, Daniel whispered to Cornelius that he was going to bolt away down the sandbar and for Cornelius to jump in the boat, push off, and "make his escape." Accordingly, they made their departure, leaving Brimage, Smith, and the "lieutenant" on the beach. Two days later the brothers were in Edenton before Chowan County justices, deposing their accounts of the day's happenings.[37]

Lieutenant Fulcher and his militia detachment proceeded to Ocracoke, where they learned that Brimage, Smith, and "Lieutenant Campbell" had been at the village but had departed. John Mann, a local resident and militia officer, captured Brimage and Smith on Roanoke Island. The "lieutenant" escaped. Mann conveyed Brimage and Smith to Edenton.[38]

Robert Smith responded to Governor Caswell on July 31 with excellent news: the night before, a militia detachment had brought Brimage to Edenton, where he was placed in jail. The detachment likewise brought in John

Smith, who was confined. "Lieutenant Campbell" escaped from the militia as the detachment was making the arrests. The arrest of Brimage caused Robert Smith to become somewhat alarmed; he reported to Governor Caswell that "Tyrrell, and Bertie counties, are not likely long to be quiet." Smith obviously surmised that the two counties contained enough devout Loyalists that they might rise up in protest and unrest. Smith placed a "strong guard" on the arms and munitions magazine in Edenton. He expressed the belief that officials [in the Edenton District] had not "yet had reason to doubt any person in this County [Chowan], Perquimans, Pasquotank, or Currituck having any hand in the conspiracy, at least no one had yet been 'impeached or even suspected.'" He added: "We shall have many unhappy devils to take their trial for their life next Oyer Court."[39] Indeed, quite a few "unhappy devils" had been implicated in John Llewelyn's "religious" conspiracy.

As news of the detention of William Brimage spread throughout the state, Whig leaders reveled in his capture and the downfall of the conspiracy. Brig. Gen. Allen Jones (Halifax District) wrote to Thomas Burke on August 6 that, while "some of the most atrocious [leaders of the conspiracy] are not yet taken[,] . . . the great Mr. Brimage is in Edenton jail, being one of the heads of these Cut throats." Jones felt that only one fate was appropriate for the conspirators; he suggested to Burke that "no doubt but hanging, about a dozen, will have exceedingly good effect, in this State, and give stability to our new government. They seem to have been designed for this purpose by Providence."[40]

Rumors quickly spread throughout the coastal region that James Rawlins was on the run and likely headed toward the coast. On Friday, August 1, Hyde County militia officer Abraham Jones was especially vigilant, having received a report that "one of the Heads amongst the tories . . . was expected to pass by the settlement of Mattamuskeet." Jones, a Whig who had represented Hyde County in the Fifth Provincial Congress, was determined to apprehend Rawlins, if possible. As Jones maintained his vigil of Pamlico Sound, he "spied a small sail off in the Sound." He quickly "fitted out a Boat" and gathered up four men (probably members of the militia) and sailed out into the sound to intercept the vessel. Upon nearing the craft, he ascertained that it was carrying Rawlins and his family. Jones and his assistants commandeered the vessel, apprehended Rawlins, and brought him ashore to a magistrate.[41]

By August 10 Rawlins had been transported to New Bern. On that day, he appeared before Craven County justice James Davis. In a detailed deposition, Rawlins provided an account of the history and workings of the conspiracy, from his initial discussion with John Llewelyn regarding the Roman "religion"

Allen Jones (1739–1798) was a member of the Continental Congress, a delegate to five provincial congresses, and rose to a rank of brigadier general. He favored harsh punishment for the conspirators. Engraving from a portrait by Albert Rosenthal. Image provided courtesy of the N.C. Museum of History.

on March 28 until his flight from Martin County on July 5 and subsequent capture in Hyde County. He informed Justice Davis that he was "certain [that] none of the . . . vile proceeding[s]" he had recounted were included in the writings of the conspiracy. Rawlins, now exposed and contrite in thought, stated that some of the aims of the plot were "very Repugnant" but, apparently indirectly defending himself, also noted that "the Express words in their writings were those to Govern their Lives and actions By the Just Laws of Morality and . . . the Scriptures of old and New Testament, to which they were sworn." Then, passing blame to his former leader and confidant, John Llewelyn, Rawlins concluded: "Many [of the actions] to be Cald [called] in the proceedings of Cruelty, I believe altho first proposed by John Lewelling."[42]

On an undisclosed date sometime after giving his deposition, Rawlins was still confined in New Bern, where he met with George Wainwright, a resident of Martin County and "Great Friend to John Lewelling." The two men discussed "some News" of what Rawlins had conveyed to Justice Davis. Rawlins, clearly having attempted to affix blame and responsibility upon Llewelyn, must have been apprised by Wainwright that Llewelyn had insinuated that Rawlins was not truthful. Following his conversation with Wainwright, Rawlins wrote to the "Worshipful Justices of New Bern" to confirm his deposition. He wrote: "I knowing the Great Influence Capt. Lewelling has over that neighborhood [in Martin County] have Great Reason to fear he will make any attempts to invalidate my Testimony, and though no other person but myself could have discovered the Beginning of the Scheeme, unless himself."[43]

In early September, after the excitement and fervor of the news related to the collapse of John Llewelyn's conspiracy had subsided, Governor Caswell wrote to Cornelius Harnett that he and others "have been alarmed with the rising of tories, and forming of conspiracies: the former among the Highlanders & Regulators and in the County in which you had the honor to draw your first breath, and in Bertie and Martin." Referencing the Llewelyn conspiracy, he advised Harnett that "many of them have been apprehended and committed to gaol, in order to take their trials in the Courts of Oyer. Among them is Mr. Brimage, who attempted to escape, got as far as Ocacock [sic] . . . [and] was apprehended." Brimage had written to Caswell and requested to be granted bail and let out of the "poisonous and noisome dungeon" (the Edenton jail). The governor advised Harnett that he "did not think [it] proper to meddle in" the affair, the Chowan County justices having refused to grant Brimage bail. Nevertheless, by October 11 Brimage had been released from confinement and had returned to his residence ("Westbrooks") in Bertie County, when he wrote to Caswell and requested the governor to order a Captain Anderson at Ocracoke to return his portmanteau, which the captain had confiscated in late July when Brimage was apprehended.[44]

On Tuesday, August 12, 1777, amid the excitement and discourse associated with the revelation of the Llewelyn conspiracy, the Bertie County Court of Pleas and Quarter Sessions convened in Windsor. On this day two Bertie County residents—Peleg Belote and Samuel Hyman—along with John Clifton of Anson County, gave depositions regarding the Llewelyn conspiracy. Belote and Hyman were accused of "being concerned in a Conspiracy against the State." They testified regarding their involvement as participants. As a result of Hyman's deposition, the justices ordered him to appear as a witness against John Garrett, one of the principals in the Llewelyn conspiracy, at the next court of oyer and terminer, to be held in Edenton. Clifton testified that he had been approached by Martin County men to be a "reader" but that he never "attempted to influence any one to join the Association." He revealed that on July 23 he informed his brother, Peter Clifton, a Bertie County justice, regarding the "circumstances" of his involvement with the plot and that on the twenty-fourth he gave a sworn statement to Thomas Pugh, another Bertie County justice.[45]

Also during the session, the justices administered the statutorily mandated oath of allegiance to the state of North Carolina to county residents. The various justices were assigned to individually attend "private musters" of the county's militia companies within each company's district. The following table presents the justices and companies to which they were designated to administer the oath of allegiance. Each company represented a distinct district within the county for which the inhabitants were to be administered the oath.[46]

TABLE 3
Bertie County Justices Designated to Administer the Oath of Allegiance
to North Carolina, by Militia Company/District, August 1777

Justice	Company/District
William Bryan	Capt. Rhodes
James Campbell	Capt. Askew
William Cherry	Capt. Wynns
Jonathan Jacocks	Capt. Ryan
Andrew Oliver	Capt. Oliver
William Pugh	Capt. Pugh
David Standley	Capt. Ballard
Zedekiah Stone	Capt. King
Thomas Ward	Capt. Freeman

The law mandating the oath of allegiance for North Carolina residents also stipulated that those persons who refused to subscribe to the oath were to depart the state for Europe or the West Indies within sixty days. The Bertie County justices, immediately upon beginning to administer the oath, identified various persons who refused to submit to it. In accordance with the subject law, the justices ordered the persons to depart the state within the time period specified by the law. On August 13 Bertie County justices ordered Richard Jones to "depart this state within Sixty days" for having "refused to take" the subject oath. The next day, the justices similarly ordered Thomas Bogg, James

Buchanan, Thomas Clarke, and Rev. Francis Johnston to depart. Before the session concluded, Dr. Robert Lenox was likewise ordered to leave.[47]

Almost six weeks later, the six men were completing their preparations to leave. On September 22 James Buchanan wrote to Governor Caswell and requested a pass for Lenox, Johnston, and himself to allow them to sail to the West Indies without "being molested." Buchanan also sought gubernatorial documentation to "hinder American cruisers, from making a prize" of his vessel, the brigantine *Tryal*, which was loaded with barrel staves, tobacco, and "a bundle of Deer skins." Thomas Clarke wrote to the governor on the twenty-third and likewise requested "passports" for Thomas Bogg, Richard Jones, and himself to leave aboard the sloop *Free Mason*. Bogg was the master of the vessel, which was loaded with tobacco, flaxseed, barrel staves, and beeswax.[48]

The statute respecting the oath of allegiance further stipulated that all persons ordered to depart North Carolina for refusing to subscribe to the oath would be at "Liberty to sell and dispose of . . . their Estates." Such persons were also permitted to appoint attorneys to sell and dispose of their properties, but any real estate that had not been sold within three months after an individual departed the state was to be forfeited to the state. On September 27 Thomas Bogg, a devout Loyalist, transferred ownership of his real and personal property to his father-in-law, Benjamin Blount Sr., of Tyrrell County. Bogg, recognizing that "the situation of my affairs makes it necessary that I should leave this state," consummated a deed of "special trust," with Blount stipulating that the transferred property be used "for the benefit and support of his wife [Hannah Blount Bogg] and children." Three days later Bogg sold thirty-five acres of land situated on the east side of Cashie River in Bertie County to William Williams.[49] Sometime thereafter, Bogg, clearly demonstrating his deep devotion to the British Crown, left his "Dearly Beloved" wife and young children to endure their fates in Whig-dominated northeastern North Carolina.

Trials for a number of the "Llewelyn conspirators" took place in Edenton District Superior Court in September 1777. Llewelyn stood trial and was found guilty of the "Crime of high Treason." He was sentenced to death but was never executed. A number of other Llewelyn Loyalists were found guilty of "Misprision of Treason." These "lesser offenders" were released from the Edenton jail on bail, which was set as high as £1,000. William Brimage was indicted for treason and misprision of treason, but the charges could not be sustained, and he was released from confinement in the Edenton "dungeon."[50]

When the Bertie County Court of Pleas and Quarter Sessions next convened in November 1777, a number of other Loyalists who had refused to take the oath of allegiance to the state were ordered to depart within sixty days.

William Brimage was one of them. Constable Josiah Redditt was directed to serve a copy of the court's order on Brimage, since he had failed to appear in person before the justices. James Blake, Solomon Pender, William Mitchell, and Josiah Nichols were likewise ordered to leave the state.[51]

By early January 1778 William Brimage was fully preparing to depart Bertie County pursuant to the county court's order. On Thursday, January 8, he and his wife Elizabeth transferred ownership of nearly 1,900 acres of land in Bertie and Carteret counties to their three children—daughters Mary F. and Elizabeth P. Brimage and son William West Brimage. Also on this day, the Brimages conveyed to William title to their slaves and personal property.[52]

Brimage left Bertie County in April 1778 and traveled to New York. There he was welcomed by former royal North Carolina governors William Tryon and Josiah Martin. Both men considered Brimage "a respectable man." Brimage was later appointed attorney general for Bermuda. With the British invasion of the Carolinas in 1780–1781, he attempted to return to Charleston, but British forces evacuated the South, and Brimage journeyed to England, arriving in June 1782. His family continued to reside on his property in Bertie County near the mouth of the Cashie River.[53] (That area is still commonly known today by local residents as "Brimage's").

The dates that Pender, Mitchell, and Nichols departed Bertie County are not evident from extant records. On March 1, 1778, Governor Caswell granted permission to James Blake and Colin Clark (who also had refused the oath of allegiance and had been ordered by Bertie County justices to depart the state) to leave. Caswell stipulated that Blake and Clark depart with their property from the Port of Roanoke (Edenton) aboard the schooner *Nancy*, which was to sail "shortly."[54]

Subsequent to James Buchanan's September 22, 1777, letter, Dr. Robert Lenox had a change of heart and decided that he wanted to remain in North Carolina. He initiated legal proceedings and went to Chowan County, where he took the oath of allegiance to the state "agreeably" to law. In November 1778 Lenox presented to the Bertie County justices a petition "praying" that the previously issued order "for sending him out of the State be rescinded." The highly influential Chowan County lawyer James Iredell pleaded Lenox's case before the court and produced a certificate from Chowan County justices that Lenox had indeed taken the oath of allegiance. But the Bertie County justices were not moved—they rejected Lenox's petition but did grant a motion for him to appeal to the Edenton District Superior Court. Lenox did appeal to the district court. In May 1779 the justices of that body ruled that the Bertie County court's orders (for Lenox to depart North Carolina) "were not warranted by the Laws of this State." Since Lenox had taken the oath of allegiance in August 1778 (confirmed by a certificate from Joseph Hewes), they were "of the Opinion that the said Robert Lenox is . . . entitled to all the Privleges of a Citizen in virture of a late Act of Assembly."[55] The Whig justices in Bertie County were staunch in their renderings and dealings with those individuals who were Loyalists or who had exhibited Loyalist proclivities. Dr. Lenox, having prevailed in his appeal, was not forced to depart Bertie County. He died there about the fall of 1789. At the time of his death, he owned 1,100 acres of land and substantial personal properties.[56] His landholdings had not been confiscated by Bertie County Whig authorities.

The year 1777 was tumultuous and trying for those Bertie County Loyalists who supported King George III by affiliating with the Llewelyn conspiracy or refusing to submit to the oath of allegiance to the state of North Carolina. Undoubtedly, some of the Loyalists felt that the king's military forces would overwhelm the American rebels and that royal rule would be reasserted. Other persons surely were passive Loyalists who privately supported the Crown without any public displays. The matter of allegiance was often not an easy choice, and a number of Bertie County's residents who stood up for the king paid the price of banishment from the community, disruption of their life-styles, and loss of property. Still others, unknown to history, anguished silently with their Loyalist sentiments in a community dominated and controlled by revolutionary Whigs.

Notes

1. Hugh T. Lefler, *History of North Carolina*, 4 vols. (New York: Lewis Historical Publishing Company, [1956]), 1:233. The Fourth and Fifth Provincial Congresses dealt with a number of items related to Tory activities within the province. The fourth congress (April–May 1776) addressed controlling, accounting for, and disposing of property that had been confiscated from Tories, as well as granting relief and assistance to a few residents who had suffered property losses and personal injuries at the hands of Tories. The delegates also considered a request from Guilford County citizens to be reimbursed for costs associated with disarming Tories of that community. By the end of the year, the fifth congress was forced to deal with some Tory violence and discontent in the southeastern region, mostly in Bladen County. Rewards were offered and orders dispatched to detain and bring to justice the Tories responsible for killing a Bladen County citizen. Residents of that county had seized a number of firearms from Tories in the area, and the congress directed that Thomas Robeson be authorized to hire gunsmiths to repair all confiscated guns thus seized that were "not fit for

service." Overall, the congresses were not inclined to address ongoing uprisings, violence, or insurrections by Tories or Loyalists within the colony following the Moores Creek affair. William L. Saunders, ed., *The Colonial Records of North Carolina*, 10 vols. (Raleigh: State of North Carolina, 1886–1890), 10:503, 524, 526, 535, 545, 551, 555, 566, 585, 935, 939, 1002.

2. Saunders, *Colonial Records*, 10:585. On March 14, 1776, the Continental Congress had resolved that "it be recommended" to the colonial provincial congresses, conventions, assemblies, and councils of committees of safety of the "United Colonies" to "immediately . . . cause all persons to be disarmed within their respective colonies, who are notoriously disaffected to the cause of America, or who have not associated, and shall refuse to associate, to defend, by arms, these United Colonies, against the hostile attempts of the British fleets and armies." Worthington Chauncey Ford, ed., *Journals of the Continental Congress*, 34 vols. (Washington, D.C.: Government Printing Office, 1904–1937), 4:205.

3. Jeffrey J. Crow, "Tory Plots and Anglican Loyalty: The Llewelyn Conspiracy of 1777," *North Carolina Historical Review* 55 (January 1978):1; Lefler, *History of North Carolina*, 1:258.

4. Alan D. Watson, *Bertie County: A Brief History* (Raleigh: North Carolina Division of Archives and History, 1982), 67.

5. *The Episcopal Church in Bertie County, 1701–1990, From Its Anglican Roots to the Twentieth Century* (Windsor, N.C.: St. Thomas' Episcopal Church, 1990), 28; Paul H. Smith and Ronald M. Gephart, eds., *Letters of Delegates to Congress, 1774–1789*, 26 vols. (Washington, D.C.: Library of Congress, 1976–2000), 5:513.

6. The depositions relative to the Llewelyn conspiracy were taken in various counties before the documents were submitted to the court of oyer and terminer in Edenton. Pertinent depositions may be found in the following collections at the North Carolina State Archives: Edenton District Superior Court, Depositions Relative to Llewelyn Conspiracy, 1777; Edenton District Superior Court Papers, 1774–1779; Chowan County Papers, XV, 1772–1777, March–October. Many of the depositions were published in J. R. B. Hathaway, ed., *North Carolina Historical and Genealogical Register II* (April 1901): 208–217; (July 1901): 390–405; (October 1901): 566–577. Hereafter, the author identifies the individuals who submitted cited depositions, as well as the dates and counties in which the depositions were rendered.

On July 1, 1777, Bertie County justices held a court in Windsor "for the Purpose of Enquiring into Sundrey Suspicions ag[ains]t" a number of persons rumored to be involved with alleged conspiracy. On that date William Skiles deposed that he had been informed that the "Scheme took its rise in Virginia and thence was forwarded to Luellan [John Llewelyn]." William Skiles, deposition dated July 1, 1777, Bertie County; Walter Clark, ed., *The State Records of North Carolina*, 16 vols. (11–26) (Raleigh: State of North Carolina, 1895–1906), 23:994; Crow, "The Llewelyn Conspiracy," 4.

7. James Rawlins, deposition dated August 10, 1777, Craven County.

8. Crow, "The Llewelyn Conspiracy," 2–5; Clark, S*tate Records*, 23:994. In addition to Hill and Llewelyn, the Provincial Congress appointed the following men as justices in Martin County: John Hardison, Edward Smithwick, William Slade, William Sherrod, John Everitt, Thomas Wiggins, Thomas Hunter, Kenneth McKenzie, Francis Ward, Samuel Smithwick,

Samuel Williams, John Ross, John Kennedy, John Griffin, Nathan Mayo, Blake Baker Wiggins, Joshua Taylor, John Perry, James Moore, and Thomas Riddick.

9. Saunders, *Colonial Records*, 10:1011; Crow, "The Llewelyn Conspiracy," 6.

10. Crow, "The Llewelyn Conspiracy," 4, 9.

11. William Skiles, deposition dated July 1, 1777, Bertie County.

12. Clark, *State Records*, 12:1; 24:1, 3, 5, 9–11; Saunders, *Colonial Records*, 10:558. The General Assembly adjourned on May 9, 1777.

13. Michael Ward, deposition dated July 9, 1777, Samuel Hyman, deposition dated August 12, 1777, Bertie County; William May Jr., deposition dated June 19, 1777, Pitt County; William Hyman and John Wheatley, depositions dated July 4, 1777, Martin County.

14. Clark, *State Records*, 24:10.

15. William Hyman, deposition dated July 4, 1777, Martin County; Benjamin Harrison, position dated July 16, 1777, Tyrrell County.

16. Thomas Harrison, deposition dated July 14, 1777, Tyrrell County.

17. Peleg Belote, deposition dated August 12, 1777, Bertie County.

18. William Skiles, deposition dated July 1, 1777, Bertie County.

19. Michael Ward, deposition dated July 9, 1777, Bertie County.

20. John Allen, deposition dated July 1, 1777, Samuel Hyman, deposition dated August 12, 1777, William Burkett ["Berket"], deposition dated July 1, 1777, Bertie County.

21. James Rawlins, deposition dated August 10, 1777, Craven County; Crow, "The Llewelyn Conspiracy," 10.

22. John Brogden, William Skiles, and William Brogden, depositions dated July 1, 1777, Bertie County. Petition of the Inhabitants of Bertie County in favour of Wm. Burkitt [Burkett], January 27, 1779, General Assembly Session Records, January-February 1779, State Archives. By early 1779 William Burkett, a member of the Bertie County militia, had been drafted to serve in a detached militia company that was ordered to "go to the Southward" (most likely South Carolina). However, he was "apprehensive" about serving in the detached unit since he felt he was in "Continual Danger for his Life." He, having exposed the Llewelyn conspiracy to Whig authorities, subsequently was reportedly the target of retributive threats from individuals who were involved in the plot. Therefore, he sought help from Whig officials to dismiss him from active military duty. On January 27, 1779, twenty-seven prominent Whigs of Bertie and Martin counties petitioned the North Carolina General Assembly that Burkett be excused from serving in the detached militia company that was being organized as a favorable consideration for the "Meritorious . . . Service rendered to [Bertie] County & [the] State" for divulging the subversive scheme. The petition was apparently presented to the General Assembly on February 2, 1779.

According to various depositions, Daniel Leggett met with William Durance, James Harrison, Thomas Harrison, Bird Land, John Stewart, and Jonathan Davis on July 1. He also met with "others," who were unnamed in subject depositions. William Durrance, James Harrison, and Thomas Harrison, depositions dated July 14, 1777; Bird Land, deposition dated July 16, 1777, all in Tyrrell County; John Stewart, deposition dated July 12, 1777, Martin County.

23. Clark, *State Records*, 22:861, 907; Saunders, *Colonial Records*, 8:507–511, 10:164–165.

24. Thomas Harrison Sr., deposition dated July 14, 1777, Tyrrell County.

25. William May Jr. submitted a deposition in Pitt County on June 19, 1777. William Skiles, John Allen, and William Burkett submitted depositions on July 1, 1777, in Bertie County. On June 4, 1777, David Taylor and Joseph Taylor submitted depositions in Martin County. William Skiles, John Allen, and William Burkett, depositions dated July 1, 1777, Bertie County; David Taylor and Joseph Taylor, depositions dated June 4, 1777, Martin County; Michael Ward, deposition dated July 9, 1777, Bertie County; Peleg Belote, deposition dated August 12, 1777, Bertie County; William Hyman, John Hodge, Solomon Pippen, John Wheatley, and Nathan Hathaway, depositions dated July 4, 1777, Martin County; Saunders, *Colonial Records*, 10:164–167.

26. James Rawlins, deposition dated August 10, 1777, Craven County; David Taylor and Joseph Taylor, depositions dated June 4, 1777, Martin County; Crow, "The Llewelyn Conspiracy," 11.

27. Thomas Stubbs Sr., deposition dated July 14, 1777, Tyrrell County.

28. John Clifton, deposition dated August 12, 1777, Bertie County; Bertie County Criminal Action Papers, C.R.010.326, folder 1771–1780, State Archives.

29. Clark, *State Records*, 11:521.

30. The author computed the number of depositions given, as well as the number acknowledged by deponents with their marks (X's), in the three cited counties during the period July 1–16, per the depositions noted in previous notes to this chapter. Of the twenty-four persons who gave depositions, eleven (ten men and one woman) affirmed the documents with X's.

31. John Clifton, deposition dated August 12, 1777, Bertie County; Wynnette Parks Haun, comp., *Bertie County, North Carolina, Court Minutes, 1772–1780, Book IV* (Durham: the compiler, 1979), 74 (hereafter cited as Haun, *Bertie County Court Minutes, IV*).

32. Thomas Harrison and Benjamin Harrison, in their Tyrrell County depositions dated July 4, 1777, and July 16, 1777, and John Stewart in his July 19, 1777, Martin County deposition, gave accounts of William Brimage's involvement in the conspiracy. It should be noted that no Bertie County men who were associated with the plot and provided depositions indicated that Brimage had solicited them. Absalom Leggett of Martin County generally

recruited the Bertie County men before Brimage was appointed senior warden. The author concludes that Brimage had very little, if any, impact on the membership of the conspiracy, since he was not appointed senior warden for Bertie County until July 4, when the conspiracy was quickly dissolving as its members had given depositions before various counties' justices. Brimage fled from Bertie County within a few weeks of becoming senior warden. The author is of the opinion that Brimage would not have been able to recruit persons to join a conspiracy that was already exposed to state and county officials and whose members were daily being called before justices. Given the circumstances that existed in July 1777, the author doubts that Brimage would have endeavored to solicit men for the conspiracy. Furthermore, the author found no information indicating that any of the Bertie County confirmed participants in the conspiracy were brought into the plot by Brimage. The author believes his opinion is further borne out by the fact that charges of treason and misprision of treason levied against Brimage were not sustained in Edenton District court in September 1777. Memorial of William Brimage to the Honorable Thomas Townshend, one of his Majesty's Principal Secretaries of State, November 23, 1782 [Brimage Memorial], English Records, Box 3, "Brimage, William" folder, State Archives (hereafter cited as "Brimage Records").

33. Clark, *State Records*, 11:539.

34. Clark, *State Records*, 11:537–538.

35. Clark, *State Records*, 11:543.

36. Clark, *State* Records, 11:551–552; John Smith, deposition dated July 31, 1777, Chowan County.

37. Daniel Austin and Cornelius Austin, depositions dated July 30, 1777, Chowan County.
    John Smith testified on July 31, 1777, that he was at Ocracoke when he met William Brimage. Smith reportedly told Brimage that he was surprised to see him, since he had heard before he (Smith) left Bertie County that Brimage had been arrested and was in the Halifax jail. Brimage reportedly said to Smith that he had departed Bertie County because "he might not take the oath prescribed by the last [North Carolina General] Assembly." (Brimage referred to the oath of allegiance to the state of North Carolina mandated in law by the General Assembly in May 1777.) John Smith, deposition dated July 31, 1777, Chowan County.

38. Clark, *State Records*, 11:555–556.

39. Clark, *State Records*, 11:551–552.

40. Clark, *State* Records, 11:561–562.

41. Abram [Abraham] Jones, deposition dated August 9, 1777, Hyde County.

42. James Rawlins, deposition dated August 10, 1777, Craven County.

43. James Rawlins to the Worshipful Justices of New Bern, undated letter.

44. Clark, *State Records*, 11:602–604, 22:755.

45. Haun, *Bertie County Court Minutes, IV*, 74–75; Peleg Belote, Samuel Hyman, and John Clifton, depositions dated August 12, 1777, Bertie County.

46. Haun, *Bertie County Court Minutes, IV*, 78.

47. Clark, *State Records*, 24:9–12; Richard Jones, court order to depart North Carolina, August 13, 1777, Thomas Bogg, James Buchanan, Thomas Clarke, and Francis Johnston, court orders to depart North Carolina, August 14, 1777, Bertie County Miscellaneous Records, Revolutionary War Papers, C.R.010.928.12, State Archives (hereafter cited as Bertie County Revolutionary War Papers); Haun, *Bertie County Court Minutes, IV*, 87–88.

48. Clark, *State Records*, 11:633–634, 776. Rev. Francis Johnston settled in Jamaica and became pastor of a church. See Robert O. DeMond, *The Loyalists in North Carolina during the Revolution* (Baltimore: Genealogical Publishing Co., 1979), 184.

49. Clark, *State Records*, 24:11–12, 706; Deed M-376, Bertie County Register of Deeds Office, Windsor (hereafter cited as Bertie County deed(s), with book and page of the subject document[s]); Deed 7-191, Tyrrell County Register of Deeds Office, Columbia.
   Thomas Bogg married Hannah Blount in Tyrrell County on November 3, 1770. The Boggs were residing in Bertie County in 1773 when Thomas, along with other county residents, signed a petition to the North Carolina General Assembly for the county's new courthouse to be constructed in Windsor. By October 1784 Hannah Bogg was deceased, leaving her three children "in some measure . . . destitute." Thomas Bogg likewise had died by that date, thereby rendering the children orphans. During the October–November 1784 session of the North Carolina General Assembly, the legislators passed a law authorizing Benjamin Blount to sue and recover for the use of Bogg's children all debts due and owing to Bogg. Several suits had been filed against Bogg's estate, which threatened to further impoverish the children. The North Carolina assemblymen exhibited compassion by authorizing Benjamin Blount to sue others with outstanding debts to Thomas Bogg. "Marriage Bonds of Tyrrell County, North Carolina," online at www.ncgenweb.us/tyrrell/TYRMARBB.HTM; Saunders, *Colonial Records*, 9:804–806; Clark, *State Records*, 24:706; Benjamin Blount Senior's will (1–158), November 4, 1786, Tyrrell County Office of the Clerk of Court, Columbia. In his will, Blount bequeathed to his grandchildren—Janet Bogg, Hannah Bogg, and James Bogg—"ten pounds each lawful money."

50. Crow, "The Llewelyn Conspiracy," 14–15; Brimage Memorial, November 23, 1782, in "Brimage Records." According to Crow, eighteen Loyalists (including John Llewelyn) were tried. No Bertie County men were included. See Crow, "The Llewelyn Conspiracy," 14n.

51. Haun, *Bertie County Court Minutes, IV*, 83.

52. Bertie County deeds, M-356, M-357, M-358, and M-359.

53. Crow, "The Llewelyn Conspiracy," 15–16. Upon Brimage's departure from Bertie County, he left his wife and children to continue to reside on his plantation near the mouth of the Cashie River. About late 1780 or early 1781, however, he had his family join him in Bermuda; his wife and children arrived there in January 1781. With his property in Bertie County being vacated, Brimage was justifiably concerned that his landholding would be

confiscated. Therefore, during the summer of 1781 he and his family, with their possessions, sailed to Charleston and then to Portsmouth, Virginia. At that time General Cornwallis's forces were situated in southeastern Virginia, and Brimage surmised that he would be able to return to Bertie County. But upon his arrival at Portsmouth, Brimage discovered that communications with Bertie County were "totally barred." Following Cornwallis's surrender on October 19, Brimage concluded that he must send his wife and children back to his vacated plantation in Bertie or the Whig leaders would surely confiscate the property. He hired a flag-of-truce schooner, the *Three Friends*, which sailed for the port of Edenton, arriving in February. The vessel and its contents were immediately seized by the commanding officer and crew of a brigantine with Virginia registry. Brimage's possessions, including a number of slaves, were sold at a court of admiralty held in Williamsburg in April 1782. See Brimage Memorial, November 23, 1782; Statement by Jo[siah] Martin, May 1, 1783; Inventory of William Brimage's property seized aboard the schooner *Three Friends*, a Flag of Truce, and attached statements, June 19, 1786; Memorial of Thomas West Brimage, October 25, 1784; Memorial of William Brimage, April 17, 1788; all in "Brimage Records."

54. Clark, *State Records*, 13:373.

55. Haun, *Bertie County Court Minutes, IV*, 87–88; James Blake, court order to depart North Carolina, November 14, 1777, Bertie County Revolutionary War Papers; Edenton District Superior Court, Minute Docket, April 1769–November 1781, D.C.R. 2.001, State Archives.

56. Bertie County Estate Records, 1730–1920, C.R.010.508.61, file for Robert Lennox [Lenox], State Archives.

CONTINENTAL VOLUNTEERS
AND "DRAFTED MILITIA"

The thirteen independent states, acting as a unified entity, required a singular army so that the Continental Congress, through the generals and other commanders whom it appointed, could prosecute the American war effort against Great Britain. In order to assemble such an army, the Congress on September 16, 1776, resolved that each state raise a specified number of regiments. It required the colonies to enlist a total of eighty-eight regiments. North Carolina's quota was nine regiments, all of which the Congress assigned to the Continental army's Southern Department.[1]

On November 12, 1776, the Fifth (and final) Provincial Congress convened at Halifax.[2] On November 28 that body authorized three regiments—the Seventh, Eighth and Ninth—to be raised pursuant to the direction of the Continental Congress. The provincial congress appointed James Hogun (Halifax County) colonel of the Seventh Regiment, James Armstrong (Pitt County) colonel of the Eighth, and John Williams (Craven County) colonel of the Ninth. The congress also appointed John McGlaughon of Bertie County as a captain in the Seventh Regiment and fellow county resident Thomas Watson as a first lieutenant under McGlaughon's command.[3]

Once McGlaughon and Watson received their appointments, they began recruiting residents of Bertie County for their company. On December 10

William White enlisted to serve in the company as a sergeant. Sixteen days later, county resident Hardy Keel likewise enlisted as a sergeant. White and Keel, being the first men to enlist and being authorized as noncommissioned officers, obviously assisted Captain McGlaughon and Lieutenant Watson with recruiting and organizational activities. On April 27, 1777, Benjamin Bryer of Bertie County was appointed an ensign in the company and further assisted in recruiting for the unit. By the spring of 1777, more than two dozen Bertie County men had enlisted in the Seventh North Carolina Regiment, predominantly in McGlaughon's company.[4]

North Carolina leaders designated the town of Halifax as the central rendezvous for the state's Continental regiments. There, during the spring of 1777, the Seventh, Eighth, and Ninth Regiments were organized. The Seventh Regiment was comprised of eight companies, including McGlaughon's unit, from the Edenton and Halifax districts. The Eighth Regiment was comprised of companies from the New Bern and Wilmington districts, while companies from the Hillsborough and Salisbury districts constituted the Ninth.[5]

The Continental Congress initially assigned North Carolina's nine regiments to the Southern Department, but on February 5, 1777, it directed that all of the state's regiments be relieved from the Southern Department and assigned to Gen. George Washington's main army, then encamped in winter quarters at Morristown, New Jersey. Also on this day, the Continental Congress elected Col. Francis Nash of the First North Carolina Regiment to be a brigadier general in the Continental army. The Congress directed brigadier generals James Moore and Nash to utilize their personal influence to recruit men from across North Carolina to fill the state's regiments "to their full complement [of troops]" before March 15, at which time they were to begin marching northward. The two generals were directed to "proceed with the nine continental regiments . . . to join General Washington."[6]

The date that Capt. John McGlaughon, along with his subordinate officers and recruits, departed Windsor for the regimental rendezvous at Halifax is not evident from existing records. Bertie County men enlisted in McGlaughon's company throughout the winter and spring of 1777. It is quite likely that Benjamin Bryer, an ensign, remained in Windsor to recruit for the company after McGlaughon and his contingent had departed the town.

General Moore's North Carolina brigade, comprised of the state's older regiments, was situated in South Carolina. One contingent was under Nash's command at Beaufort, and another was under Moore's immediate control at Charleston. By March 15 the regiments' ranks had not been filled with recruits, and the units had not assembled at Halifax. No march to join

Brig. Gen. James Moore (1737–1777) commanded Whig forces at Moores Creek Bridge and the North Carolina Brigade at Charleston. His untimely death in 1777 deprived the state of its leading candidate for higher rank and responsibility in the Continental Line. Image courtesy of the North Carolina Collection, University of North Carolina at Chapel Hill Library.

General Washington's command would commence within the time frame previously stipulated by the Continental Congress. The march northward was impeded by a number of factors, including a lack of money to pay the troops, inadequate provisions, and changing directions from Congress. Moreover, Maj. Gen. Robert Howe (commander of the Southern Department) refused to allow the North Carolina regiments to leave South Carolina. Then, on April 15, General Moore—the primary catalyst for organizing the North Carolina troops—died suddenly. His death deprived North Carolina of probably its greatest military mind of the era.[7]

By early April General Howe had released the North Carolina troops in Charleston, from which they marched to Wilmington. General Nash, busy recruiting men in the backcountry of North Carolina, abandoned those efforts and hurried to Wilmington to assume command of the troops. From Wilmington the soldiers trekked to Halifax, just south of the Virginia border. The Third North Carolina Regiment, commanded by Col. Jethro Sumner, was the first unit to arrive at Halifax. Slowly, the units under Nash's command began gathering at the rendezvous, where an outbreak of smallpox occurred. Finally, in early May the North Carolina regiments began marching northward. Included in Nash's brigade were a number of Bertie County men. Residents of the county were serving in seven of the nine regiments. General Nash remained at Halifax for a few days to establish recruiting procedures. He assigned Col. John Williams of the Ninth North Carolina Regiment to remain at the Halifax camp and oversee the recruitment activities of twenty-seven officers (three from each of the nine regiments). Williams was to organize and forward recruits to the army in the north as fast as they were enlisted and brought to the rendezvous.[8]

The North Carolina troops trudged across Virginia through Petersburg, Richmond, and Fredericksburg to Alexandria, where they arrived by May 21. At Alexandria the soldiers who had not already had smallpox were inoculated for the disease. About two hundred of the North Carolinians had previously suffered the disease and were placed under the command of Col. Jethro Sumner and Lt. Col. Archibald Lytle and immediately marched to join Washington's army. Those men who were inoculated remained at Alexandria until they contracted mild cases of smallpox (from the inoculations) and recovered. They then departed the inoculation site, crossed the Potomac River at Georgetown (upriver about eight miles from Alexandria), and marched through Baltimore to Trenton, New Jersey, arriving in early July. On July 8 the Continental Congress directed that Nash's troops repair to Billingsport, New Jersey, and remain there while awaiting further orders. General Washington soon ordered Nash's command, which had been reinforced by local militia, some Virginia soldiers, and an artillery company, to remain at Trenton. Before ordering Nash's command to move further, General Washington awaited British general Sir William Howe's next move.[9]

Howe's British force, estimated at 18,000 men, began embarking aboard a fleet of vessels in New York harbor on July 8. General Washington assumed that Howe's troops were destined to meet up with Gen. John Burgoyne's command, then driving southward from Canada through New York. Washington surmised that the two British forces would rendezvous at a point on the Hudson River. On July 10 Washington began moving his baggage wagons and ordered his army to march early the next morning. That night, the North Carolina troops—then assigned to Maj. Gen. Nathanael Greene's division—camped with the remainder of the army at Pompton Plains, New Jersey. Inclement weather moved in for the next several days, but by July 14 Washington's army was at Smith's Clove, in the New York highlands. In the meantime, Howe's British troops were still aboard naval vessels in New York harbor. They eventually sailed on July 23—to the southward, not up the Hudson River. Philadelphia appeared to be the most likely objective, despite what appeared to be Howe's illogical abandonment of Burgoyne in New York.[10]

For more than three weeks, General Washington's army maneuvered while the British troops remained aboard naval vessels at sea. On August 22 Washington received news that the British fleet was standing in the mouth of Chesapeake Bay. Howe's intended movement was now obvious—he was about to land his army at the head of Chesapeake Bay and march for Philadelphia. Washington began moving his main army to Philadelphia but stationed Brig. Gen. Francis Nash's North Carolinians at Trenton. Nash's troops were to remain encamped there, pending further confirmation of Howe's intentions. The troops under Jethro Sumner and Archibald Lytle's command who had marched in advance from Alexandria to join Washington's army were merged back into Nash's force in early August. Washington's army marched into Philadelphia on the twenty-fourth; the following day Nash's troops marched through the city, having been ordered to join the main army. Two days later the army was at Wilmington, Delaware. Battle was imminent between Washington's and Howe's armies.[11]

Brandywine Creek meanders through the Pennsylvania countryside about thirty miles south of Philadelphia. General Washington concluded that the creek seemed a logical site to make a stand against Howe's British forces moving toward Philadelphia. The terrain around Chadds Ford favored defensive operations. Washington decided to center his line on the high ground above the ford, where the creek was about fifty yards wide. The center of the American line was anchored by Gen. Nathanael Greene's division, which included Francis Nash's North Carolina brigade. The North Carolinians were placed in reserve behind the main body of the division, however. Thomas Burke, North Carolina delegate to the Continental Congress, rode out to Chadds Ford from Philadelphia to survey the battle preparations. On September 10 he wrote to Gov. Richard Caswell that "Our army is disposed to receive the Enemy who are about three miles distance & advancing, every person is in high spirits, and expect a very important engagement. Our army is supposed superior."[12]

Shortly after daybreak on Thursday, September 11, the firing of American alarm guns along the heights announced that British regulars and Loyalist soldiers had been sighted approaching Brandywine Creek. The British vanguard soon encountered a contingent of light infantry, including select members of the Third North Carolina Regiment, posted on the south side of the tributary under the command of Brig. Gen. William Maxwell. A brisk engagement ensued, but by midmorning the sheer number of British troops forced Maxwell's soldiers to splash back across the creek to the American line. Nevertheless, the British made no concerted efforts to cross the creek and engage the Americans—their approach to Chadds Ford was merely diversionary. Howe's main assaulting force was marching upstream, where it intended to cross the creek, turn Washington's right flank, and fall in upon the rear of the American line. By late morning reports reached Washington that a large number of enemy troops were marching upstream on the opposite side of the creek. Washington immediately ordered troops to march to meet the reported force; but, in short order a note arrived from Maj. Gen. John Sullivan, commanding officer of the American right wing (upstream from Greene's division), that he had received information from a scout who had been posted on the "British" side of the Brandywine that no large body of troops was moving. Sullivan surmised, and conveyed to Washington, that the previous intelligence was false. Washington, relying on Sullivan's communication, recalled his troops, still anticipating an all-out frontal assault at Chadds Ford.[13]

About midafternoon chaos engulfed the Americans—news reached General Washington that the British had crossed the creek upstream. General Sullivan moved his men to meet the advancing enemy troops, and Washington dispatched three divisions in that direction. Washington remained with General Greene near Chadds Ford, still of the opinion that the primary assault would come at that location. Nevertheless, around 4:30 in the afternoon the rumble of artillery fire and the crackle of rifles and muskets convinced Washington that his forces had been outflanked. He immediately ordered Greene, with Nash's North Carolinians in support, to march to Sullivan's aid. Outnumbered in fierce combat, the Americans time and again were forced to pull back, only to rally and surge forward again. Finally, before nightfall, the angry fighting took its toll, and the Americans were forced to retreat. Sullivan's soldiers who had been face-to-face with the British fell backward into Greene's division. Greene's men opened their ranks to allow Sullivan's men to pass through and then reformed into a defensive position. General Nash's brigade was not involved in the day's actions, having been held in reserve. That night the Americans fell back about fifteen miles to Chester, their designated rendezvous site.[14]

Bertie County soldiers, members of the regiments that comprised the North Carolina brigade, experienced the sounds, stress, and anxiety that accompany close-quarters combat, even though they were not directly involved in the day's fighting. At one point British warriors came to within about fifty yards of the Carolinians. Nash's troops—with bayonets fixed—were preparing to engage the British soldiers, when they (the British) were repelled. Lt. Thomas Blount Whitmell and Pvt. Joseph Lawrence, both residents of Bertie County, were wounded during the battle. James Anderson served as a guard over the army's baggage. Other residents of Bertie—John Barrow, Ezekiel White, Solomon Howard, Abraham Jenkins, Charles Rhodes, and William White—later stated that they were present during the battle.[15]

Thomas Burke, who had visited the American forces on the eve of the confrontation, returned to Philadelphia, where on the seventeenth he wrote to Governor Caswell. Burke, referring to his correspondence of September 10, noted: "I wrote you a few Lines from Head Quarters on Brandywine near Chads Ford on the Tenth Instant, and in them gave you the hopes I then Entertained of seeing in a few hours our Arms triumphant over our Enemies. I am sorry I can not now tell you those hopes were realised." Burke was "grieved to his Soul" over the defeat of Washington's army. Also on this day, Burke and the two other North Carolina delegates to the Continental Congress—Cornelius Harnett and John Penn—jointly wrote to Caswell, informing him that the American losses were about 700 men killed and wounded. The delegates, obviously adopting an optimistic, even propagandist, view of the circumstances, noted that "[British] General Howe is making his last effort. If he meets with a defeat, his is undone, as he is a considerable distance from his ships, his situation is truly critical." The delegates concluded their correspondence by advising the governor that the "North Carolina Troops were not ingaged in the late action."[16]

On Friday, September 12, Washington, having the evening before written to the Continental Congress that the British were "masters of the field," marched his army away from Chester and encamped near Germantown. For the next three weeks the two armies maneuvered about the region immediately near Philadelphia. On September 26 Howe's troops marched into Philadelphia, the members of the Continental Congress having vacated the city on the twentieth and established their temporary seat of government at Lancaster before moving to York. Washington eventually moved his army nearer to the British until on October 3 combat was again imminent.[17]

Near dusk on the third, the American troops were to begin marching toward the British forces at Germantown. According to Washington's intricate and involved battle plan, the troops were to approach to within about two miles of the British in the early hours of the fourth, make final dispositions, and attack before daybreak. The American plan called for the army to envelope Howe's British in a pincer movement: four columns of Washington's soldiers would move simultaneously in a concerted approach spread across seven miles.

The Battle of Germantown was fought on October 4, 1777. Even though North Carolina's troops fought valiantly, they were forced to retreat, and Gen. Francis Nash was
mortally wounded. General Howe's "redcoats" defeated General Washington's army.
This print, from an engraving by Lossing & Barritt, is reproduced from the September
1853 issue of *Harper's Magazine*.

Success rested on precision and coordinated timing of movements—a doubtful prospect given the American officers' scarcity of training, experience, and
discipline. Moreover, British patrols alerted their officers about 3:00 A.M. that
the Americans were on the move.[18]

About six o'clock on the fourth, Gen. John Sullivan's command, which
formed the center of the American line, attacked British positions in his front.
Although many delegates in the Continental Congress had blamed Sullivan for
the American defeat at Brandywine Creek, Washington nonetheless selected
him to lead the frontal attack. Because of various delays, Sullivan's assault was
an hour late in commencing, but his troops drove the British before them. At
the commencement of the action, General Nash's North Carolina brigade was
held in reserve, but sometime after nine o'clock the North Carolinians were
ordered to move out to Sullivan's flank. Nash's troops pushed forward and
fell into the thick of the fighting. But overall delays, problems, and mistakes

by the American officers began to diminish the troops' ability to engage the British. American units broke and ran from the field. Although General Washington early in the action had felt that victory was achievable, Sullivan's troops—believing they had been surrounded by enemy soldiers—began running to the rear.[19]

The North Carolinians did not break and run with their comrades. Even though Nash's men had not been thrown into the most intense action, they had gone forward at the point of their bayonets and engaged British troops. As Sullivan's men rushed backward, General Nash moved his brigade into position to stem the retreat and initiated a stubborn resistance, while slowly pulling back. His men had earlier captured seven pieces of artillery from the British, but as they pulled back had to relinquish possession of the weapons in order not to inordinately hinder their withdrawal. As Nash sat astride his mount directing his men, a cannonball slammed into his left thigh, mangling the limb and killing the horse. A musket ball hit him in the head, causing blindness. His men fashioned a stretcher from limbs and poles and carried their gravely wounded commander from the field. Nash's troops had "behaved well" and "with great resolution" during the battle but were now jolted by the reality that their commander was likely mortally wounded. Other North Carolina officers—Col. Henry Irwin, Capt. Jacob Turner, Adjt. David Lucas, and Lt. John McCann—were killed. An undocumented number of North Carolinians were wounded, including Col. Thomas Polk (Fourth North Carolina), who was shot through the jaws.[20] Bertie County's soldiers in the North Carolina brigade were involved in the day's frenzied action, in which Pvt. Isaac Sholar of Capt. John Pugh Williams's company, Fifth North Carolina Regiment, was killed. General Nash died on October 7.[21]

By ten o'clock—a mere four hours after Sullivan's initial attack—the Americans were routed and in full retreat. The men did not curtail their retreat until they had gone about twenty miles from the battlefield.[22] For the second time in a little over three weeks, General Washington's army had been defeated by General Howe's "redcoats." The defeat ensured that Philadelphia, the seat of the Continental Congress, would remain occupied by the British. Despite the defeat, certain American leaders remained encouraged at the war effort, and General Washington was committed to carry on. On October 6, John Penn wrote to Governor Caswell that the Continental Congress (then reassembled at York, Pennsylvania) had received from General Washington's headquarters an express letter in which the commander stated that he "had harangued his army, who promised to follow him where he pleased." The soldiers were reported to

North Carolina's Continental Line regiments (collectively, brigade) were relieved from the Southern Department on February 5, 1777, and assigned to Gen. George Washington's main army. Not until the early summer of 1777, however, did all of the state's regiments join up with Washington's army. Brig. Gen. Francis Nash commanded the North Carolinians until he was mortally wounded at Germantown, Pennsylvania, on October 4, 1777. On December 20, 1777—two days after Washington's army arrived at its winter camp at Valley Forge, Pennsylvania—General Washington (*left*) placed Brig. Gen. Lachlan McIntosh (*right*) of Georgia in command of the North Carolina brigade. McIntosh commanded the vastly understrength brigade until May 15, 1778, when Washington transferred him to another command. Images from the Prints and Photographs Division, Library of Congress.

be "in high spirits," and according to Penn, Washington was "determined" to attack Howe's British forces again.[23]

With the death of Francis Nash, no general officer was left with the North Carolina brigade to assume its command. General Washington initially gave command of the brigade to Brig. Gen. Alexander McDougall of New York. On October 13 the troops were inspected for the purpose of ascertaining clothing needs. The troops of the brigade were pathetic in their current attire: the inspection revealed that cumulatively they desperately needed 415 coats, 461 waistcoats, 752 pairs of pants, 779 pairs of socks, 456 pairs of shoes, 599 shirts, 618 blankets, and other items.[24] Winter in the northern clime was quickly approaching, and the soldiers' exposed state invited misery, suffering, illness, and death.

Two and a half years into the war, American successes in battle were few, and the Continental army's ranks, including the North Carolina regiments, were not filled. The Continental Congress resolved that each state should implement measures to recruit men for the army from every county/jurisdiction. Because North Carolina's Continental Line regiments were substantially undermanned, the North Carolina Council of State in early September 1777 resolved that every county in the state be deemed a distinct district for recruiting purposes. The council appointed an influential citizen of each county to oversee and manage recruiting activities; it appointed Thomas Pugh to the requisite duties for Bertie County.[25]

Throughout the remainder of October into mid-December, Washington and Howe's armies did not engage in another major action. While foraging parties and patrols periodically encountered each other, by December 15 Washington was ready to encamp his troops in their winter quarters. He selected Valley Forge, a bleak and desolate site on Valley Creek about twenty miles northwest of Philadelphia, from which the Americans would be in sufficiently close proximity to monitor the British army. On December 16 Washington issued orders to his troops that "tents are to be carried to the encampment [at Valley Forge] . . . and pitched immediately." Washington's Continental army arrived at Valley Forge on Thursday, December 18.[26]

The North Carolinians remained under the command of a general officer not from their home state. On December 20 Washington designated Brig. Gen. Lachlan McIntosh of Georgia to command the North Carolina brigade. The brigade's nine regiments that arrived at the winter encampment consisted of only 1,051 men. The units were drastically under full strength. Furthermore, of the men who arrived at Valley Forge, 517, or nearly half, were unavailable for duty—353 men were reported sick, and another 164 were deemed unfit for service because of the lack of adequate clothing. Among the North Carolinians was an undetermined number of Bertie County men. The primary task to be undertaken by the troops was to build huts for their protection from the brutal cold of the Pennsylvania winter.[27]

The area about the encampment was well timbered, offering ample raw material with which to construct huts. On the other hand, a sufficient number of haul animals (horses, oxen, or mules) was not available to drag logs into the camp. Men were forced to harness themselves to fallen trees and manually drag and heave them to the locations at which their huts were to be situated. Each hut was to be fourteen by sixteen feet and to house twelve men.[28] Quarters would be cramped.

The Continental soldiers in Gen. George Washington's army endured the harsh winter of 1777–1778 at Valley Forge, Pennsylvania. Extreme cold and snow contributed to the soldiers' suffering and even death for a significant number, including an undetermined number of Bertie County men. This artist's depiction shows officers and men in the cold, snowy conditions at the encampment. Image courtesy of Google images.

The winter of 1777–1778 in southeastern Pennsylvania was brutal. Bitter cold, wind, and snow made life miserable and dangerous for the poorly clad and inadequately provisioned Continental troops. Undernourished and poorly clothed, living in crowded, damp quarters, the army was ravaged by sickness and disease. Typhoid, jaundice, dysentery, and pneumonia were among the various diseases that killed an estimated 2,500 men that winter. Although Washington repeatedly petitioned for relief, the Continental Congress was unable to provide it, and the soldiers suffered intolerably.[29]

Bertie County's Continental soldiers at Valley Forge suffered equally with their comrades. Jeremiah Cooper and David Broadwell died on undisclosed dates. Jeremiah McGlaughon passed away on April 21, 1778 (having suffered through the winter only to succumb once spring had arrived). A number of other Bertie County men also likely died while encamped along Valley Creek. The men were "omitted" (i.e., dropped) from the rolls of their units while the North Carolina brigade remained at Valley Forge. Joseph Boon, Jacob Pearce, John Liscombe, and Abraham Green were omitted in January 1778. Willis Boon, James Hicks, Shadrach Holmes, William Pearce, Ephraim Todd, and William Todd were omitted from the rolls in February 1778—Holmes, Pearce, and Ephraim Todd had died on undetermined dates. Jeremiah Cooper was omitted in April 1778, also likely having passed away on an undisclosed date.[30]

Unfortunately, sickness and death were realities within the army encampment. Many of the soldiers who became desperately sick or ill at Valley Forge were transported to outlying hospitals in nearby communities. Men who died at those locations were most often buried in church cemeteries near the hospitals. The burial sites for the Bertie County men who died at Valley Forge were not noted in official records.[31]

In April a few additional men from North Carolina arrived at Valley Forge to be incorporated into the state's brigade. The men were members of the Tenth North Carolina Regiment, commanded by Col. Abraham Sheppard. The North Carolina General Assembly had authorized the regiment a year earlier, and the Continental Congress had placed the unit in the "Continental establishment" on June 12, 1777. Sheppard encountered inordinate difficulties in recruiting men for the unit. While a deadline of July 1, 1777, had been established for Sheppard and his subordinate officers to recruit three hundred men for the regiment, they failed to reach that goal by the stipulated date. Not until early August did the officers finally assemble the quota of men; but then only three organized companies appeared at Kinston, the regimental rendezvous site. By late August—nearly two months after the recruitment deadline—Sheppard still had not begun to march northward. On September 15 Gov. Richard Caswell ordered the colonel to march to Richmond. By October 6, Sheppard and his men had proceeded to a point only two miles north of Halifax, and at that point Sheppard absented himself to visit his home in Dobbs County. Caswell, exasperated, ordered Sheppard to return to his regiment and move out. By the time the colonel returned to his unit and began its northerly march, he was obliged to leave behind forty-seven men who were too ill for the trek. By mid-February the Tenth Regiment had only covered about 150 miles, reaching Hanover, Virginia. Finally, in early March, Sheppard and his men arrived at the smallpox inoculation station on the Potomac River. Six men died as a result of the inoculations, but more succumbed to measles. Meanwhile, two Bertie County men—John Conner and Malachi Wiggins— had enlisted in the regiment.[32]

North Carolina's Continental troops at Valley Forge were in dire need of clothing; therefore, in early May 1778 the General Assembly resolved that the citizens of each of the North Carolina counties provide various articles of clothing for those troops. Bertie County residents were to furnish 55 hats, 220 yards of linen, 110 yards of woolen or double-woven cloth, 110 pairs of shoes, and 110 pairs of stockings. The county justices and militia field officers were responsible for allocating the county's quota of articles to the various companies. The company captains were further responsible for identifying the persons in their districts who would provide particular items. All items were to be valued by three freeholders, and persons providing the items were to receive certificates of valuation from the colonel or commanding officer to be used to offset taxes due. The colonel or commanding officer was empowered to hire wagons to deliver the clothing to the state commissary of stores in Halifax by September. The commissary would be responsible for transporting the clothing to the North Carolina troops serving in the Continental army.[33]

Winter gradually yielded to more moderate temperatures and springtime conditions at Valley Forge. The time for a military campaign, defensive or offensive, against the British was quickly approaching, and General Washington was making plans. On May 15 Washington transferred Brig. Gen. Lachlan McIntosh to a separate command and appointed Col. Thomas Clark to command the egregiously undermanned North Carolina brigade. The regiments of the brigade were so vastly below full strength that the state's General Assembly in April passed a bill intended to bring them up to full complement. The law stipulated that throughout the state, militiamen were to be drafted to serve in the Continental army. The legislature chose to draft members of militias inasmuch as previous efforts to recruit volunteer Continental soldiers within the state had failed to meet the lawmakers' expectations.

The Continental Congress, independent of the state General Assembly's directions, decided in late May to consolidate the regiments then at Valley Forge rather than await reinforcements from North Carolina. That body directed General Washington to form the North Carolinians into as many regiments as there were men to complete them. Supernumerary officers were to be immediately dispatched to North Carolina to assist in raising and organizing the militiamen being drafted for Continental duty. Congress further stipulated that North Carolina, in addition to recruiting militiamen for the regiments reorganized at Valley Forge, fill four new regiments with draftees from within the state. Those four new regiments were to remain within North Carolina, pending further orders from the Continental Congress. Officers in excess of those needed for the reorganized regiments at Valley Forge and the draftee regiments raised in North Carolina were to be dismissed from the army.[34]

On June 2 General Washington wrote to Henry Laurens, president of the Continental Congress, that he would "undertake the reform of the North Carolina Batallions [regiments] in Camp, as soon as circumstances will admit."[35] The ten North Carolina regiments were reduced and consolidated in short order. Rank-and-file members of the disbanded and reduced units were transferred, generally to the First and Second Regiments. Col. Thomas Clark retained command of the North Carolina brigade. The following table delineates the actions taken with the North Carolina regiments.

TABLE 4
Reduction and Consolidation Actions,
Regiments of the North Carolina Brigade,
Valley Forge, Pennsylvania, Early June 1778[36]

Regiment	Action(s) Taken
First	Reorganized to consist of nine companies (previously comprised of eight companies)
Second	Reorganized to consist of nine companies (previously comprised of eight companies)
Third	Reduced to a cadre and relieved from the North Carolina brigade
Fourth	Reduced to a cadre, relieved from the main Continental army, and assigned to the Southern Department
Fifth	Reduced to a cadre, relieved from the main Continental army, and assigned to the Southern Department
Sixth	Reduced to a cadre, relieved from the main Continental army, and assigned to the Southern Department
Seventh	Disbanded
Eighth	Disbanded
Ninth	Disbanded
Tenth	Disbanded

Four Bertie County residents—Capt. John Pugh Williams (Fifth Regiment), Adjt. Benjamin Coffield (Sixth), and Lts. Benjamin Bryer and William Walton (both of the Seventh)—were still serving as officers with the North Carolina regiments on June 1, 1778. Williams and Bryer resigned their commissions (they likely were deemed to be supernumeraries), leaving only Coffield and Walton as county residents serving as officers in the regular army after early June 1778.

On June 18 elements of Washington's army began departing Valley Forge, having learned that the British had evacuated Philadelphia and were moving overland in the direction of New York. At Valley Forge on the eighteenth, General Washington issued orders that directed six brigades to march that day. The remainder of the army was to march at five o'clock the following morning. Col. Thomas Clark's North Carolina regiments were assigned to Gen. Marquis de Lafayette's brigade, which departed the winter quarters during the early hours of the nineteenth. Detachments of Washington's command began annoying and popping at the British's left flank. The Second North Carolina Regiment had been included in Brig. Gen. Charles Scott's command, which was ordered to perform that duty. Two companies of North Carolinians were ordered to harass the British right flank as part of Brig. Gen. Daniel Morgan's command. Gen. Sir Henry Clinton now commanded the king's forces, having replaced General Howe. The British arrived at Monmouth Court House, New Jersey, during the night of the twenty-sixth and halted there.[37]

On the morning of the twenty-eighth, Clinton's forces began departing Monmouth in two columns. General Washington ordered Maj. Gen. Charles Lee to attack. No concerted battle plan was drawn up, but a rough battle line was formed in the rear of the British—Lafayette's command on the right, Brig. Gen. Anthony Wayne's in the center, and Scott's on the left. The North Carolina regiments were assigned to the right wing with General Scott's troops. The Americans repulsed an enemy cavalry charge, but soon elements on the right of the line began to fall back, exposing the line to being flanked by British troops. Lafayette ordered his troops to pull back rather than be outflanked. Clinton reportedly began moving "heavy columns" toward the Americans. Washington rode forward to find fleeing soldiers from Lee's command. Appalled at the situation, he caught up with Lee and heatedly demanded an explanation. Upon receiving no satisfactory answer, he dismissed his subordinate and set about personally trying to rally Lee's men. The Americans established a new line along a hedgerow and held off the British long enough for their comrades to take up a defensive position to the west. Late in the day, both armies were bloodied and drained from the summer heat and the tension of combat. Clinton ordered his troops to break off from the battle and withdraw toward New York. Washington wished to continue the pursuit, but his men were too exhausted. Consequently, Clinton's redcoats were able to reach the safety of Sandy Hook, New Jersey.[38]

Clark's North Carolinians behaved well during the day's action. A number of Bertie County men—Ezekiel White, Solomon Howard, Abraham Jenkins, and William White—later stated that they participated in the day's combat. Pvt. John Barrow declared that he was held out of the action and served as a "baggage guard."[39]

The Continental Congress, while representing the thirteen states, did not have the unilateral authority to draft men within the states to raise army units (companies, regiments, and so on). Therefore, the Congress appealed to the states to raise regiments to serve in the national army. On May 1, 1777, North Carolina's General Assembly passed "An Act to Establish a Militia in this State," a statute that provided for a militia for "Defending and securing the Liberties of a free State." The law stipulated that "all persons within the ages of sixteen and fifty shall be liable to be drafted, and every person so drafted, obliged to serve or find an able bodied person in room." With the enactment of that measure, the state could thenceforth draft militiamen to fill regiments for which volunteers did not come forth in sufficient numbers. The "drafted militia" could be assembled and, at the direction of the General Assembly, designated for Continental service.[40]

A May 1778 act by the General Assembly directed that 2,648 men from across the state be "raised and detached from the Militia." A specified quota was apportioned to each county, and that number was again apportioned by the colonel of the county among its militia companies. As a result, every militia company in the state had to furnish its "proper share" of the troops. Those men who became Continental soldiers and faithfully served their nine months of actual service were, thereafter, to be exempt from military service for a period of three years. Of the statewide total, 411 men were to be raised in the Edenton District, with 76 to come from Bertie County. County militia commanders were responsible for ensuring that their quotas were raised, whether through volunteerism or draft. (Generally, county commanders first sought volunteers and then resorted to drafts by ballot to fill any deficit in reaching stipulated quotas.)

The law required the colonel or commanding officer in each county to order the field officers and captains of his regiment to meet at the courthouse on or before May 25, and "apportion the Men to be raised in the County" to companies in proportion to the number of militia requested. Each volunteer was to be paid a $100 bounty, whereas each draftee was to receive $50. Moreover, each volunteer or draftee was entitled to receive from the commanding officer of the county a pair of shoes, a pair of stockings, two shirts, a hunting shirt, a waistcoat with sleeves, a pair of breeches and trousers, a hat, a blanket, and five yards of tent cloth. Every sixth man was to receive an ax and a pot or camp kettle. The clothing and camp items were to be obtained from county residents, who were to receive receipts and valuation certificates endorsed by the county's commanding officer. The commander could demand that needed items be seized from citizens if sufficient numbers of items were not voluntarily provided. (Tax gatherers were to deduct the value of any such seized item from future tax collections.) Each district's brigadier general was responsible for obtaining "good and sufficient" arms from the populace and having them distributed to the troops.[41]

Bertie County's "drafted militia," along with other Edenton District troops, were to march to the rendezvous site at Halifax. The troops from the Halifax, New Bern, and Wilmington districts were likewise to assemble at Halifax. Militiamen raised in the Hillsborough and Salisbury districts were to march to Peytonsburg, Virginia. While the men were originally intended to be assembled and marched northward to join the North Carolina brigade, the Continental Congress directed that they be organized into "new" regiments and remain in North Carolina until needed and requested by the Congress.[42]

Bertie County's militia officers set about raising men to be detached from their regiment. Some men volunteered, while others were drafted for the nine-month tour of duty. Lewis Boon and Uriah Dunning "enlisted" together. Peter White, a member of Capt. James Campbell's company, similarly enlisted, as did John Hoggard, William Watford, Hardy Robinson, Amos Thomas, William Freeman, and others. Thomas Tart's company was designated to furnish six men for the detached service. The company, "in order not to stand [a] draft," collected $200 in "Continental money" to provide to anyone who would volunteer. Tart, "[r]ather than be drafted[,] . . . took the money & volunteered." He, along with the other Bertie volunteers and draftees, rendezvoused at Windsor.[43]

By Saturday, June 13, Bertie County militia officers had designated the seventy-six men to be detached from the county's militia for Continental service. Capt. William Williams was "chosen" to command the contingent; Lt. Col. Thomas Pugh certified that Williams was the designated commander. Williams wrote to Governor Caswell on the thirteenth that he and his men were "preparing to march as soon as possible." Williams requested the governor to send his commission by the bearer of Williams's correspondence, "should [he] lose time" waiting for the document.[44]

Sometime after mid-June, Captain Williams marched his Bertie County contingent from Windsor to Col. Nicholas Long's "old field," near the town of Halifax. (Colonel Long was serving as North Carolina's deputy quartermaster general). There the Bertie County troops joined hundreds of detached militia from other counties waiting to be organized into companies and mustered into the Continental army. While the Bertie County troops were encamped near Halifax, Captain Williams "resigned his commission and returned home."[45]

By July 6 Col. James Hogun, former commander of the Seventh North Carolina Regiment, had assembled volunteers and draftees from eleven counties into a regiment. According to Col. Jethro Sumner, who had arrived at the Halifax camp three days previously, Hogun had nearly achieved "the proper establishment" of the unit but needed Gov. Richard Caswell's approval of the recommended subordinate officers. Hogun also required "some money to purchase forage" and other items before the regiment could depart for its northern assignment.[46]

On July 20 more than 520 "drafted militia" were mustered into the Third North Carolina Regiment ("Second Organization") at Halifax.[47] The regiment was comprised of nine companies. The company commanders—John Baker, Keder Ballard, Reading Blount, Gee Bradley, Francis Child, Henry Dixon, Thomas Hogg, Joseph Montfort, and Michael Quinn—had served as officers in six different regiments prior to the regimental consolidations at Valley Forge in early June. The majority of the Bertie County troops were assigned to Maj. Reading Blount's company. (Blount was likely a familiar character to at least some of the Bertie County troops, in that his uncle was the influential William Gray of the county.) But since there were more county militiamen than authorized for one company, some men were assigned to other companies, including those of Capts. John Baker and Francis Child.[48]

Colonel Hogun and his regiment, upward of 550 men strong (including officers and field staff), departed the camp near Halifax and marched northward through Virginia, Maryland, and New Jersey, arriving in Philadelphia about August 27. Hogun then trooped his command to General Washington's headquarters at White Plains, New York. When within six miles of the North Carolina brigade at headquarters, Hogun, to his great "Mortification," received orders to march his regiment to West Point, on the Hudson River. He and his men were assigned as a "working party." Disappointed, Hogun, in compliance with his orders, marched his men to West Point, where they were

Reading Blount (1757–1807) was commissioned as a captain in the Third N.C. Regiment in 1776 and became a major in 1778. The majority of the troops from Bertie County were assigned to his company. He commanded troops at the Battles of Guilford Courthouse and Eutaw Springs. Image provided courtesy of the North Carolina State Archives.

(according to Hogun) "disagreeably situated, being hemmed in by the River on one side, and a chain of broken rocky mountains on the other."[49]

While the remainder of the North Carolina brigade was assigned to Washington's headquarters, Hogun and his band of nine-month drafted militia labored at West Point through the end of summer and into autumn. Constructing fortifications was not Hogun's desired duty. Commanding a regiment of men whose tools of endeavor were picks, spades, shovels, axes, saws, mallets, and hammers, rather than rifles, muskets, and bayonets, displeased the colonel. The disposition of the army about the New York region seemed "a little curious" to Hogun, who found displeasure in a number of aspects of his and his men's assignment. Bertie County residents and regimental members John Hoggard and William Watford later stated that they and their comrades marched to West Point "and worked on the Fort." Fellow county resident Hardy Robinson similarly recalled that "while in the Regular Service . . . he was employed the greater part of the . . . time . . . working on a Fort [Fort Putnam] at West Point."[50]

Washington's assignment of Hogun's drafted militia to work details at West Point stemmed at least partly from the fact that the men were poorly armed. The weapons the men had lugged from North Carolina were generally in such a poor state of repair that they were useless for combat. General Washington had to procure four hundred muskets from the armory at Albany to provide to the men. It is likely that Washington consciously did Colonel Hogun a favor by not exposing his inadequately armed regiment to potential combat.[51]

Hogun's troops, laboring in the pleasant New York highland autumn weather, were not immune to illness and camp sickness. On Thursday, October 22, Hogun held a general muster of his regiment, during which ninety (more than one in five) of the rank-and-file members present were sick. Another sixty-seven men were reported as sick-absent at undisclosed locations. In all, more than one-fourth of the members of the regiment were incapacitated because of illness.[52]

Hogun's nine-month men labored at West Point until about mid-December. At that time, a regiment was needed in Philadelphia to perform garrison duty, and Washington chose Hogun's unit for that assignment. In Washington's words, Hogun's North Carolinians were "a tender set of people . . . illy provided with Cloathing and therefore require warm quarters." Again, Washington was exhibiting conciliatory gestures to Hogun and his men, assigning them to a locale in which they would be less apt to suffer during the dead of winter. Hogun immediately withdrew his regiment from West Point and marched the troops the roughly 140 miles to Philadelphia, arriving by January 16, 1779. Hogun's troops immediately "settled in the Barracks" at the end of "a severe march" in weather that was "excessively cold." Upon arriving in Philadelphia, the troops were "in reasonable heath and good spirits." Only three months remained in their terms of service.[53]

On January 9, 1779, the Continental Congress appointed James Hogun and fellow North Carolinian Jethro Sumner brigadier generals in the Continental army. Hogun's regiment of drafted militia remained in Philadelphia until about early April, when the troops were ordered to return to Halifax, where they would be discharged. Lt. Col. Robert Mebane was placed in command of the regiment. The troops who were physically able to travel were transported by ship from the "head" of Elk River (present-day Elkton, Maryland) to Suffolk, Virginia. From Suffolk they marched to Halifax, where they were discharged on April 20, having not been involved in any combat during their tour of duty. The men, including those from Bertie County, would not again be liable for active military service until April 1782. At least seven Bertie County men—Arthur Britt, Nathaniel Cooper, James Hubbard, David James, Thomas Sorrell, Burrell White, and Caleb Woodward—died while serving in the regiment, most of them at West Point. James Asbett [Asbell] may also have died, as he was "omitted" from the regiment's rolls in October 1778. Thomas Ryan was discharged in late October or early November at West Point.[54]

By the summer of 1779, nearly all the Bertie County men who had volunteered or had been drafted from the militia for service in the Continental army were no longer in the army's ranks. The men who had enlisted at Windsor in April and May 1776 for terms of service of three years or two and one-half years had been discharged, as had been the nine-month drafted militia of Colonel Hogun's regiment. In all, more than 80 men had been discharged; 8 (officers) had resigned; more than 30 men had died in service; one man (Isaac Sholar) had been killed in action; and one (Pvt. Cader Raby) had deserted. As of early autumn 1779, the relatively few county men still serving in the North Carolina brigade (First and Second North Carolina Regiments) were assigned to the army's Highlands Department (in New York) and stationed at West Point.[55]

The situation in South Carolina, however, was an important matter to American leaders in the spring and early summer of 1779. As early as May 7, 1779, the Continental Congress was concerned over the state of affairs in the South. The Congress, fearing a British invasion of South Carolina, was of the opinion that the southern army needed to be reinforced. The Congress resolved that recently raised Virginia troops be ordered to immediately join the army in South Carolina. On July 12 the Congress resolved that North Carolina "afford the army in South Carolina the reinforcements of which they stand in need." On July 7 Governor Caswell wrote to Brig. Gen. Isaac Gregory (of the North Carolina militia) at Kinston and provided him with a "scheme of a Draft" to be made from the Edenton District militia brigade. The purpose of the draft was to complete raising a militia force of two thousand men, as directed by the state's General Assembly in May. The legislature had passed an act to raise "regular forces" (soldiers for the Continental army) for the defense of North Carolina and its neighboring states. The law provided that on or before July 1, 1779, if ten militiamen would persuade one able-bodied man to enlist in the Continental army for a term of service of eighteen months or longer, then the ten men would, during the subject period of enlistment, be exempt "from all military duties or drafts whatsoever," except should North Carolina be invaded, or a case of domestic insurrection should arise. The General Assembly desired that two thousand soldiers be raised pursuant to the act's provisions. In the event that the stated quota of men was not enlisted in the Continental service by July 1, then the governor, with the advice of the Council of State, would be empowered to "embody [draft] a number of militia equal to the deficiency." The deficiency (if any) was to be made up from all of the counties of the state, in proportion to the numbers of men they furnished by enlistment under the act.[56]

Obviously, by early July two thousand men had not been raised across the state, and the quota for the Edenton District had not been attained. Therefore, Caswell ordered Gregory to have the Edenton District draftees (including those from Bertie County) rendezvous at Edenton on August 1, as the "situation of affairs to the Southward [in South Carolina]" made it necessary for the "matter" to receive the general's prompt attention. Caswell directed that the force be marched immediately to South Carolina and placed under the command of Brig. Gen. Alexander Lillington.[57] It is unknown how many Bertie County men enlisted under the act's provisions, or how many were drafted to fill the county's stipulated quota (also unknown). John Clemmons and William Johnston enlisted in the Third North Carolina Regiment on July 1, 1779. Other county men likely were forced into service pursuant to the "scheme" that Governor Caswell furnished General Gregory.

On November 11, 1779, the Continental Congress relieved the North Carolina brigade (commanded by Brigadier General Hogun) from the Highlands Department and assigned it to the Southern Department. Thirteen days later, Hogun's troops departed West Point and arrived in Philadelphia by December 5. At Philadelphia the troops sought water transportation to the south, but the Continental Congress was unable to provide the necessary vessels; nevertheless, vessels were made available to ferry Hogun's men across Chesapeake Bay. On February 19, 1780, Hogun's North Carolinians reached Wilmington, North Carolina, having marched in horrible winter conditions—bitter cold and snow in drifts three feet deep in some locations along their route. During the evening of March 3, Hogun's two-regiment brigade—approximately six hundred members strong (and approximately 40 percent under strength)—finally marched into Charleston more than three months after departing West Point. A handful of Bertie County men—including James Anderson, James Farmer, Absalom Wiley, Lewis Williford, and William Wren—were present in Hogun's command when it arrived at Charleston.[58]

Hogun's men joined the American forces under the command of Maj. Gen. Benjamin Lincoln, commander of the Southern Department. Included in the Charleston garrison were other North Carolinians, predominantly nine-month soldiers of the reconstituted Third North Carolina Regiment (Lt. Col. Robert Mebane, commanding) and detached militia. Among the militiamen was Capt. Allen Ramsay's company, which included Bertie County men. Lincoln's force eventually totaled about 5,400 Continental soldiers and militia from South Carolina, North Carolina, Virginia, and Georgia, as well as some armed citizens. British naval and army forces besieged Charleston in March. Throughout April and into May the British tightened their siege lines about Lincoln's garrison. Unable to withstand the deprivation of essential items (food, provisions, forage, arms, and so on) created by the siege and unable to withdraw and escape, Lincoln called a council of general officers during the evening of May 11. The council suggested capitulation. Shortly before noon the following day, Lincoln surrendered his entire command—the largest surrender of an American force during the war. The Americans were quite weary and worn from the two-plus-months' siege. One British officer referred to the men as a "most ragged rabble," while another termed them "a ragged dirty looking set of People."[59]

Pvt. James Anderson of Bertie County eluded the British and escaped capture at Charleston, but other of his Bertie comrades were not so fortunate. James Farmer, Absalom Wiley, Lewis Williford, and William Wren were captured. Wren later died as a prisoner of war. Their brigade commander, General Hogun, was likewise captured, as were more than four dozen other North Carolina officers. Hogun would later die as a prisoner of war.

Surrender of the North Carolina brigade en masse on May 12 essentially destroyed the entire North Carolina Continental Line. Only those officers who happened to be on furloughs to their homes escaped. Furthermore, four regiments of the state's militia had also surrendered. The surrender of the southern army at Charleston, as well as other recent setbacks within the Southern Department, caused great dismay among the Patriots in North Carolina. Surely the citizens of Bertie County were similarly distressed. The few county sons who remained on active duty in the Continental army were now prisoners of war facing uncertain fates. Moreover, members of the county's militia in Captain Ramsey's company were likewise prisoners.[60] The conflict had been ongoing for more than five years, and no decisive war-ending victory appeared to be within the capability of American forces.

Furthermore, by the fall of 1780 more than five and one-half years of war had drained North Carolina's financial and other resources. The state was encountering extreme obstacles in providing rations and desperately needed commodities to its troops. When the state's General Assembly convened at Hillsborough in early September, the legislators fully recognized that "the operations of war" had made it difficult to purchase provisions sufficient to supply North Carolina's military forces. Therefore, the General Assembly passed a statute that imposed a "specific provision tax" on all state inhabitants. Each person, for every one hundred pounds' value of their taxable property, was to contribute a stipulated amount of specified agricultural commodities. For each base valuation ($£100$ value), a person was "bound and obliged" to provide to state commissary agents any of the following: one peck of Indian corn; a half-peck of wheat; 5 pounds good flour; one and one-fourth peck of clean oats; three-fourths peck of rye; one peck of rough rice; one-third peck of clean, merchantable rice; three pounds of good pork; two pounds of fatted pork; or four and one-half pounds of good beef. Citizens were further obligated to deliver the items to warehouses designated within each county. Within Bertie County, a warehouse was designated in Windsor. Further, the justices of each county were mandated to appoint a commissioner "for collecting provision taxes"; Bertie County justices appointed Peter Clifton.[61]

Clifton immediately set about gathering hundreds of hogs and cattle; thousands of pounds of fresh and salted pork, bacon, and beef; and thousands of barrels and bushels of grain, principally corn. Clifton's accounts reveal that Bertie County's citizens individually contributed livestock and commodities valued at from a few shillings up to hundreds of pounds.[62]

When the North Carolina General Assembly next convened on January 18, 1781, a principal item of business was to reconstitute the state's Continental Line regiments. While six regiments were currently authorized in accordance with prior mandates, the Continental Congress, in consideration of the reduced number of officers, on October 21, 1780, had recommended that North Carolina complete only two regiments. Members of the legislature realized that attempting to recruit volunteers for the Continental army on the basis of prior experiences and in consideration of the mass troop surrender at Charleston was "impracticable." Therefore, the legislators decided to once again mandate that the state's militia units furnish the necessary men. A total of 2,724 men were to be raised statewide and organized into four regiments. The colonel or commanding officer of each county's regiment(s) was directed to muster his command on or before March 20, 1781, and to raise, through volunteerism and/or draft, the county's quota of men. Those men who had served nine months pursuant to the May 1778 statute were exempt from having to serve. The men subject to military service were to be divided into "classes" of fifteen men each. Each class was to provide at least one individual (volunteer or draftee) to serve. Each man who volunteered or was drafted was obliged to perform a twelve-month term of duty. Each was authorized to receive a bounty of two thousand pounds and "the same clothing as Continental soldiers." Despite the bounties to be paid to soldiers and some support to be provided to their families, the draft law proved to be unpopular. Further, it appeared improbable that 2,700-plus soldiers could be raised pursuant to the statute's provisions.[63]

James Campbell was serving as commander of the Bertie County militia inasmuch as Arthur Brown, the former colonel, had, about December 1780 or January 1781, "refused to act any longer." The number of men under Campbell's command who were subject to Continental military service in accordance with the provisions of the 1781 militia law is not ascertainable from extant records. Nonetheless, almost three dozen county men were enlisted in the Continental army for twelve-month terms of service during 1781; the majority of the men were enlisted about mid-April. The men were assigned to the First, Second, Third, and Fourth North Carolina Regiments. The men, along with the month in which each enlisted, were: Benjamin Baker, James Bates, Richard Billups, Thomas Billups, William Bonner, Jethro Butler, John Butler, James Davidson, Hugh Dundelow, Charles Evans, James Hall, Micajah Hoard, Jeremiah James, Elijah Jenkins, Hardy Keel, Moses Manley, William Mitchell, Abraham Morris, Henry Nichols, James Outlaw, William Smith, Amos Thomas, Thomas Thomas, and William Wilson—April; Richard Richardson, James Thomas, Absalom Wiley, and Josiah Wilson—May; James Gregory—June; Aaron Freeman—August; Henry Cobb and John Weston—September; and Josiah Nowell and Israel Outhouse—undisclosed month (enlisted in "1781").[64]

The men drafted into the Continental service were ultimately destined to join Maj. Gen. Nathanael Greene's army. On October 30, 1780, the Continental Congress appointed Greene to command the Southern Department and its army, relieving Maj. Gen. Horatio Gates of that duty. Gates, who briefly succeeded General Lincoln as commander of the Southern Department, had led the southern army into a disastrous defeat at Camden, South Carolina, in August. That disaster directly led the Continental Congress to dismiss Gates and to appoint Greene. By early December Greene arrived in North Carolina to assume his command. After several months of strengthening his army and maneuvering throughout the Piedmont and into Virginia, Greene's forces met Gen. Lord Charles Cornwallis's British army at Guilford Courthouse on March 15, 1781.[65]

Cornwallis, commander of British forces in the South, had marched his army of redcoats from South Carolina into North Carolina in January. A British force commanded by Gen. Banastre Tarleton had been decisively defeated at Cowpens, South Carolina, on January 17, 1781, by Americans commanded by Brig. Gen. Daniel Morgan, one of Greene's subordinates. Cornwallis was

Hardy Murfree (1752–1809) rose to the rank of lieutenant colonel. He successfully led troops of the Second N.C. Regiment against British forces near Murfree's Landing. Image provided courtesy of the North Carolina Collection, University of North Carolina at Chapel Hill Library.

consumed with destroying Greene's army and chasing the American forces across North Carolina into Virginia. On March 15 Cornwallis's army moved on Greene's force, which was encamped at Guilford Courthouse. The British arrived on the field about midday. The two armies clashed ferociously for about ninety minutes. When the fighting ended, Cornwallis's forces held the field, although Greene's army had exacted heavy casualties on the British.[66]

The Bertie County militia draftees for the Continental Line regiments were marched to Winton (Hertford County), where they, along with other drafted men from the region, were placed under the purview of Continental army major Hardy Murfree (Hertford County). Murfree was endeavoring to organize the drafted troops from the Edenton District preparatory to marching them to Halifax, where the troops from the Edenton and Halifax districts were to rendezvous. Those men, once assembled at Halifax, were then to march into the Piedmont region of North Carolina, where they would be merged with troops from other districts. A smallpox epidemic was raging at Halifax, so Murfree placed the drafted troops under the command of Lts. Richard Andrews and Thomas Finney (both of the Second North Carolina

Regiment), who marched them into the Piedmont. Brig. Gen. Jethro Sumner, who was in charge of organizing all of North Carolina's drafted Continental soldiers, designated Halifax (initial rendezvous site for the Edenton and Halifax districts) and Harrisburg (near Charlotte) as the rendezvous sites. (Troops from the Salisbury, Hillsborough, New Bern, and Wilmington districts were directed to assemble at Harrisburg.)

On June 15 Murfree, then at Winton, wrote to Sumner: "I have sent Lieuts. [Richard] Andrews and [Thomas] Finn[e]y with the 12 months drafts . . . received from the counties of Bertie, Hertford and Gates." Almost seven weeks later, Murfree and the troops he had assembled were at Murfree's Landing (present-day Murfreesboro) on the Meherrin River. On August 1 Murfree again wrote to Sumner that he had "a few drafts" from Bertie, Hertford, and Gates counties. Apparently, the draftees were ill-clad, inasmuch as Murfree penned that he had "frequently applied for the mens cloathing but can't get but very little." Furthermore, with Gen. Cornwallis's forces in southeastern Virginia, Murfree was concerned that Loyalists in the northeastern region of North Carolina might become aroused. He wrote that "we are frequently alarmed expecting the enemy and plundering parties of tories among us." He concluded his correspondence by assuring Sumner that "if I can do anything in this part of the country to serve the Troops I will with pleasure do it."[67]

The draftees from the Edenton District were apparently quite tardy in joining Sumner's force. On July 14 Sumner was encamped near Salisbury "with five hundred rank and file badly equip[pe]d." His drafted Continentals lacked arms, equipment, and clothes. By "every industry possible," Sumner had managed to obtain almost three hundred "good arms . . . without bayonets," along with some cartridge boxes. He had distributed the arms to "some good men." Sumner wrote to Maj. Gen. Nathanael Greene that "difficulties" in timely marching the reinforcement of troops to Greene's command had "arisen" because the colonels of a number of counties had "been very tardy in making their drafts, and having them Cloathed." He continued that he "thought it more prudent" to remain at the camp for a few days so that he could further equip more of his men. He obviously was also awaiting the arrival of militia draftees from the east, noting to Greene that "Major Murfree of [the] Edenton District and Capt. [George] Doherty from Wilmington, must be far advanced on their march to join us, with a number of the drafts of those districts." On July 20 Gov. Thomas Burke wrote to Sumner that "a party of the drafts were immediately to march from Duplin County and another is on its way from Bertie."[68] The date on which the Bertie County troops joined up with Sumner's command is not evident from extant records.

About three weeks following the Battle of Guilford Courthouse, Greene had begun marching his army toward South Carolina and had ordered General Sumner to keep a close surveillance on the movement of Cornwallis's troops. Greene would no longer pursue and confront Cornwallis's forces—who marched to Wilmington—but he still needed to maintain a strong vigilance over the locations and movements of those forces. Greene also ordered Sumner to "collect and forward on the remaining troops [militia draftees] raised for the Southern Army." Sumner eventually raised a number of men sufficient to form into a regiment—the Second North Carolina Regiment, as the general termed the unit. Two other regiments were organized, yielding an undersized brigade for Sumner to command. Sumner and his men rejoined Greene's army about early August.[69]

During the early morning of Saturday, September 8, a British foraging party encountered a scouting party from Greene's army near Eutaw Springs, South Carolina. The British pursued the Americans and were led into an ambush, in which a number of men were killed and others captured. A nearby British camp contained a detachment of about 2,000 soldiers from the Charleston garrison. General Greene's force, estimated at 2,200 men, approached the British camp, which had been warned of the American's approach by an officer who escaped the earlier ambush. As the Americans moved on the camp, they formed two assault lines, with the militia in the first line and North Carolina, Virginia, and Maryland regulars in the second. The British charged the Americans and broke the first line. Sumner's North Carolina Continentals in the second line reinforced the first and temporarily held off the British charge until they, too, were broken. The Virginia and Maryland regulars then came to the aid of their comrades, stopping the British advance. The British began retreating in disorder while being pursued by the Americans. A majority of the Americans stopped to plunder British supplies. Soon a British officer was able to restore discipline to the remainder of the British force and launched a counterattack that drove the Americans from the British camp.[70]

The few Bertie County drafted Continentals who were serving with Sumner's command were involved in the day's action. Pvt. Absalom Wiley was wounded in the right arm. Jethro Butler, William Smith, James Outlaw, and Josiah Wilson later recalled that they participated in the confrontation. Rebecca James, widow of Pvt. Jeremiah James, stated that her husband also participated in the fight. Lt. Richard Andrews, who had marched with the Bertie County troops from Winton, was wounded.[71]

Following the affair at Eutaw Springs, Sumner's drafted Continentals were involved in no additional battles. By the spring of 1782, approximately two-thirds of the North Carolina Continental Line troops' terms of enlistments were nearing their expirations. During the three-month period from April through June, 766 of the 1,154 Continentals were slated to be discharged. Included in this number were Bertie County troops, who were discharged at or near Charleston at the expirations of their one-year terms of service (mostly April and May 1782). Pvt. Hugh Dundelow died in January, apparently of sickness, and John Murter, who had enlisted or been drafted in 1781, also "died in the Service."[72]

Gen. Charles Cornwallis had marched his army to the coast for resupply at Wilmington following the Battle of Guilford Courthouse. On April 25 Cornwallis's force, having rested but finding supplies severely limited, marched northward out of Wilmington, destined for Virginia, a replenishing source of men and supplies for his weary army. Cornwallis hoped to "conquer" Virginia and hasten the end of the war. On May 10 Cornwallis's army reached Halifax, where on the following day his troops skirmished with local militia before marching onward into Virginia that evening. Cornwallis and his army marched to Petersburg, then Richmond. Responding to orders from Gen. Henry Clinton, Cornwallis moved eastward toward the coast to take up a defensive position between the York and James rivers. At that location Cornwallis believed that his army could be resupplied by Clinton or evacuated for action elsewhere, if necessary. The British army arrived at Yorktown on August 1 and began to fortify its position there and also across the York River on Gloucester Point. All the while, Cornwallis anticipated assistance from Clinton's troops in New York and the British fleet in American waters. Unfortunately for Cornwallis, Gen. George Washington, with assistance from French troops and a naval force, surrounded Cornwallis's position, effectively bottling up his army. Following an American and French bombardment of five days, Cornwallis, having fatefully blundered by encamping his troops at Yorktown, surrendered his army on Friday, October 19. The British capitulation at Yorktown ended the major combat of the Revolutionary War. For all practical purposes, the war was over; nevertheless, almost two years would pass before the final peace treaty would be signed.[73]

While major combat may have concluded, North Carolina still had a responsibility to field its four Continental Line regiments. Nonetheless, by May 1782 the state's regiments were but a shadow of their previous strengths. The twelve-month draftees of the spring of 1781 were discharged from service, and few men were willing to enlist. In May every twentieth man in the militia was drafted in order to raise two thousand men to serve eighteen months in the Continental service.[74] Across the state it was time to plant crops for the upcoming growing season. Peace negotiations between the Americans and British were ongoing, but the war was not officially over. After seven years of combat and strife, most North Carolinians seemingly had lost interest in the conflict.

In April the General Assembly had passed a bill to raise troops for completing the state's Continental regiments. The law, similar to previous statutes, mandated that the colonels and commanding officers raise the necessary troops from the ranks of the counties' militia regiments. The commanders were to hold musters of their troops on or before June 15 in order to raise their quotas of men for service. Free males ages sixteen to fifty who were not exempt from service (based on prior Continental service and other factors) were liable for army duty. Men who enlisted either by volunteering or being drafted were to serve for eighteen months, and they were to rendezvous at stipulated points within the state's military districts by or before August 1. Bertie County's contingent was to assemble at Edenton along with other levies from the district. The district's troops then were to march from the Edenton rendezvous by August 10 and join up with Halifax District levies at Warrenton on or by August 15, "if possible."[75]

During the fall of 1782, Bertie County native William Walton—a captain in the First North Carolina Regiment—was situated at Winton, where he was overseeing the gathering of provisions and clothing for Continental soldiers. On September 10 Walton wrote to Peter Clifton, the Bertie County commissioner for provision taxes, that he was "Once More Oblige[d] to Call on You for some Publick Corn, as there is None to be had in this County [Hertford]." Walton had dispatched two wagons to Windsor to transport the requested grain back to Winton, although he was unsure whether Clifton would be capable of supplying the scarce commodity. Variously during the autumn, Captain Walton requisitioned grain and livestock from his home county to furnish to Continental soldiers.[76] In Bertie and other northeastern North Carolina counties, citizens and soldiers suffered considerably for the want of basic food items and daily provisions.

As late as September, the organization of the militia was still in progress, and efforts were still being made to complete the draft of "18 months men." On September 10, 1782, twenty Bertie County men were enlisted in the Continental army pursuant to the most recent militia law. The men—Dempsey Baker, James Farmer, Jesse Farmer, John Fields, Willis Fryar, William James, John Kennedy, James Lassiter, Oliver Mitchell, Solomon Page, Lewis Powell, William Sowell, Matthew Tennison, William Thurston, John Tranton, George White, Arthur Wiggins, Matthew Wiggins, Archibald Williford, and James Williford—were assigned variously to the First, Second, and Third North Carolina Regiments. Those men were the last county residents to enlist, or be drafted, into the state's Continental Line regiments prior to the formal conclusion of the war. They were ordered to the Ashley River region of South Carolina (British forces remained in and about Charleston while peace negotiations were under way between American and British officials). The Continental Congress resolved that regular troops were not to remain in the field, except those who had enlisted for three years. On May 26, 1783, the Congress resolved that the commander in chief, Gen. George Washington, be instructed to grant furloughs to the noncommissioned officers and soldiers who had enlisted to serve for the duration of the war. Thus, the Bertie County soldiers were likely furloughed or discharged prior to the expiration of the eighteen-month terms of service—except for Privates Dempsey Baker and Matthew Tennison: both men deserted on June 21, 1783.[77]

The final peace treaty between the United States of America and Great Britain was formally executed on September 3, 1783. Eight and one-half years of conflict by rebellious Patriots had finally come to a conclusion.

Notes

1. The Continental Congress stipulated that each state furnish its respective quota of regiments, as follows: New Hampshire, 3; Massachusetts, 15; Rhode Island, 2; Connecticut, 8; New York, 4; New Jersey, 4; Pennsylvania, 12; Delaware, 1; Maryland, 8; Virginia, 15; North Carolina, 9; South Carolina, 6; and Georgia, 1. The Congress had established the Southern Department on February 27, 1776. The department encompassed the colonies (later states) of Virginia, North Carolina, South Carolina, and Georgia and the western frontiers of those colonies (states). Maj. Gen. Charles Lee was appointed commander of the department on March 1, 1776. He was succeeded on September 9, 1776, by Maj. Gen. Robert Howe, a North Carolinian. The field army of the department was known as the Southern Army. While the Continental Congress authorized for North Carolina a total of nine regiments, it had previously authorized five regiments for the colony to be incorporated into the Continental army. The North Carolina Provincial Congress had authorized six regiments as of April 17, 1776, the Sixth North Carolina Regiment being considered a "provincial" unit since the Continental Congress had not officially sanctioned it for the Continental army. The Continental Congress "adopted" the Sixth Regiment into the Continental army on May 7, 1776, and assigned it to the Southern Department. Worthington Chauncey Ford, ed., *Journals of the Continental Congress*, 34 vols. (Washington, D.C.: Government Printing Office, 1904–1937), 2:107, 4:59, 174, 237, 331, 5:762; Robert K. Wright Jr., *The Continental Army*

(Washington, D.C.: Center of Military History, United States Army, 1963), 82, 299–303, 431; William L. Saunders, ed., *The Colonial Records of North* Carolina, 10 vols. (Raleigh: State of North Carolina, 1886–1890), 10:186, 187, 513, 520.

2. Saunders, *Colonial Records*, 10:913. Since the thirteen American colonies had declared their independence from Great Britain on July 4, 1776, the author refers to North Carolina as a "state" in passages within this book related to events after that date. Such treatment is consist-ent with nomenclature and presentation in Walter Clark, *The State Records of North Carolina*, even though the assembly held in November and December 1776 was officially termed a "Provincial Congress" rather than a "state assembly" or "general assembly." Clark addresses this subject in his "Preface Notes" to volume 11 (the initial volume) of his *State Records*:

> Colonel [William L.] Saunders, in arranging THE RECORDS relating to the Colo-nial period of our history, thought it well to regard that period as extending to the adoption of the State Constitution in December, 1776. . . . THE COLONIAL RE-CORDS ends with the close of the year 1776 [Volume 10]. It seems, however, more in accordance with historical events to consider that the Colonial period was ter-minated by the Declaration of Independence; for then North Carolina disavowed further connection with the mother country and, solemnly asserting that her Co-lonial life had ceased, declared her title to full Statehood in the face of the world.
>
> Indeed, the date of adopting a Constitution providing for a permanent govern-ment will appear to be of less moment when we recall that Colonial dependence had then long ceased, that the last Colonial Assembly met in April, 1775, that a month later the Royal governor had fled, and that the powers of government were being regularly exercised by the revolutionary authorities that had supplanted the Colonial system. The government by the Provincial Congress and the Committee of Thirteen, when the Congress was not in session, was as certain and autonomous in its character as any other could have been, and the new State did not arise on the adoption of a written constitution, or depend on the particular form of gov-ernment established, but rather dates from the declaration that the people were no longer subjects of Great Britain, but were independent and sovereign, and that the Colony had now become the State of North Carolina. Therefore the Editor of this volume has regarded the Fourth of July, 1776, as the birthday of our Statehood, and he has treated it as the dividing point between the COLONIAL and State RECORDS.

Walter Clark, *The State Records of North Carolina*, 16 vols. (11–26) (Raleigh: State of North Carolina, 1895–1906), 11:vii.

3. Saunders, *Colonial Records*, 10:943–944, 946, 949.

4. Clark, *State Records*, 16:1015,1185, 1098; Francis B. Heitman, *Historical Register of Of-ficers of the Continental Army during the War of the Revolution, April, 1775 to December, 1783* (Washington, D.C.: The Rare Book Shop Publishing Co., 1914), 129; William White, declaration dated May 4, 1822, Revolutionary War pension file for William White (S42071); James Anderson, declaration dated July 18, 1834, Revolutionary War pension file for James Anderson (S12930), Revolutionary War Pension and Bounty Land Warrant Files, 1800–1900,

(microfilm, M804), Record Group 15, National Archives, Washington, D.C. (hereafter cited as Revolutionary War pension files).

5. Wright, *The Continental Army*, 302–303.

6. Ford, *Journals of the Continental Congress*, 4:174, 237, 331, 5:762, 7:89–90.

7. Hugh F. Rankin, *The North Carolina Continentals* (Chapel Hill: University of North Carolina Press, 1971), 86–88.

8. Rankin, *North Carolina Continentals*, 89–90. Throughout this chapter, any lists of Bertie County soldiers who served in North Carolina's Continental Line regiments and any statistics or general statements related to such soldiers were developed by the author based on information gathered for the roster presented in Appendix 1. Hereafter in the chapter the author generally has not included separate notes referencing the appendix for such lists, statistics, or statements. Full endnotes for the appendixes are found at www.ncpublications.com/bertie.html.

9. Rankin, *North Carolina Continentals*, 90–92; Ford, *Journals of the Continental Congress*, 8:538.

10. Rankin, *North Carolina Continentals*, 93–94.

11. Rankin, *North Carolina Continentals*, 94–95, 97–98.

12. Rankin, *North Carolina Continentals*, 100–101; Thomas Burke to Richard Caswell, September 10, 1777, Paul H. Smith and Ronald M. Gephart, eds., *Letters of Delegates to Congress, 1774–1789*, 26 vols. (Washington, D.C.: Library of Congress, 1976–2000), 7:640.

13. Rankin, *North Carolina Continentals*, 102–103.

14. Rankin, *North Carolina Continentals*, 104–105.

15. Rankin, *North Carolina Continentals*, 105; Joshua Lawrence and Salley Lawrence (children of Joseph Lawrence), joint declaration dated February 8, 1853, Revolutionary War pension file for Joseph Lawrence (R6194); James Anderson, declaration dated July 18, 1834, Revolutionary War pension file for James Anderson (S12930); John Barrow, declaration dated August 13, 1821, Revolutionary War pension file for John Barrow (R566); Ezekiel White, declaration dated November 13, 1820, Bertie County Miscellaneous Records, Revolutionary War Papers, C.R. 010.928.12, State Archives (hereafter cited as Bertie County Revolutionary War Papers); Revolutionary War pension file for Ezekiel White (S42070); Solomon Howard, declaration dated July 11, 1833, Revolutionary War pension file for Solomon Howard (S31757); Abraham Jenkins, declaration dated May 18, 1821, Revolutionary War pension file for Abraham Jenkins (W20180) and Bertie County Revolutionary War Papers; Charles Rhodes, declaration dated February 18, 1833, Revolutionary War pension file for Charles Rhodes (S7386); William White, declaration dated May 14, 1822, Revolutionary War pension file for William White (S42071) and Bertie County Revolutionary War Papers.

The author identified more than eighty Bertie County residents who had enlisted, or were appointed officers, in North Carolina Continental Line regiments prior to the Battle of Brandywine and who were possibly present on September 11, 1777. Because of the lack of detailed muster rolls and other records, the author could not substantiate with certainty that all of the county residents who had enlisted were present at Brandywine Creek. For example, some men may have been on command assignments, absent by reason of sickness, on furlough, and so on.

16. Burke to Caswell, September 17, 1777, Burke, Cornelius Harnett, and John Penn to Caswell, September 17, 1777, Smith and Gephart, *Letters of Delegates*, 6:678–679, 690–691.

17. Ford, *Journals of the Continental Congress*, 8:735; Rankin, *North Carolina Continentals*, 106–110; Penn to Caswell, October 5, 1777, Smith and Gephart, *Letters of Delegates*, 8:59–60.

18. Rankin, *North Carolina Continentals*, 110–111.

19. Rankin, *North Carolina Continentals*, 110–114.

20. Rankin, *North Carolina Continentals*, 114–115, 117–118.

21. Clark, *State Records*, 16:1155; Abraham Jenkins, declaration dated October 23, 1819, in Bertie County, Secretary of State Revolutionary War Military Papers, folder 54.2, State Archives, Office of Archives and History, Raleigh (hereafter cited as State Military Papers with specific county where given); Heitman, *Historical Register of Officers*, 409.

22. Rankin, *North Carolina Continentals*, 114.

23. Penn to Caswell, October 6, 1777, Smith and Gephart, *Letters of Delegates*, 8:70.

24. Rankin, *North Carolina Continentals*, 119, 122.

25. Clark, *State Records*, 22:926–928.

26. Rankin, *North Carolina Continentals*, 121–122, 136; General Orders, December 16, 1777, W. W. Abbott et al., eds., *The Papers of George Washington*, 20 vols. to date (Charlottesville and London: University Press of Virginia, 1985–2010), 12:613–614 (hereafter cited as *Papers of George Washington*).

27. Rankin, *North Carolina Continentals*, 122–123.

28. Rankin, *North Carolina Continentals*, 139.

29. Rankin, *North Carolina Continentals*, 124–148. See generally chapter 6, ("Valley Forge, 1777–1778,") of Rankin's study.

30. The author compiled the names of the Bertie County men who died at Valley Forge and/or were omitted from the rolls while the North Carolina brigade was at that location (December 18, 1777 to June 18, 1778) from the information he compiled for the putative roster of Bertie County Continental Line soldiers (Appendix 1). Because of the incompleteness of rolls and records for North Carolina troops, the author cannot be certain that he was able to identify all Bertie County men who were: (1) present at Valley Forge, (2) died at Valley Forge, or (3) omitted from the rolls during the cited period. Additionally, when the North Carolina troops departed Valley Forge on June 19, 1778, at least two Bertie

County soldiers—William Fryar and Arthur Pugh—were left at the camp, too sick to march. Pvt. Hardy Pierce was likewise left at the camp as an orderly. Pierce later died, presumably at the camp.

31. Marc Brier, park ranger, Valley Forge National Historic Park, "Revolutionary Resting Place" (undated information paper); William Lange, park ranger, Valley Forge National Historic Park, telephone conversation with author, December 10, 2011. The author discovered no records that identified burial locations for North Carolina's deceased soldiers, including those from Bertie County.

32. Rankin, *North Carolina Continentals*, 87, 89–90, 129–131, 138; Clark, *State Records*, 16:1033, 1187; Prudence Johnston, declaration dated June 16, 1820, in Bertie County, State Military Papers, folder 101-A.7; Thomas Conner, Wright Conner, and Patsey Conner, brothers and sister (heirs) of John Conner, power of attorney to Joseph H. Bryan to seek a military land warrant based on John Conner's Revolutionary War service, June 16, 1820, in Bertie County, State Military Papers, folder 101-A.6; Thomas Wiggins and others, heirs of Malachi Wiggins, power of attorney to Darling Cherry or William Harrell to seek a military land warrant based on Malachi Wiggins's Revolutionary War service, November 10, 1819, in Currituck County, State Military Papers, folder 86.1.

33. Clark, *State Records*, 12:638–640.

34. General Orders, May 15, 1778, Headquarters, Valley Forge, *Papers of George Washington*, 15:123–124; Clark, *State Records*, 24:154–157; Ford, *Journals of the Continental Congress*, 11:550–551.

35. George Washington to President of Congress [Henry Laurens], June 2, 1778, *Papers of George Washington*, 15:302–303.

36. Wright, *The Continental Army*, 299–303; Rankin, *North Carolina Continentals*, 147.

37. General Orders, Headquarters, Valley Forge, June 18, 1778, *Papers of George Washington*, 15:429–431; Rankin, *North Carolina Continentals*, 150–153.

38. Rankin, *North Carolina Continentals*, 154–158.

39. Rankin, *North Carolina Continentals*, 158, 396; John Barrow, declaration dated August 13, 1821, Revolutionary War pension file for John Barrow (R566); Ezekiel White, declaration dated November 13, 1820, Revolutionary War pension file for Ezekiel White (S42070); Solomon Howard, declaration dated July 11, 1833, Revolutionary War pension file for Solomon Howard (S3175); Abraham Jenkins, declaration dated May 18, 1821, Revolutionary War pension file for Abraham Jenkins (W20180); William White, declaration dated May 14, 1822, Revolutionary War pension file for William White (S42071).

40. Clark, *State Records*, 12:57, 62, 24:1, 3.

41. Clark, *State Records*, 13:viii–ix, 24:154–157.

42. Clark, *State Records*, 24:154–157; Ford, *Journals of the Continental Congress*, 11:550.

43. Lewis Boon, declaration dated August 16, 1843, Revolutionary War pension file for Lewis Boon (S6683); Peter White, declaration dated May 17, 1819, Revolutionary War pension file for Peter White (S42066); John Hoggard, declaration dated November 13, 1833, Revolutionary War pension file for John Hoggard (R4804); William Watford, declaration dated September 21, 1832, Revolutionary War pension file for William Watford (S34631); Hardy Robinson, declaration dated November 3, 1818, Revolutionary War pension file for Hardy Robinson (S41992); Amos Thomas, declaration dated November 14, 1820, Revolutionary War pension file for Amos Thomas (S42041); William Freeman, declaration dated July 23, 1832, Revolutionary War pension file for William Freeman (W10042); Thomas Tart, declaration dated August 15, 1833, Revolutionary War pension file for Thomas Tart (S7676).

44. Clark, *State* Records, 13:160–161.

45. Lewis Boon, declaration dated August 16, 1843, Revolutionary War pension file for Lewis Boon (S6683); John Hoggard, declaration dated November 13, 1833, Revolutionary War pension file for John Hoggard (S4804).

46. Clark, *State Records*, 13:189–190.

47. The official designation for the regiment that Col. James Hogun organized at Halifax in July 1778 is unclear from extant records. Hogun had originally served as colonel of the Seventh North Carolina Regiment. That regiment was disbanded by Gen. George Washington at Valley Forge in early June 1778. Hogun, being considered a supernumerary officer, was ordered to North Carolina to recruit and organize volunteers and militia drafts for the Continental Line. Hugh F. Rankin referred to the regiment that Hogun raised in July 1778 as the "Seventh Regiment from North Carolina" and the "new Seventh Regiment." (Rankin, *North Carolina Continentals*, 162, 164, 180, 181.) Apparently no official action was taken by the North Carolina General Assembly to transfer Hogun's colonelcy to another regiment following General Washington's actions at Valley Forge. Washington had consolidated and disbanded the North Carolina regiments at the direction of the Continental Congress, not that of the North Carolina General Assembly. In addition, Washington (or his designated subordinate or subordinates) had reassigned officers and identified supernumeraries. The majority of the officers who were assigned to command companies in Hogun's newly organized regiment had originally been appointed to, and served in, the Third North Carolina Regiment. The Third Regiment, commanded by Col. Jethro Sumner, was reduced to a cadre at Valley Forge and relieved from the North Carolina brigade. The regiment was not officially disbanded, and Colonel Sumner was not "officially" appointed to the colonelship of another regiment. Indeed, on November 7, 1778, Colonel Hogun dispatched to Colonel Sumner a letter that he signed as colonel of the Seventh North Carolina Regiment. (Clark, *State Records*, 13:495–496).

Francis Bernard Heitman recorded inconsistent information regarding Hogun. On page 46 Heitman noted that Hogun was colonel of the Seventh North Carolina Regiment from November 26, 1776, until January 9, 1779. On page 291, however, he noted that Hogun served as colonel of the Seventh North Carolina until June 1, 1778, when he was transferred to the Third North Carolina Regiment. (Heitman, *Historical Register of Officers*, 46, 291.) "James Hogun, Col." is listed on a 1778 roster of commissioned and noncommissioned officers belonging to the Third North Carolina Battalion [Regiment]. The roster is from the orderly book of Sgt. Isaac Rowel of the North Carolina Line. See Clark, *State Records*, 13:343–344; "Names of commissioned and non-commissioned officers belonging to the 3d N.C. Battalion," Revolutionary War Rolls, 1775–1783 (microfilm, M246), Record Group 93, National Archives. Sergeant Rowel served on the staff of the Third North Carolina Regiment. (Clark, *State Records*, 16:1148.) Additionally, the roster of North Carolina's Continental Line soldiers erroneously lists all of the men who were enlisted in Hogun's regiment in July 1778 as members of the Tenth North Carolina Regiment. (Clark, *State Records*, 16:1002–1197, various entries throughout.) Walter Clark, in the preface of volume 14 of his *State Records*, referred to the regiment as "the [T]hird (originally the 7th) Regiment." (Clark, *State Records*, 14:vii.) Finally, some veterans of Hogun's regiment stated in their pension declarations that they had served in the Third North Carolina Regiment. Therefore, given the inconsistent designations (in official records and published works) for Hogun's regiment raised in July 1778, the author chose to identify the unit as the "Third North Carolina Regiment (Second Organization—Hogun's)." In the author's view such identification distinguishes Hogun's regiment from Col. Jethro Sumner's Third Regiment (original or first organization) and a later Third North Carolina Regiment designated by Sumner in 1781. Hogun's regiment, under the command of Lt. Col. Robert Mebane, was discharged in totality (except for a few men who were sick and left at locations in the North) at Halifax at the end of its nine-month term of service (April 20, 1779).

48. Clark, *State Records*, 16:1002–1197 (various entries); Heitman, *Historical Register of Officers*, 82, 84, 108, 117, 153, 198, 244, 396, 456. Ballard, Blount, Bradley, Dixon, and Montfort had served in the Third North Carolina Regiment; Hogg in the First and Fifth Regiments; Child in the Sixth Regiment; Baker in the Seventh Regiment; and Quinn in the Eighth Regiment.

The author was unable to identify all seventy-six Bertie County militiamen who volunteered or were drafted to serve in Hogun's regiment. The roster of North Carolina Continental Line soldiers does not include information regarding residences of the soldiers. The lack of such information, along with the commonality of surnames in Bertie County with those in other areas of North Carolina, prevented the author from identifying all county members of the regiment. An inordinate amount of genealogical research and analyses would be required to identify the counties of residence of North Carolina Continental Line soldiers in order to more fully document Bertie County's troops.

Reading Blount's parents were Jacob Blount and Barbara Gray (sister of William Gray). The Blounts and Grays were devout Whigs and highly involved in the Revolutionary movement. Jacob Blount was a member of the provincial congresses of April 1775, August–September 1775, and April–May 1776. William Gray represented Bertie County at the provincial congress of August–September 1775 and November–December 1776. Gray was also a member of the Edenton District Committee of Safety and a justice of the peace for Bertie County. Saunders, *Colonial Records*, 9:1178, 10:164, 500, 913, 992.

49. Clark, *State Records*, 13:viii, 211, 495–496. On August 27 Cornelius Harnett (North Carolina delegate to the Continental Congress) wrote to Governor Caswell that "Col. Hogun is just arrived with 500 and odd [number of] men."

50. Clark, *State Records*, 13:496; John Hoggard, declaration dated November 13, 1833, Revolutionary War pension file for John Hoggard (R4804); William Watford, declaration dated

September 21, 1832, Revolutionary War pension file for William Watford (S3463); Hardy Robinson, declaration dated November 3, 1818, Revolutionary War pension file for Hardy Robinson (S41992).

51. *Dictionary of North Carolina Biography*, s.v. "Hogun, James"; Rankin, *North Carolina Continentals*, 163.

52. Clark, *State Records*, 13:488.

53. Gen. George Washington to Maj. Gen. Alexander McDougall, December 7, 1778, Washington to Maj. Gen. Benedict Arnold, December 13, 1778, Washington to Lt. Col. William Lee Davidson, December 19, 1778, *Papers of George Washington*, 18:379–380, 399, 466; Clark, *State Records*, 14:15–16; Rankin, *North Carolina Continentals*, 165.

54. Ford, *Journals of the Continental Congress*, 13:46; John Hoggard, declaration dated November 13, 1833, Revolutionary War pension file for John Hoggard (R4804). Hoggard stated that "about the first of April 1779, he [along with his regimental comrades] was ordered to Halifax, N.C. to which place he marched with . . . Captain Reading Blount and there he arrived . . . and was discharged."

On Friday, January 1, 1779, the Continental Congress considered a Board of War report dated December 26, 1778, concerning clothing needs of the men in Colonel Hogun's regiment. The board reported that there was no provision made for supplying clothing to those troops. Taking into consideration that the term of service for Hogun's men was to expire in a few months, the board noted: "That as to the articles wanted by the regiment, some may be spared without inconvenience and others cannot *without depriving the men enlisted during the war of them* [emphasis added by author]. Of coats vests and breeches there are more than are wanted; of hose [socks] a few may be spared, but shoes are scarce and not to be had but at most extravagant rates; and of blankets there is not nearly a supply for the troops at camp." The board recommended to Congress that it [the board] "supply, on application of the delegates of North Carolina, to the men of Colonel Hogan's regiment, which chiefly consists of draughts from the militia of that State, such articles of cloathing as in the opinion of the Board may be spared from the continental stock, *without detriment to the service* [emphasis added]; the articles received by the regiment by order of the Board to be charged to the said State." The Continental Congress concurred with the board's recommendation. The men under Hogun's command had been compelled to depend on their own pay for supplies and clothing while stationed at West Point. Ford, *Journals of the Continental Congress*, 13:14; Smith and Gephart, *Letters of Delegates*, 11:371n. Clark, *State Records*, 14:viii.

55. Wright, *The Continental Army*, 299.

56. Clark, *State Records*, 24:254–255; Ford, *Journals of the Continental Congress*, 14:559–560, 820.

57. Richard Caswell to Brig. Gen. Isaac Gregory, July 7, 1779, Richard Caswell, Governors Letter Books, State Archives.

58. Ford, *Journals of the Continental Congress*, 15:1256; Wright, *The Continental Army*, 299; Rankin, *North Carolina Continentals*, 213–214, 219.

59. Rankin, *North Carolina Continentals*, 222–232. The quotations of the two unidentified British officers are from page 231 of the cited source.

60. Clark, *State Records*, 14:xi–xii. Historian Hugh T. Lefler noted that the surrender of Charleston "was disastrous" for the army in that 7 generals, 290 other officers, and more than 6,000 men (including 815 North Carolina Continental Line troops and about 600 North Carolina militia) became prisoners of war. See Hugh T. Lefler, *History of North Carolina*, 4 vols. (New York: Lewis Historical Publishing Company, [1956]), 1:244.

61. Clark, *State Records*, 24:344–345. Provision taxes were also known as "taxes in kind." Clifton served as the county commissioner during 1780 and 1781; John Wolfenden succeeded him in 1782. See Weynette Parks Haun, comp., *North Carolina Revolutionary Army Accounts, Treasurer, State, Books E–G, H, J, Part XVIII* (Durham: the compiler, 2004), 2445.

62. Weynette Parks Haun, comp., *North Carolina Revolutionary Army Accounts, Treasurer: State, Book K, Part XVIII* (Durham: the compiler, 2004), 2617–2622 (hereafter cited as Haun, *North Carolina Revolutionary Army Accounts, Part XVIII*).

63. Clark, *State Records*, 24:358, 367–373; Ford, *Journals of the Continental Congress*, 24:960; Rankin, *North Carolina Continentals*, 324, 343.

64. Clark, *State Records*, 14:847, 22:593–594; Haun, *North Carolina Revolutionary Army Accounts, Part XVIII*, 2709. James Campbell wrote to Gov. Thomas Burke on September 5, 1781, that the "Colonel of this County refused to act any longer in the Military Department." Campbell apparently referred to Arthur Brown, who appears to have succeeded James Moore as colonel of the county's militia by June 1780, at which time he penned a letter to Gov. Abner Nash and signed it as "Colonel." Campbell further reported that "I have acted only by Appointment these nine months past." Based on Campbell's statement, the author concluded that Arthur Brown had abdicated the colonelship of the Bertie County militia about December 1780 or January 1781 (approximately nine months prior to the date of Campbell's letter).

65. Ford, *Journals of the Continental Congress*, 18:994–995; Rankin, *North Carolina Continentals*, 259; Clark, *State Records*, 14:765; Jeffrey J. Crow, *A Chronicle of North Carolina during the American Revolution, 1763–1789* (Raleigh: Department of Cultural Resources, Division of Archives and History, 1975), 40–41, 43.

66. Clark, *State Records*, 17:vi; Crow, *A Chronicle of North Carolina*, 44, 46.

67. Clark, *State Records*, 15:111, 118–119, 183, 591; William Smith, declaration dated August 29, 1832, Revolutionary War pension file for William Smith (W17828); Josiah Wilson, declaration dated August 13, 1832, Revolutionary War pension file for Josiah Wilson (S14855).

68. Clark, *State Records*, 15:530–531, 556–557.

69. Clark, *State Records*, 17:1048; Rankin, *North Carolina Continentals*, 316–317, 346–347.

70. Rankin, *North Carolina Continentals*, 351–359.

71. Jethro Butler, declaration dated November 14, 1820, Revolutionary War pension file for Jethro Butler (S41465); Rebecca James, declaration dated September 14, 1846, Revolutionary War pension file for Jeremiah James (W467); James Outlaw, declaration dated March 24, 1820, Revolutionary War pension file for James Outlaw (S41929); William Smith, declaration dated August 29, 1832, Revolutionary War pension file for William Smith (W17828); Absalom Wiley, declaration dated March 26, 1824, Revolutionary War pension file for Absalom Wiley (Wilday) (S38473); Josiah Wilson, declaration dated August 13, 1832, Revolutionary War pension file for Josiah Wilson (S14855); Rankin, *North Carolina Continentals*, 360.

72. Clark, *State Records*, 16:271,1048, 1131; John Butler, declaration dated May 17, 1820, in Bertie County, State Military Papers, folder 89.5; Clark, *State Records*, 16:1118; Jethro Butler, declaration dated September 24, 1821, in Bertie County, State Military Papers, folder 469.4; Nancy Murter and Elisha Murter, heirs of John Murter, power of attorney to James Freeman to seek a military land warrant based on John Murter's Revolutionary War service, October 5, 1821, Bertie County Revolutionary War Papers.

73. Crow, *A Chronicle of North Carolina*, 47–48; William S. Powell, *North Carolina: A History* (Chapel Hill and London: University of North Carolina Press, 1977), 76–77.
   Peace negotiations began in Paris in April 1782. On November 30, 1782, the parties reached a preliminary peace treaty, which was to become effective once Great Britain had reached terms with its other enemies. The United States Congress ratified the preliminary peace treaty on April 15, 1783. American peace commissioners Benjamin Franklin, John Jay, and John Adams signed the final treaty on September 3, ending the American Revolution. Alan Axelrod, *The Real History of the American Revolution: A New Look at the Past* (New York: Sterling Publishing Co., 2007), 344–347.

74. Rankin, *North Carolina Continentals*, 377; Clark, *State Records*, 16:xi.

75. Clark, *State Records*, 16:634–635, 24:413–417.

76. Capt. William Walton to Peter Clifton, September 30, 1782, Andrew Oliver to Peter Clifton, November 18, 1782, Treasurer's and Comptroller's Papers, Military Papers, Box 10, 1782–1783, Receipts, Orders, Accounts for salt, corn, etc., State Archives. Oliver apparently succeeded James Campbell as colonel of the Bertie County militia (although no appointment document is found in Clark, *State Records*).

77. Clark, *State Records*, 16:xi; Rankin, *North Carolina Continentals*, 384; Dempsey Baker, declaration dated March 10, 1834, Revolutionary War pension file for Dempsey Baker (R408); Ford, *Journals of the Continental Congress*, 24:364.

DETACHED MILITIA

From August 1776, when Capt. Andrew Oliver's militia company returned home to Bertie County, until November 1778, the county's militiamen experienced a hiatus from deployed service. The fledgling state government did not call for any militia companies from the county to confront Tories or British forces. Indeed during this period no British forces were threatening the state or its neighbors, Virginia and South Carolina, and the Tories had subdued their activities within North Carolina. The British military campaign was being carried out in the northern states. By the fall of 1778, however, the British were exhibiting signs that they intended to move the war front to the southern states, prompting the Continental Congress to act.

On September 25 the Continental Congress concluded that, based on intelligence it had received, there was "reason to believe a formidable attack" was being contemplated by the British against South Carolina, and probably Georgia. The Congress adopted the position that "every precaution ought to be taken to guard against" the presumed attack. The body resolved that North Carolina governor Richard Caswell immediately be requested to march three thousand troops "to the assistance of South Carolina and Georgia." All troops sent to the two states pursuant to the Congress's request would be at the expense of the Continental establishment and were to be placed under the command of a Continental army officer. The Congress also determined that Virginia should send one thousand troops to South Carolina. It decreed that the three-thousand-man contingent to be marched from North Carolina was to include militia, levies (draftees), and all the Continental troops in the state.

The militia and levies were to continue in the service and pay of the United States for five months from the time that they marched from the state. The Continental Congress requested Governor Caswell "to take the most vigorous measures to carry this resolution into full and immediate effect" and resolved that if Caswell desired to "march . . . at the head of the North Carolina forces," he would "have the rank and pay of [a] major general in the army of the United States."[1]

To prepare for the defense of the South, the Congress changed commanders of the Southern Department. It resolved that Maj. Gen. Robert Howe, a North Carolinian who had commanded the department since March 1776, report to Gen. George Washington at his headquarters near West Point, New York. Simultaneously, it ordered Maj. Gen. Benjamin Lincoln to take command of the department and to "repair immediately to Charleston."[2] Notwithstanding the desire of the Congress promptly to change the leadership of the department, Howe did not depart the South for General Washington's headquarters. Congress's orders were delayed in reaching Howe, and when the general finally received them, a British invasion of Georgia appeared imminent. Howe, being of the opinion that he could not vacate the command until General Lincoln arrived, quickly relocated to Georgia to take command of that state's defenses.[3]

Henry Laurens, president of the Continental Congress, wrote to Governor Caswell on September 26 and conveyed a copy of the act of Congress of the previous day, which called for "the immediate defence of South Carolina and Georgia." Laurens advised Caswell that "an attack by an Army of ten thousand troops," supported by "a sufficient number of ships-of-the-line was intended upon South Carolina at Charlestown and Beaufort-Port-Royal, or both." Laurens further asserted that the "recovery of South Carolina and Georgia is a project of the first magnitude to Great Britain." (On this same day Laurens wrote nearly an identical letter to Governor Patrick Henry of Virginia.)[4]

Cornelius Harnett, one of North Carolina's delegates to the Continental Congress, likewise wrote to Caswell on the twenty-sixth and informed the governor that a warrant in the amount of $400,000 had been obtained from the Continental treasury to pay expenses "of the new[ly] raised Levies." He further advised the governor that Congress had resolved to send "1000 Men from Virginia, and 3000 from North Carolina, to March immediately to So. Carolina," on the apprehension that British general Sir Henry Clinton was about to evacuate his forces from New York and Rhode Island and move on Charleston. Harnett declared that the South Carolina congressional delegates desired that Caswell assume command of the North Carolina troops to be sent to Charleston. Regarding the overall command of all the troops in the Department of the South, Harnett informed the governor that the South Carolina and Georgia congressional delegates "were so incensed against Genl. Rob. Howe" that the Congress had directed him to immediately join General Washington at his headquarters and placed General Lincoln in command of the Southern Department.[5]

On October 16 Governor Caswell, having received Laurens and Harnett's communications, issued orders to the brigadier generals of the state's six military districts to immediately raise militiamen from their brigades to be marched to South Carolina. Caswell informed the generals that the drafted militiamen were to rendezvous at various locations. The militiamen from the eastern section were to assemble at Kinston by Tuesday, November 10, with their arms, accouterments, and equipment.[6]

On October 17, more than three weeks after it resolved that North Carolina and Virginia troops should be sent to South Carolina and Georgia, Congress directed Henry Laurens, president of the body, to write Governors Caswell and Henry to "forward, with all possible expedition" the troops "required by Congress" to be sent to the two states. The Congress instructed Laurens to request Caswell to include "an addition of two thousand men" (five thousand troops in all). Laurens's letter to Caswell was dated October 18. Laurens informed the governor that the Congress had received "repeated intelligence" of the British "design" to attack South Carolina and that enemy troops had already begun embarking "for that purpose" at New York. He implored Caswell quickly to send to South Carolina and Georgia the three thousand troops that the Congress had requested on September 25. Laurens then suggested that two thousand troops, in addition to "the 3000 men," be sent to the states. In order for Governor Caswell to comply fully with the Continental Congress's directive, he would have to quickly raise and organize five thousand men from throughout the state—not three thousand, the number he had ordered the state's brigadiers to raise just the day before —and march them to Charleston.[7]

The state's brigadier generals were surprised by Caswell's orders to organize and march so many troops on such short notice. Brig. Gen. Allen Jones (Halifax District) wrote to Caswell on October 21 that he was "apprehensive" that the militiamen detached from his district's brigade would "hardly get" to Kinston by November 10, and he was sure that they would be "badly accoutered." The following day, Brig. Gen. John Butler (Hillsborough District) dispatched to the governor a letter in which he noted that the orders came "very unexpectedly." Butler further commented that he had "never heard of the Enemy's movements to the Southward." Brig. Gen. William Skinner (who had succeeded Brig. Gen. Edward Vail as commandant of the Edenton District in December 1777) wrote on the twenty-fifth that the "notice is so short, [I] am doubtful that the Militia can scarcely have time to be at Kingston [Kinston] by 10th Nov[ember]." Col. Gideon Lamb (Currituck County), a supernumerary officer of the Sixth North Carolina Regiment who had likewise received Caswell's orders and was assisting in raising troops, wrote the governor that the Edenton District was extensive in area and "cut in pieces" by swamps, rivers, and waters. As such, Lamb was "doubtful" that the drafted militiamen would be assembled "as may be expected." Brig. Gen. Griffith Rutherford (Salisbury District) wrote on October 25 that the "time is very short, but the matter requires diligence."[8]

General Skinner issued orders to the colonels of the county militia regiments within the Edenton District to organize their quotas of drafted militia. Skinner advised Caswell that he would "leave nothing in my power undone to hasten their march." Skinner was unable to accompany the men from his brigade, inasmuch as his health was such that he was mostly confined to his bed. Command of the regiment of men detached from the Edenton brigade would fall to Col. Solomon Perkins of Currituck County.[9]

Thomas Whitmell had resigned as colonel of Bertie County's militia in August, and overall responsibility for raising and organizing the county's company of militiamen apparently fell to Lt. Col. Thomas Pugh. But Pugh, like his predecessor, resigned as a general officer in the regiment in November 1778, just as efforts to organize the Bertie County company were under way. The General Assembly accepted Pugh's resignation on December 1 and immediately appointed John Pugh Williams, a former captain in the Fifth North Carolina Regiment, to fill the position (lieutenant colonel).

While Thomas Pugh had resigned as the officer second in command of the county's militia, he initially assumed command (with the rank of captain) of the company raised to accompany the other units of the Edenton District. After "a short period," however, Capt. John Wolfenden assumed control of the unit. William Davis served as lieutenant.[10]

Raising, organizing, and preparing the Edenton District militia draftees to march did not progress quickly or efficiently. On Friday, November 13, General Skinner wrote Governor Caswell that the draftees from the district were "very backward in marching." Several of the counties (unidentified) did not hold their drafts until November 5—only five days prior to the date the governor had established for the militiamen to rendezvous at Kinston. Skinner, writing from his home county of Perquimans, advised that the detached militia from Currituck County had passed through the area two days previously. Bertie County militia leaders were apparently impeded in organizing and marching the county's militia, in that Skinner did not mention that the Bertie company was on the march. Skinner was at the time personally "urging the officers of the other regiments to hasten their march." He concluded his letter by advising Caswell that his health was "in some measure restored," and he announced his intention to set out for Kinston "in about six days."[11]

Despite Skinner's "urging," the drafted militia from his district was not forthcoming to Kinston, where Governor Caswell was waiting. The Edenton regiment was not the only unit that failed to arrive at designated rendezvous sites by Caswell's stipulated date. By November 13 Gen. Allen Jones's Halifax District regiment had not made its appearance at Kinston. General Butler's Hillsborough District regiment had not assembled (at Hillsborough, its site), but several contingents of men from the district were marching. General Rutherford's Salisbury regiment was not present on the thirteenth, when Caswell wrote to Rutherford and requested him "to make me as early a return as you possibly can as well of the Continental Troops and New Levies as of the Militia forming your Brigade." Caswell noted that the militia and Continental troops who were present at Kinston would be marched for Charleston in about three days "without waiting for the Halifax and Edenton Militia," which Caswell "fear[ed]" would be longer in arriving.[12]

By November 18 the Edenton and Halifax districts' militia regiments still had not arrived in Kinston. On that day Caswell wrote to Gen. John Ashe, commander of the Wilmington District militia brigade and soon to be commander of the North Carolina militia forces to be marched to South Carolina, that "[t]here are none of the Militia from the District of Edenton and Halifax yet arrived" in Kinston. He reflectively declared: "How long it may be before they get here I know not." Considering the uncertainty surrounding the matter of when the two districts' militiamen might arrive at the rendezvous location, Caswell concluded that "whether they come or not between this and Monday next [November 23] . . . I think then to send on such of the regulars and Militia which may then be here." Caswell enclosed Ashe's commission as major general in command of the North Carolina militia forces in South Carolina and Georgia. He concluded his letter by noting that he had learned that Maj. Gen. Benjamin Lincoln (who would be Ashe's superior officer at Charleston) was at Williamsburg on November 7, en route to take command of the troops in the Southern Department.[13]

By November 19 General Lincoln had reached Kinston, where he met with Caswell and Col. Jethro Sumner (Third North Carolina Regiment). Also on this day, Caswell wrote to General Skinner: "I am much concerned to find the Militia in general is so tardy in marching. None of them are arrived except from the Hillsboro district. These with the Continental Troops must march from hence on Monday next. Let me entreat you Sir, to forward your Drafts to this place with all expedition." Caswell's message was exceedingly clear: he wanted Skinner to get the Edenton District militia regiment (including the Bertie County company) to Kinston absolutely without any further delay. The following day, he wrote to General Butler that "it gives me pain [that] many Militia officers are tardy in the discharge of their respective duties." Eight weeks had passed since the Continental Congress had resolved that North Carolina forces be marched to South Carolina "with all possible dispatch."[14] Nonetheless, Governor Caswell had not been able to assemble the forces despite his repeated pleadings and directives.

Caswell, still awaiting Skinner's regiment from Edenton, on Wednesday, November 25, wrote General Rutherford that the troops then at Kinston had not marched from the rendezvous, but that he expected them to depart in a few days. According to the governor, their delay was "entirely owing to the tardiness of the Edenton and Halifax Militia." The next day the governor, in a seemingly irritated tone, sent one more letter to General Skinner, advising him that "I have several days past been looking for you and the Detachment from your Brigade." Caswell recognized that Skinner, serving in the dual capacities of a brigadier general and a state treasurer, was "much wanted on the business of the Treasury." He informed Skinner that his militiamen could continue on to South Carolina (once they reached Kinston). Unaware of where Skinner and the Edenton District troops were, he wrote: "Pray let me hear by the return of Capt. [Manlove] Tarrant or some person to be sent by you or Col. Lamb, immediately on the receipt of this where your men are, their Numbers, arms and Camp necessaries, and also the time they may be expected to arrive at this place." Caswell concluded that the troops who were then in camp at Kinston "must move on" without the Edenton District troops "unless they arrive in a very few days." During the day, Col. Solomon Perkins passed through Mackey's Ferry in Tyrrell County (present-day Washington County) with a party of Edenton District militia that was estimated at about 150 men. Perkins and his party had reached Kinston by November 29.[15]

A company of detached militia from Gates County marched to Windsor. The unit, commanded by Capt. William Figure, fell under Lt. Col. John Pugh Williams's overall command upon reaching the town. Pvt. William Brooks recalled that from Windsor the company marched "through North Carolina to South Carolina" to the Savannah River near Augusta. Upon reaching the river, the militiamen found that "British [soldiers] were encamped just across the river."[16]

The Bertie County militia company was pitifully tardy in marching for the rendezvous site. Capt. Thomas Pugh with eighty-five men finally arrived at Kinston on Saturday, January 2. Lt. Col. John Pugh Williams intended to accompany his Bertie County men but was still at his home when Captain Pugh and the company marched from the county. Pugh reported to Col. Gideon Lamb that about one hundred men were marching toward Kinston from Hertford County, having departed "about the same time" that Pugh and his men had marched away from Windsor. (Lamb had also been informed that about fifty militiamen from the counties of Pasquotank, Currituck, and Perquimans were expected to reach Kinston "in four or five days.") The following day (January 3), Lamb wrote to Governor Caswell that the troops presently at the rendezvous site, including Captain's Pugh's company, would begin their march toward Cross Creek the next day. Lamb advised Caswell that the "addition of Capt. Pugh's Company" to the troops already at Kinston rendered the funds he had on hand for commissary and quartermaster expenses "insufficient." He advised Caswell that he required "no less sum than fifteen hundred pounds" for the commissary and quartermaster, who were to march with the militiamen toward Cross Creek.[17] Presumably, Captain Pugh with his Bertie County company marched from the rendezvous site on January 4. (Lieutenant Colonel Williams eventually joined the North Carolina militia force on the march, likely at Elizabethtown, Bladen County, but the date he joined is unknown.)

Major General Lincoln arrived in Charleston in early December to find that the North Carolina militia was not yet on location. With the predominant component of his defensive force not present, Lincoln was obviously concerned, since British warships loaded with assault troops were sailing to the south. Four days before Christmas, more than forty enemy ships sailed past Charleston Harbor on a southward course. The next day Lincoln wrote to Caswell and advised him of the enemy ships. Lincoln wrote: "I hope, Sir, the Troops from your State are nigh, but lest they may have been halted, on an idea that all was safe, I have sent to Genl. Ashe to urge them on as fast as possible, and now request if they have not left the State, that your Excellency would order them forward." On the last day of December, Lincoln reported to Caswell that only about nine hundred North Carolina troops had arrived and that his total force was about fourteen hundred combatants—"a small force to act against an Enemy so much superior."[18]

About the last of December, General Lincoln moved out of Charleston and was marching with his troops southward toward Savannah when a letter from Maj. Gen. Robert Howe reached him. Howe reported distressing news: on December 29, a British force of about 3,500 men under Col. Archibald Campbell had routed his much smaller American contingent and captured Savannah. Howe, who was unpopular in the state and who had been ordered northward

Robert Howe (1732–1786), a major general from. N.C., was forced to abandon Savannah in late December 1778 after a brief but decisive battle with British forces. Howe failed to garner sufficient support from the Georgians, particularly from their militia forces. Image from the Prints and Photographs Division, Library of Congress.

more than three months previously by the Continental Congress, had now been taken aback by the loss of Georgia's major port city. While Howe did not receive sufficient cooperation and support from Georgian authorities, he bore the brunt of the blame for the loss of Savannah. He was later exonerated in a court-martial.[19]

The early months of 1779 found Lincoln's southern army in control of South Carolina and Campbell's British forces dominating Georgia. By early February additional troops, including Continental soldiers and militia, had joined Lincoln's command, which would eventually total more than 6,000 men. The two armies skirmished and maneuvered, and by late February Lincoln was positioning his forces to flank the British around Augusta. Lincoln, as part of his battle plan, sent Gen. John Ashe, along with an estimated 1,200 militia and 200 Continental soldiers, south of Augusta to Brier Creek, a tributary of the Savannah River. Ashe's force was further strengthened by the addition of 270 Georgians (Continental soldiers and militia). Ashe's command included Col. Solomon Perkins's Edenton District regiment of militia. Capt. John Wolfenden's Bertie County company was a constituent unit in Perkins's regiment.[20]

Ashe's patrols had sighted British infantry in the area of Brier Creek, and one group had even exchanged fire with the redcoats; but, incredibly, no one had informed Ashe. During the afternoon of Tuesday, March 2, groups of British soldiers were sighted in the vicinity, across the creek from Ashe's position. Ashe did not undertake defensive precautions, however, but relying upon the advice of two subordinate officers (Brig. Gen. William Bryan and Col. Samuel Elbert), decided to march out and disperse what he and other officers believed to be nothing more than small parties of the enemy. The following day Ashe formed his command into two lines and moved out to push the British out of the area. About three o'clock in the afternoon, American cavalrymen gave the alarm that British forces had been sighted. Within a few minutes after General Ashe received the report, a formidable column of British soldiers suddenly appeared in the rear of the Americans. Three columns of redcoats, six men abreast, approached to within about 150 yards of the Americans and methodically deployed right and left into a line of battle. Ashe's troops, mostly farmboy militia, hurriedly reversed their front and assembled in a loose formation. Confusion and hysteria reigned among the troops. Perkins's Edenton District militiamen, including Wolfenden's Bertie County men, were positioned on the right side of the front line. Approximately 200 Georgia Continentals were to the left of Perkins's regiment, and the New Bern District militia regiment was to the left of the Georgians.[21]

The Edenton Regiment and the Georgia Continentals fired as the British opened on the American center with cannon. After firing several volleys, the Georgians began to advance but drifted to the left in front of the New Bern regiment and obstructed that unit's line of fire. Perkins's Edenton regiment was forced to move to the right, opening a hole in the line. The Halifax regiment, occupying a position in the second line, broke and ran without firing a shot. The Wilmington regiment moved to its right to prevent being flanked and, along with the New Bern men, fired several volleys. Americans began falling dead and wounded throughout the American lines. About that time the Edenton regiment broke and fled. As the Georgia Continentals held their ground, the American lines disintegrated into chaos as the militiamen streaked for safety in the nearby swamps. British soldiers poured into the hole in the American center. The "battle" lasted but about five minutes.[22]

Perkins's Edenton militiamen frantically scattered to the swamps along with other troops. Captain Wolfenden was captured, while Pvt. James Ward of Bertie managed to escape. Colonel Perkins later stated that "his regiment, which was for a few minutes engaged with the enemy, was entirely broken." It is unknown how many of Perkins's men, including those in the Bertie County company, were killed, wounded, or captured. General Ashe later reported that "I saw the Edenton Regiment break and take to flight. I then used my utmost exertions to get in front of the fugitives for half a mile or three-quarters, in order to rally them." Ashe further noted that he was assisted by Colonel Perkins, Lt. Col. John Pugh Williams, and other officers but found it "impossible" to impede the militiamen's retreat. According to Pvt. Henry Halsey, a Chowan County militiaman, "we were discomfited and had to make our retreat in[to] South Carolina." Halsey specifically elaborated that "Colonel John P. Williams of Bertie . . . acted bravely in this contest, & narrowly escaped being taken [prisoner] by the enemy."[23]

Once the troops broke off from the encounter, personal survival became each man's utmost concern. Americans splashed across Brier Creek and labored through the swamps; some sailed into the Savannah River to swim to the opposite bank. An unknown number flailed about in the river and drowned. Samuel Reed, a militiaman from Rowan County, was one of the men who dove into the river. He later recalled that "a large number tried to get back to the Main Army which lay across the [Savannah] River. There were a good many drowned. I swam the river & got back safe."[24]

Before the day's end, General Ashe, who had fled the battle scene with his terrified troops, wrote to General Lincoln and conveyed the woeful news. "I am sorry to inform you that [at] 3 o'clock P. M. the enemy came down upon us in force, what number I know not. The troops in my division did not stand fire five minutes; many fled without discharging their pieces; I went with the fugitives half a mile, and finding it impossible to rally the troops, I made my escape into the river swamp, and made up in the evening to this place; 2 officers and 2 soldiers came off with me. The rest of the troops, I am afraid, have fallen into the enemy's hands."[25]

With Captain Wolfenden having been captured, command of the Bertie County militia company devolved to Lt. William Davis. The company apparently served out the remainder of its five-month term of service and was discharged in April 1779. Pvt. James Ward later stated that "he served the whole term for which he was drafted" and that he was discharged by Lieutenant Davis per the order of Lt. Col. John Pugh Williams. Ward returned to Bertie County after being discharged. William Brooks, a member of a Gates County company that marched to the Savannah River, marched back through South and North Carolina to Windsor, where he was discharged from detached service.[26]

BATTLE OF BRIER CREEK - MARCH 3, 1779

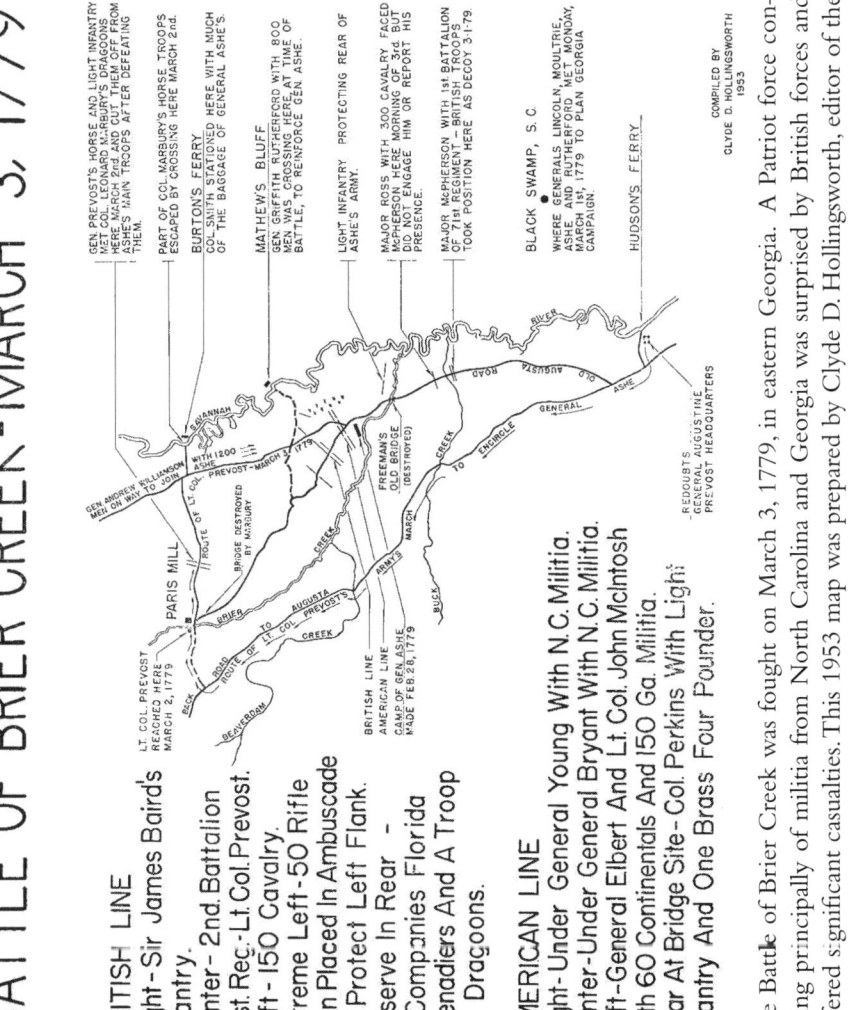

BRITISH LINE
Right - Sir James Baird's Infantry.
Center - 2nd. Battalion
71st. Reg. - Lt. Col. Prevost.
Left - 150 Cavalry.
Extreme Left - 50 Rifle Men Placed In Ambuscade To Protect Left Flank.
Reserve In Rear — 3 Companies Florida Grenadiers And A Troop Of Dragoons.

AMERICAN LINE
Right - Under General Young With N.C. Militia.
Center - Under General Bryant With N.C. Militia.
Left - General Elbert And Lt. Col. John McIntosh With 60 Continentals And 150 Ga. Militia.
Rear At Bridge Site - Col. Perkins With Light Infantry And One Brass Four Pounder.

GEN PREVOST'S HORSE AND LIGHT INFANTRY AND COLONEL LEONARD McGIRTH'S DRAGOONS HERE MARCH 2nd AND CUT THEM OFF FROM ASHE'S MAIN TROOPS AFTER DEFEATING THEM.

PART OF COL. MARBURY'S HORSE TROOPS ESCAPED BY CROSSING HERE MARCH 2nd.

BURTON'S FERRY
COL SMITH STATIONED HERE WITH MUCH OF THE BAGGAGE OF GENERAL ASHE'S.

MATHEW'S BLUFF
GEN GRIFFITH RUTHERFORD WITH 800 MEN WAS CROSSING HERE AT TIME OF BATTLE, TO REINFORCE GEN ASHE.

LIGHT INFANTRY PROTECTING REAR OF ASHE'S ARMY.

MAJOR ROSS WITH 300 CAVALRY FACED McPHERSON HERE MORNING OF 3rd BUT DID NOT ENGAGE HIM OR REPORT HIS PRESENCE.

MAJOR McPHERSON WITH 1st BATTALION OF 71st REGIMENT — BRITISH TROOPS TOOK POSITION HERE AS DECOY 3-1-79

BLACK SWAMP, S. C.
WHERE GENERALS LINCOLN, MOULTRIE, ASHE, AND RUTHERFORD MET MONDAY, MARCH 1st, 1779 TO PLAN GEORGIA CAMPAIGN.

HUDSON'S FERRY

COMPILED BY
CLYDE D. HOLLINGSWORTH
1953

GEN ANDREW WILLIAMSON WITH 1200 MEN ON WAY TO JOIN ASHE

PARIS MILL

LT. COL PREVOST REACHED HERE MARCH 2, 1779

ROUTE OF LT. COL. PREVOST

PREVOST - MARCH 2 1779

BRIDGE DESTROYED BY MARBURY

FREEMAN'S OLD BRIDGE (DESTROYED)

BRIER CREEK

AUGUSTA CREEK

ROAD OF TO LT. COL. PREVOST'S

BEAVERDAM CREEK

ARMY'S

BUCK CREEK

BRITISH LINE
AMERICAN LINE
CAMP OF GEN. ASHE MADE FEB. 28, 1779

MARCH CREEK

TO ENCIRCLE

SAVANNAH RIVER

OLD AUGUSTA ROAD

GENERAL ASHE

REDOUBTS
GENERAL AUGUSTINE PREVOST HEADQUARTERS

The Battle of Brier Creek was fought on March 3, 1779, in eastern Georgia. A Patriot force consisting principally of militia from North Carolina and Georgia was surprised by British forces and suffered significant casualties. This 1953 map was prepared by Clyde D. Hollingsworth, editor of the *Sylvania Telephone* newspaper. It shows the movements of Loyalist and Patriot forces along the Savannah River and Brier Creek. A similar map is displayed on a Georgia historical marker at the battle site.

The North Carolina General Assembly met from January 19 to February 13, 1779. During the session the legislators took up the issue of raising sufficient forces to defend the state and assist in the defense of neighboring states. The assembly, recognizing that the terms of service of the state's militiamen on duty in South Carolina would expire in April, passed a law that, among other provisions, authorized Governor Caswell to promptly raise another body of militia to replace those men who were to be discharged. The law directed Caswell to "immediately issue orders" to the colonels of militia across the state to hold musters of their regiments and enlist able-bodied men who were to serve terms of three months from the date(s) on which they were to depart the state. All volunteers were to be paid bounties of $300, plus they were to receive their daily pay while in service. If sufficient numbers of volunteers were not obtained to fill the counties' stipulated quotas of troops, then the colonels were authorized to hold drafts in order to satisfy the deficiencies. Draftees were entitled to a $150 bounty, plus their regular pay. The law mandated that 1,500 troops be raised and that each county furnish its established quota, according to the laws regulating the state's militia. Further, the law stipulated that the "volunteers and drafted men" who were raised pursuant to the act be organized into two regiments. One regiment was to be formed from the militiamen raised in the districts of Halifax, Edenton, New Bern, and Wilmington. Militiamen from the Hillsborough and Salisbury districts were to comprise the second regiment. Both regiments were to be commanded by North Carolina militia officers.[27]

In early March Governor Caswell issued orders to the state's brigadier generals and colonels to call general musters and raise the militiamen mandated by the recently enacted statute. Caswell provided to the colonels the respective quotas of troops to be furnished. Militiamen from the eastern section of the state were to assemble in Kinston on March 15 and from there march for South Carolina.[28]

Within Bertie County, Capt. Charles Rhodes was elected or appointed to command the county's company. Rhodes had previously served as a sergeant in Capt. John Pugh Williams's company of the Fifth North Carolina Regiment. His subordinate officers were William Rascoe (lieutenant) and William Goodman (ensign). Rhodes's company was comprised of forty-two "vol[unteer]s and drafts." Amos Rayner, a nineteen-year-old county resident, was drafted. John Rhodes volunteered because he "was unwilling to stand a draft." As a volunteer, Rhodes was entitled to the $300 "volunteer" bounty. The company was assigned to the regiment commanded by Col. Jonas Johnston (Edgecombe County). Brig. Gen. John Butler was the overall commander of the North Carolina militia.[29]

Captain Rhodes and his company of drafted militia marched to South Carolina by way of Martin, Edgecombe, Lenoir (in which Kinston, the designated militia rendezvous site was situated), and Duplin counties. They marched across South Carolina and joined the southern army under General Lincoln a short distance into Georgia on April 26 but soon crossed back into South Carolina. Lincoln and his force arrived in the vicinity of Charleston shortly after British forces pulled away from the outskirts of the city on May 12. British forces under the command of Gen. Augustine Prevost had moved toward Charleston, which Brig. Gen. William Moultrie occupied on May 7 with a contingent of South Carolinians. Prevost, upon learning that Lincoln and his army were marching toward Charleston, moved to the coast and encamped his command on John's Island.[30]

Over the next week, the American and British forces maneuvered, skirmished, and constructed defensive lines and redoubts. Lincoln concluded that a nearby British garrison at Stono Ferry, less than ten miles from Charleston, appeared to be poorly defended and was vulnerable. During the evening of June 19, 1779, Lincoln held a council of war with his commanders, during which they decided to attack the Stono garrison the following morning. General Moultrie was to march from Charleston with a detachment and ferry across the Stono River to James Island. Moultrie's advance was diversionary in purpose; it was intended to provoke Prevost to observe the movement and maintain his position—and therefore send no reinforcements to Stono. Lincoln would march to Stono with Butler's North Carolina militia and Brig. Gen. Jethro Sumner's Continentals, all under Sumner's overall command, comprising Lincoln's "right wing." Brig. Gen. Isaac Huger, a South Carolinian, commanded the "left wing," comprised of Georgia and South Carolina Continentals. Lincoln's total force was estimated at 1,200 men.[31]

As happens so often in war, Lincoln and his commanders' plans hurriedly made during the council soon fell apart. First, General Moultrie did not depart Charleston in a timely manner; and by the time his men reached boats prepositioned on the Stono River, the tide was lost and the river current was too strong to accommodate ferriage by the small vessels. Lincoln marched his command shortly after midnight (the morning of June 20), but incompetence and confusion among his scouts led him to form his battle line nearly a mile from the enemy. Sumner's "right wing" of Butler's militia (including Colonel Johnston's regiment, of which Captain Rhodes's Bertie County company was a component) and his regulars encountered thickets of scrub oak and pine saplings, greatly encumbering their advance. Huger's command advanced through more open terrain and thus moved more quickly than Sumner's men.

About seven o'clock in the morning, Sumner's troops engaged a line of British pickets but quickly dispersed them toward the main body of enemy troops. About the same time, a contingent of Huger's light infantry on the left flank engaged a British unit in desperate and bloody close-quarters combat. Fewer than a dozen British soldiers escaped from Huger's men and fell back inside their Stono fortifications.[32]

Rhodes's Bertie County company was engaged during the battle and "partook of the dangers" associated with infantry combat. As British pickets and forward detachments fell back within their defensive lines, the Americans advanced. They quickly realized, however, that the British redoubts and lines were far stronger than General Lincoln had expected. Furthermore, a deep creek—of which Lincoln was unaware—protected the right side of the enemy's line. When the Americans advanced to within about sixty yards of the British, the redcoats unleashed a devastating volley. While some British defenders fled from in front of Sumner's troops by jumping in small boats to cross Stono Inlet, Lincoln held the North Carolinians back from pursuing the enemy, being of the opinion that they were not sufficiently battle tested to charge British regulars at the point of a bayonet.[33]

The Americans soon began to run low on ammunition, while British reinforcements were sighted approaching from across Stono Inlet. (Moultrie's delayed diversionary movement had failed to hold the reinforcements.) Lincoln ordered his men to pull back, which they did in a disciplined manner. The actual battle had lasted less than an hour. John Rhodes, a member of the Bertie County company, recalled that "we attacked the British forces" situated within their "entrenched camp—we stormed the fortifications but failed." American casualties numbered 155 men killed and wounded, along with nine soldiers reported as missing in action. The number of casualties suffered by Captain Rhodes's Bertie County company is unknown.[34]

Following the battle, Rhodes's company remained with Lincoln's army for a few weeks. The members' terms of service were to expire on July 10, so they soon departed from the army and "marched in the direction of [their] homes" until they reached Tarboro, where they were discharged. Their regimental commander, Col. Jonas Johnston, died suddenly during the trek to Tarboro.[35]

On February 16, 1780, North Carolina officials approved a 2,000-man draft from the state's militia forces. Sixty-six rank-and-file troops, along with a captain, a lieutenant, and an ensign, were to be detached from the Bertie County militia regiment. In essence, Bertie was to furnish a force equal to a whole company, officers included. In all, the Edenton District militia brigade

Benjamin Lincoln (1733–1810), commander of the Southern Department, surrendered the entire southern army at Charleston on May 12, 1780. The capitulation represented the largest American surrender of the war and in effect virtually wiped out North Carolina's Continental Line regiments. Image from the Prints and Photographs Division, Library of Congress.

was designated to provide 320 men and twelve officers (four companies). The district's detached militia units were to rendezvous at Kinston. The action by the state officials was in accord with a May 1779 statute by the General Assembly that authorized "the governor, with the advice of the council of state, to order any number of the militia not exceeding two thousand men, to be embodied . . . and marched to the assistance of the commonwealth of Virginia . . . should [it] be invaded by the British forces, or to the state of South Carolina, if from the operations of the British troops . . . it shall appear that this state is in apparent danger of becoming the seat of war." At the time, British army and naval forces had sailed southward from New York and had invested the coastal region of South Carolina. The news that a sizable enemy fleet had sailed discouraged new enlistments in North Carolina for the Continental army.[36] South Carolina, and Charleston in particular, was about to become "the seat of war."

About the spring of 1780, Capt. Solomon Cherry Jr. commanded a company of Bertie County militia that marched to the western Piedmont region, an area of Tory activities. Cherry's subordinate officers were Lt. Hardy Watford and Ens. Thomas Rhodes. Cherry's company first deployed to the Randolph County-Uwharrie area and camped along Deep River at or near Bell's Mill. Subsequently, the company relocated to an encampment along Six Mile Creek near Charlotte, where several other militia companies were stationed. Cherry's men performed a three-month tour of duty during which they were "often sent out on scouting parties in quest of Tories." The company was involved in no combat with British forces or altercations with "parcels of Tories" and was quartered at Six Mile Creek when its term of enlistment expired, and the men were discharged on an undisclosed date.[37]

In late March 1780 the British military besieged Charleston and Maj. Gen. Benjamin Lincoln's southern army. The general needed additional troops, and he looked to North Carolina to provide them. The number of enlistments in North Carolina's Continental Line regiments had been disappointing to state officials. Lincoln, like most regular army commanders, did not desire to have militia in his command. He opined that it was a waste of time and resources to march mostly untrained men to camp for relatively short-term enlistments. But the situation at Charleston was desperate, and Lincoln would take any troops he was offered.[38]

In early April Governor Caswell (in the final days of his term as the state's chief executive) ordered North Carolina militiamen to the aid of Charleston. While Caswell specified a draft of 4,000 troops, across the state men were "slow in turning out." (It is unclear whether or not the 4,000-man draft included the 2,000 troops authorized on February 16 or was in addition to the earlier call.) The war was entering its fifth year, and the state's residents were weary of militia drafts and the constant call of recruiters for the regular army. Moreover, money to pay enlistment bounties was scarce, further prompting military-age men to shun active service. Some potential soldiers declared that they would not leave their homes unless they were first paid their enlistment bounties. Nonetheless, Caswell's brother, Brig. Gen. William Caswell of the New Bern District, was able to raise a force of about seven hundred militia and hurriedly marched southward.[39]

Governor Caswell initially designated Kinston as the rendezvous point for militiamen recruited in the eastern part of the state, but he soon changed the rendezvous location to Cross Creek in the southeastern section of the state. Cross Creek was situated closer to South Carolina and in a more direct line of march to Charleston. Time was of the essence in getting reinforcements to General Lincoln, and the most direct route was preferable.[40]

In Bertie County, a number of men were raised to serve in this latest call by the state for "drafted militia." As had become customary in such drafts, a few county residents volunteered to serve, while others waited to be drafted. Some individuals, once drafted, hired substitutes to serve in their places and thereby avoided military service altogether. The county's militiamen, committed to three-month terms of service, were not placed under the command of one of the county's militia officers but were instead combined with men raised in neighboring Hertford County to constitute a company. Capt. Allen Ramsay of Hertford County commanded the company, which marched directly to Charleston. According to Josiah Harrell, one of the Bertie County militiamen, the company marched singularly to Charleston, "joined by no other Company." Indeed, the troops were well aware that they were marching into a precarious situation. Immediately upon their arrival in the besieged port city, they were merged together with the other members of Lincoln's command of Continental soldiers and militia.[41]

On Friday, May 12, 1780, General Lincoln surrendered his entire army of about 5,400 men, including more than 1,200 militiamen from North and South Carolina. Captain Ramsay's company of Bertie and Hertford County men was captured. Bertie County residents Josiah Harrell and Isaac Hendrickson were, however, fortunate—they were discharged from service shortly before Charleston fell and did not suffer the fate of prisoners of war as did many of their comrades. The articles of capitulation between General Lincoln and Gen. Sir Henry Clinton provided that the militia in the garrison would be permitted to return to their respective homes as "Prisoners upon Parole." The members of Captain Ramsay's company were paroled on an undisclosed date(s) in 1781. The following table lists the Bertie County troops who were paroled.[42]

TABLE 5
Captured Bertie County Militiamen Paroled in 1781

Robert Calend	William Fryar	Jesse Lloyd
Samuel Deans	Joseph Hedgpeth	William Low
James Dymond	William Horton	Thomas Minton
James Farmer	Frederick James	Arthur Wiggins
John Fields	William Jernigan	Lewis Williford

Shortly after the fall of Charleston, more Bertie County militiamen were called for active duty. On June 5, 1780, Capt. Elisha Rhodes assumed command of a militia company jointly comprised of men from Bertie and Gates counties. Rhodes's subordinate officers were Lt. James Swinhow Grover and Ensigns Stephen Buck and Joseph Sanderson. In early June thirty men constituted the rank and file of the company—sixteen were Bertie County residents, and fourteen hailed from Gates County.[43]

Rhodes's company was assigned to Col. Samuel Jarvis's militia regiment. Jarvis, commandant of the Currituck County militia, organized a four-company regiment that in early June included slightly more than two hundred members from counties in the northeastern region of the state. In addition to Rhodes, Captains Alexander Whitehall (Currituck County), William Brinkley (Halifax County), and William Earl (Tyrrell County) commanded the companies under Jarvis's command, which was designated the First North Carolina Regiment of Militia.[44]

Colonel Jarvis apparently organized his understrength regiment at Halifax and on an undisclosed date began marching southward for South Carolina, intending to reinforce American forces in that state. Jarvis and his men had trekked almost all the way across North Carolina in the summer heat, when distressing news arrived: Maj. Gen. Horatio Gates, the recently instituted commander of the Southern Department, had led American forces into battle at Camden, South Carolina, on August 16, 1780, and was soundly trounced. Word was that Gates's "shattered organizations" had retreated in a "rout." Jarvis and his men had reached the Pee Dee River near the South Carolina border when the news arrived. Maj. Gen. Richard Caswell, overall commander of North Carolina's militia forces, upon learning of the fiasco at Camden, immediately dispatched messengers "to intercept" Colonel Jarvis's regiment and those of Cols. Benjamin Seawell and Benjamin Exum and to direct them to march to Ramsey's Mill on Deep River in Chatham County.[45]

Jarvis's regiment arrived at Ramsey's Mill, probably toward the end of August, and was placed under the command of Brig. Gen. Jethro Sumner, the state's ranking Continental army officer. At Ramsey's Mill on September 3, 1780, the four companies of the regiment, including Captain Rhodes's unit, mustered 216 privates, who were "fit for duty." By that time, the men had fulfilled, or were close to fulfilling, their three-month terms of service and desired to be discharged. On September 29 Sumner wrote to Gates that almost two hundred men in Jarvis and Exum's regiments "claim Discharge," having completed their terms of service. Sumner requested Gates to issue him "some orders on this matter," since he (Sumner) was "not acquainted with the Resolves of the [General] Assembly respecting the Militia." Three days later Sumner again wrote to Gates that the troops in Jarvis's regiment had for "some time" claimed that they had "a right of being discharged, having . . . served upwards of four months." Sumner advised Gates that he had written to the North Carolina Board of War to ascertain if the board's position was that the troops' time of service had expired. The men of Colonel Exum's regiment likewise claimed that their time of service had been fulfilled. The drafted militiamen whose times were up were growing impatient and rowdy in the camp at Ramsey's Mill. Sumner sent another dispatch (undated) to Gates that the men were "very turbulent and complain of their time being out. They are not to be depended on; they will not fight." Gates responded immediately and "endorsed" Sumner's first letter. The men in Jarvis and Exum's regiments whose times of service were fulfilled were "honorably discharged."[46] Captain Rhodes and his Bertie and Gates counties men presumably returned to their homes.

Almost simultaneously with Elisha Rhodes's assuming command of the joint Bertie-Gates company, another Bertie County resident was placed in command of a drafted militia company. In early June Capt. Francis Pugh was elected or appointed to command a Bertie County company assigned to Lt. Col. John Pugh Williams's regiment. The regiment was a constituent unit in Brig. Gen. Isaac Gregory's militia brigade. General Gregory, a resident of Pasquotank County, had been appointed commandant of the Edenton District militia upon the resignation of Brig. Gen. William Skinner in May 1779.[47] With the fall of Charleston on May 12, troops were desperately needed in South Carolina to forestall the British. Gregory's men were to march to South Carolina as expeditiously as they could be raised and organized.

Gov. Abner Nash inquired of Gregory what was the "situation and prospect relative to the Troops" that were raised from the Edenton District brigade for active service. On June 7 Gregory wrote to the governor that the troops from "Some Counties turn out very well," while others seemed "something Tardy." The general noted that he hoped he would raise the number of men requested by Nash, or at least assemble "very near" the district's draft quota. He further informed the governor that the colonels of some of the counties within the district had found that it was "not possible to get arms." In an attempt to assure Nash, Gregory stated that he would "do everything" within his power to forward the troops to Kinston (the designated rendezvous site for the militia from the eastern region of the state) "in a short time."[48]

Bertie was one of the counties to which General Gregory alluded in his letter to the governor. On June 9 Col. Arthur Brown, commander of the Bertie

County militia regiment, wrote to Governor Nash that the county's militia had 18 volunteers and 112 draftees for service. The men refused to march until they had received their bounties, however. Brown penned: "I under stand the treasurer has no public money in his hands, our sheriff only three thousand pounds. Would be glad if you would send the sum for that use. I have sent you a bond for the faithfull application of the money."[49]

Immediately across the Chowan River, Col. Thomas Benbury was encountering similar issues with the Chowan County militia. On June 12 Benbury wrote to Nash: "I . . . Inform you that the militia that we have Drafted under your orders have Joined with the militia Drafted in the Two Last Drafts and is Now Lying in the woods and Determined Not To March but will Defend themselves to the Utmost Rigger." Benbury was on the verge of rallying other Chowan County militiamen to curtail the rebellious actions of his drafted militia and those of other counties. He advised Nash that he had "Two Hundred men under arms now, we Shall March Tomorrow With the Militia of this County to apprehend all Such as is in this County or the adjacent Countys." He concluded: "I hope the Number will be but Few When they Know the Determination of the Counties in This District."[50] Conflict between armed militiamen in the northeastern region of North Carolina likely seemed a real possibility to local militia commanders. The constant strain of potential forced military duty was wearing down the rebellious and patriotic resolve of many citizens in the northeastern part of the state.

The number of men who eventually comprised Captain Pugh's company is not disclosed in extant records; neither is the date on which the company departed Bertie County and joined up with Colonel Williams's regiment, Gregory's brigade. On August 2 the brigade was in camp at Thompson's Creek, three miles from Cheraw, South Carolina. One other North Carolina brigade, that of Brig. Gen. Griffith Rutherford, was likewise at that site. The militiamen were experiencing a miserable stay at the locale: for the previous three days, the weather in that region had been "very wet," with deluges of rain. The creeks and rivers in the area were flooded. General Caswell reported to General Gates that the gristmills in the area had stopped grinding corn because of the floods, causing the North Carolina militiamen in camp to run short of meal and, therefore, "suffer for the want of Bread."[51]

On August 7 Gregory's brigade and the other North Carolina militiamen who earlier had been encamped at Thompson's Creek met up and joined in with the American forces under General Gates that were marching toward Camden, South Carolina. Lt. Col. John Pugh Williams (Bertie County militia) accompanied the militiamen. Gates, who had received faulty intelligence from

Following the surrender of Charleston in May 1780, the Continental Congress placed Maj. Gen. Horatio Gates in command of the Southern Department. Soon after arriving to fulfill its appointment, Gates's army was routed at Camden, South Carolina (August 16, 1780), by British forces commanded by Gen. Charles Cornwallis. Following the Camden debacle, Congress quickly relieved Gates of the command of the department and replaced him with Maj. Gen. Nathanael Greene. Image of Gates from the Prints and Photographs Division, Library of Congress.

his scouts—leading him to believe reports that British general Lord Charles Cornwallis had departed the post with troops destined for Savannah—was of the opinion that the British garrison at Camden was somewhat weakened. Just the opposite was true: Cornwallis had hurried to Camden with reinforcements upon learning that Gates was marching toward the village with his force. Coincidentally, about ten o'clock in the evening of the August 15, both Gates and Cornwallis began marching their troops toward each other, each general determined to be the aggressor in the soon-to-erupt clash. About two o'clock in the morning on Wednesday, the sixteenth, the vanguard of Gates's command ran into mounted British troops at the head of Cornwallis's column. After a few short volleys, both parties fell back to the main bodies of their comrades. Gates immediately called a council with his general officers, the majority of whom agreed that their troops should continue to move toward the British force.[52]

Before daybreak Gates advanced his troops without a battle plan and without distinct orders to his subordinate officers. Cornwallis's redcoats moved aggressively forward and hit the Americans with such ferocity that the Virginian militia units instantaneously broke. Next, the North Carolina militiamen broke from the confrontation and fled for their lives. In their terrorized state, the citizen soldiers threw down muskets, equipment, and ammunition and streaked for safety away from the battle line. Members of Gregory's brigade fought with desperation, but being abandoned by the others were too greatly outnumbered to prevail. In very short order the British victory was complete. While no accurate casualty lists were compiled for the American forces, it is estimated that between 800 and 900 men were killed and probably a thousand were made prisoners.[53]

Captain Pugh and his Bertie County militia company were caught up in the thick of the stampede of North Carolina troops. Pugh escaped from the battlefield. In evading British troops at Camden, he met up with other militiamen who similarly had escaped, two of whom were Maj. James Foy and Pvt. Jesse Brown, both from the Wilmington District. Brown later stated that "I remember . . . seeing two British light horse [troopers] cutting at Cater Harrell. I myself, after our ranks were broken & dispersed escaped beyond a fence which protected me from the pursuit of the British dragoons. Many of my Comrades were shot down by my side. After this I fell in with a Captain Pugh of Bertie & we traveled together several days when we fell in with Major [James] Foy." Pvt. Solomon Barnes of Bertie County likewise escaped and later stated: "we met the British at Camden . . . and had with them a very severe Battle . . . which contest terminated in our defeat."[54] It is not known how many casualties were suffered by the members of Pugh's company.

The surviving members of Pugh's unit who escaped at Camden and rejoined the American command apparently served until at least March 1781, and some may have participated in the Battle of Guilford Courthouse (March 15, 1781). Bertie County militiaman Solomon Barnes recounted that after the defeat at Camden:

Our Army retreated—we crossed the Pedee [Pee Dee] River at what was then called the White House and halted & remained some time at the hanging Rock. From this we proceeded to Salisbury . . . & thence to Hillsborough . . . [then] to Charlotte where we remained until late in December or early in January[.] . . . [A]bout the last of November or first of December General [Nathanael] Green [Greene] took command of the Army. On leaving this place the Army was divided. We went to Cheraw Hills where we remained until it was understood that the other detachment had fought & gained a Victory at the Cowpens. Shortly after this battle & news we joined with our friends the Victors & went into the State of Virginia, where we were joined with a reinforcement. We then returned to North Carolina and about the middle of March 1781 we arrived & stationed ourselves at Guilford Court house, at which place a few days after our arrival we had a desperate fight with the enemy, but were compelled to retreat after a severe struggle. . . . [A]fter this battle we were marched to Orange County at which place this Affiant received his discharge.[55]

The year 1780 had turned into an eventful period in Bertie County as one contingent after another of the county's militiamen was called into service and marched westward to the Piedmont region of North Carolina or southward to South Carolina. About late summer in 1780 another company was called into service. Capt. Thomas Rhodes commanded the unit, which initially marched to Kinston under the overall purview of Thomas Pugh. Little is discernible regarding the company's service. Bertie County resident John Rhodes was drafted to serve in the company. Years later he recalled that he

was drafted in the year 1780 in the month of September or August. . . . I marched from Bertie County under Captain Thomas Rhodes to Kinston, remained there a few days, and I was taken sick there and becoming better I marched one days march from Kinston under the command of Lieutenant Colonel Thomas Pugh of Bertie. I was again taken sick & was confined by a fever . . . produced as I believe by a disease called the White swelling. My Colonel [unidentified] visited me, saw my situation and told me that the Regiment must go on and I must return home, which after some time I did[.] I was absent from home on this tour one month. I had no written discharge—have no documentary evidence & knows of no person that can prove this service whose testimony I can procure. I was a true Whig.

William Brooks, a Gates County militiaman, served in the regiment commanded by Thomas Pugh. Brooks and other members of a Gates County company departed their home county on August 17, 1780, and marched to Hillsborough, where the troops assembled. From Hillsborough the regiment marched to the Yadkin River, then to Salisbury and later to Waxhaws, South Carolina, where they were placed under the overall command of Brig. Gen.William Lee Davidson (North Carolina militia). The troops eventually marched to a camp near Charlotte, where the militiamen were discharged. Brooks stated that the men's discharges were signed by Lieutenant Colonel Pugh and countersigned by General Davidson.[56]

General Cornwallis, who had retired with his army to Wilmington following the Battle of Guilford Courthouse, subsequently rushed into Virginia in the spring of 1781 and made it his new base of operations in the British southern campaign. Gen. Sir Henry Clinton, Cornwallis's superior officer, was dissatisfied with Cornwallis's move to Virginia and ordered him to adopt a defensive position along the Virginia coast and prepare to send his troops northward. Cornwallis moved to Yorktown. As had been the case a number of times during the war, North Carolina once again dispatched militia forces to assist in defending a neighboring state.[57]

As Bertie County militia commanders organized volunteers and draftees to deploy on detached service, the citizens in the Albemarle Sound region lived with continued rumors of visits from British forces and uprisings by citizens with Tory inclinations. As early as February 1779 relatives and members of James Iredell's immediate family had relocated from Edenton to Windsor, seeking to remove themselves from a perceived object of a British raid. By July 1781 anticipated raids by elements of the king's forces positioned as close by as Suffolk, Virginia (sixty or so miles from Windsor), were continually the subject of conversations and correspondences. Furthermore, Loyalist row galleys—armed watercraft propelled by oars rather than sails—appeared in Albemarle Sound and the lower Chowan River, intensifying the citizens' fears of visits from British or Tory warriors. A brief enemy foray from row galleys into Edenton in late May 1781 had destroyed some personal property but resulted in no major destruction. Robert Smith, an influential Whig and Chowan County justice, suffered "some loss" during the incursion but concluded that "it might have been worse." Some residents feared that the Tories would ascend the Cashie River to Windsor, but Smith thought not. He remarked to James Iredell that he had "Serious doubts some of these pirates may go up Cashy on information of Vessells and goods being there." Jean Johnston Blair, sister of Samuel and John Johnston, wrote to Iredell from Windsor on May 29 that she was of the opinion that the enemy "Boats . . . more than probable" would raid plantations along the area waterways rather than visit Windsor to "cut out Vessels."[58] The Tory row galleys did not visit Windsor.

The *General Arnold*, one "British Galley" that raided Edenton and destroyed a number of vessels belonging to local citizens, was itself captured by local militia. Almost twenty crew members were detained as prisoners of war. The commander of the galley, Michael Quinn of Craven County, had formerly served as an officer in the North Carolina Continental Line. He initially served in the Eighth North Carolina Regiment and later as a captain in the Third Regiment (Second Organization—Hogun's). Quinn resigned his commission in December 1779 and eventually turned against his former comrades and "went over" to the British. Quinn was immediately placed in irons and detained in the Edenton jail, but in a few days he was transferred to Halifax and confined. On June 15 Maj. Hardy Murfree wrote to Brig. Gen. Jethro Sumner that he had "sent" to Halifax the crew of the *General Arnold*, including the "traitor Michael Quin." He added: "I hope [he] will get what he deserves." Less than two weeks later, "the Guard" at the Halifax jail shot and killed Quinn. A sergeant of the guard reported that Quinn had attempted to escape as the guards were transferring him to a house. Col. William Linton of the militia was charged with ordering Quinn's murder. The Halifax County coroner conducted an inquest "on the body" of Quinn, to which the jury reported "he was Murdered by the Guard by order of Colo. William Linton." The shooter (unidentified) was "tried, convicted and pardoned." Linton was charged with being an accessory to the killing. Eventually Gov. Alexander Martin pardoned Linton; Martin likely had the charges against the colonel dropped before trial. In December 1785 the North Carolina General Assembly, pursuant to a petition from Linton, resolved that the former colonel be exonerated and reimbursed for expenses incurred related to his incarceration in the Halifax jail.[59]

Bertie County residents remained aware of General Cornwallis's movements and progress northward across North Carolina, primarily by updates brought to Windsor by militia officers, officials, and other travelers. On May 3, 1781, John Johnston advised his brother-in-law, James Iredell: "we have been alarmed by a report that the English Army under Cornwallis were expected immediately at Tarborough." Johnston, unsure whether or not the information he had received was reliable, expressed to Iredell that "most" of the reports seemed "too slender a foundation to be much depended on." By early May Cornwallis was approaching the north-central region of the state. On May 10 Jean Johnston Blair, writing from Windsor, declared to her sister, Hannah Iredell, that the "English are certainly at Halifax." Indeed they were, having arrived at the town that day. Blair, unsure of precisely where British

Galleys were small enough to maneuver the sounds, so they were used by the British for raids in the Albemarle Sound region. While a few raids occurred, residents' fears were mostly unfounded. From Jack Coggins, *Ships and Seamen of the American Revolution* (Mineola, N.Y.: Dover Publications, 2002), 52.

soldiers might venture, decided that there was no need for her to vacate Windsor. In her view, the town was "as safe as any where else." The following day she advised her brother-in-law, James Iredell, that reports had confirmed that Cornwallis's "whole" army was at Halifax. Although rumors suggested that the citizens of Windsor "were in danger," no British patrols or detachments strayed as far eastward as Bertie County.[60]

Brig. Gen. Isaac Gregory was placed in command of a contingent of militia raised in the Albemarle Sound region for the purpose of marching to the Norfolk area to bolster Virginian troops. Two Bertie county companies—one commanded by Capt. John Folk and the other by Capt. William Morris (subsequently by Capt. William Rascoe)—were organized and marched to join Gregory's command. The companies were committed to serve for three months. Both were placed under the direct command of Col. Peter Dozier, also known as Dauge, of Pasquotank County. By late May General Gregory and his force were encamped at Northwest Landing on the Northwest River in southeastern Virginia. From late May until near the end of August, the

Bertie County militiamen were stationed at Northwest Bridge, where they reconnoitered the movements of the British in the Norfolk-Portsmouth area. They were involved in no altercations with British soldiers. About the middle of August the British troops in the area evacuated to Yorktown, inasmuch as smallpox was "violently raging" about Portsmouth. Shortly thereafter, the terms of service for the two Bertie County companies were about to expire. On August 22 General Gregory wrote to Gov. Thomas Burke (who had replaced Gov. Abner Nash in June 1781) that, given the British troops' withdrawal and the prevalence of smallpox in the area, it was his opinion that it was "unnecessary" for the militia to remain in service. He informed Burke: "I . . . think it my duty to discharge the militia unless some incident Should happen, which might make it necessary to alter my present Resolutions." Before the end of the month, the Bertie County militiamen were discharged and returned to their homes.[61]

Gov. Thomas Burke was of the opinion that General Cornwallis might attempt to vacate his exposed and vulnerable position in southeastern Virginia and withdraw southward through northeastern North Carolina. On August 31, 1781, Burke wrote to General Gregory that he had "intelligence" that Cornwallis intended a retreat "through the Country in order to avoid being blocked up by the French West Indies Fleet," which was then situated along the Atlantic seaboard. Burke ordered that all boats and canoes on the Chowan River be removed to Edenton. He also directed Gregory to ensure that all similar vessels on other rivers in the vicinity of the Edenton District region—which might be of service to the British should they retreat through the region—be removed into Albemarle Sound "so as to be utterly out of their power." Burke ordered Gregory to station a force of militia at Edenton to guard the vessels and "remove them to any other place" Burke might specify.[62]

On September 1 Maj. Hardy Murfree, situated at Murfree's Landing (present-day Murfreesboro) on the Meherrin River, wrote to Burke that he would "loose [sic] no time in Securing the Boats, &c." Murfree's location made it convenient for the men under his command to scour the upper Chowan, Meherrin, and Nottaway rivers in order to secure vessels and monitor ferry crossings. Six days later Murfree was at Winton and wrote to Burke that in accordance with the governor's orders, he had collected boats and canoes in that area and had them "on their way down to Edenton." At the time, Murfree's men were traveling along the Meherrin River to gather any vessels along that tributary.[63]

On September 1 Burke dispatched orders to James Campbell, then commanding the Bertie County militia, "to collect immediately the whole force of your County and hold them in readiness to march at a moment's warning to Winton and Wright's Ferry on Chowan River." Burke requested Campbell to utilize "the utmost diligence in this affair and . . . communicate to me the earliest intelligence on every occasion." Two days later Burke sent Campbell another communication, which revealed that during the evening of September 2 Burke had "received intelligence" that "the French Fleet consisting of twenty seven sail of the Line and several Frigates with six thousand land forces on board" had arrived at Hampton Roads at the mouth of the James River. That information, in conjunction with "other intelligence" the governor had received, induced him to countermand his orders to Colonel Campbell and instead to order Campbell to march the Bertie County militia "with all possible expedition to Northampton [County] Court House and to report to Gen. Allen Jones" (Halifax District).[64]

By September 1781, the Bertie County militia regiment was a shambles of a military unit as Governor Burke ordered it to be ready to march. More than six years of war and numerous calls for detached companies from the county to march off to battle had worn down the resolve and resilience of the officers and men. Moreover, the men's families had sacrificed severely as time after time their husbands, fathers, and brothers were assembled in Windsor and contingents of the men marched away to battle. County citizens were repeatedly called upon to provide food, provisions, forage, clothing, livestock, and equipment for their militiamen. The entire county was weary of war and its seemingly never-ending demands. Thus, on September 5 Campbell replied to Burke, having returned to his home from Edenton during the previous evening and received both of the governor's communications. Campbell assured Burke that he would use his "utmost Endeavours for the speedy march" of the Bertie County militia, but he was sorry to inform the governor that the men were "badly Equipt for want of Arms." Campbell wrote that he would "collect all I can for them." He then informed Burke that the colonel (Arthur Brown) of the county "refused to act any Longer in the Military Department." Campbell faced a further dilemma in that "many Captains" in the Bertie regiment had resigned, and formal commissions from the governor were needed to appoint new officers to replace those who had done so. Even Campbell himself had not been formally commissioned but for the previous nine months had "acted by Ap[p]ointment." He requested Burke to forward a colonel's commission for him and blank commissions for the other subordinate officers.[65]

Colonel Brown had labored to keep the county's militia as efficient and functional as possible, particularly by collecting funds to pay bounties to volunteers and draftees, some of whom refused to march until they had received their due payments. By 1779 Brown was confronted with the "almost impossibility of Collecting public taxes." He collected what receipts that he could from the overburdened populace and used the funds for "public Military uses"—primarily to pay bounties to militiamen destined to march to battle and participate in expeditions. During 1780 Brown paid £180 in "depreciated Currency" to 252 Bertie County militiamen—44 volunteers and 208 draftees.[66]

Campbell, as Burke had previously requested, conveyed "intelligence" that he had received just two days earlier while in Edenton. He informed the governor that on the night of September 3, 1781, there had arrived in Edenton harbor from St. Croix a brig whose captain had informed officials that "Seven Sail of French Men of War" had put ashore at Martinico from France and that several privateers were cruising among the English Islands and had done considerable damage by "Calling out Vessells, burning houses & Carrying of[f] Negroes & Effects of the Inhabitants." The captain of the vessel, upon sailing from the West Indies, learned that only two English privateers were reportedly in the area. Campbell closed by confirming to Burke that he "Shall at all times Com[m]unicate any Intelligence."[67]

A combined American-French army force, with the cooperation of a sizable French naval fleet, was moving to envelope General Cornwallis's army at Yorktown. In Governor Burke's opinion, "His Lordship's [Cornwallis's] situation" rendered the North Carolina militia's "precautions for preventing his retreat [through northeastern North Carolina] no longer necessary." On September 5 Burke wrote to Brigadier General Gregory and conveyed that opinion.[68] Burke's change of position apparently negated the need for Colonel Campbell to march the Bertie County militia to Northampton County.

At Yorktown on Friday, October 19, 1781, Gen. Charles Cornwallis surrendered his British army to a combined American-French force commanded by Gen. George Washington and Comte de Rochambeau. This decisive victory concluded the principal combat of the Revolutionary War. Nevertheless, Bertie County militiamen were again ordered into detached service—not against British soldiers but against Tories in the western region of the state.

★ ★ ★ ★ ★

Throughout the war, eleven companies of minutemen and militia, comprised wholly or partially of Bertie County residents, marched away on varying tours of duty, as summarized in the following table.

TABLE 6
Service of Bertie County Minuteman and
Militia Companies (Detached), 1776–1781

Approximate Period of Service	Company Commander(s)	Service Rendered
Feb. 1776	Capt. Charles Worth Jacocks★	Marched to Cross Creek in Duplin County in support of Col. James Moore's North Carolinians at the Battle of Moores Creek Bridge, Feb. 27, 1776—an American victory
May–Aug. 1776	Capt. Andrew Oliver★	Marched to southeastern N.C. and participated in the defense of Wilmington—involved in no engagements with British forces
Dec. 1778– Apr. 1779	Capts. Thomas Pugh and John Wolfenden	Marched to near Augusta, Ga., and participated in the Battle of Brier Creek, Mar. 3, 1779—an American defeat
Apr.–July 1779	Capt. Charles Rhodes	Marched to S.C. and participated in the Battle of Stono Ferry, June 20, 1779—an American defeat
Spring 1780	Capt. Solomon Cherry	Marched to the Piedmont region of N.C. and participated in subduing Tories during a three-month tour—involved in no engagements with British forces
Apr.–May 1780	Capt. Allen Ramsay (Hertford County)	Company partially comprised of Bertie County men participated in the defense of Charleston until the garrison was surrendered by Maj. Gen. Benjamin Lincoln on May 12, 1780—an American defeat

★Accounts of service rendered by companies of Captains Jacocks and Oliver are presented in chapter 2.

Approximate Period of Service	Company Commander(s)	Service Rendered
June–Sept. 1780	Capt. Elisha Rhodes	Company comprised of men from Bertie and Gates counties; marched toward S.C. but diverted into the Piedmont of N.C. upon learning of defeat of Maj. Gen. Horatio Gates's American army at Camden, Aug. 16, 1780. Performed three-month tour—involved in no engagements with British forces
June 1780– March 1781	Capt. Francis Pugh	Marched to S.C. and participated in the Battle of Camden, Aug. 16, 1780—an American defeat. Some members of the company apparently served until March 1781 with General Gates's army in Piedmont N.C. and participated in the Battle of Guilford Courthouse, March 15, 1781—an American defeat.
Late summer– fall 1780	Capt. Thomas Rhodes	Marched to the Piedmont of N.C., then to S.C. and back to the Piedmont—involved in no engagements with British forces
Late May–late Aug. 1781	Capt. John Folk	Marched to southeastern Va. and participated in reconnoitering the movement of British forces in the region—involved in no engagements with British forces
Late May–late Aug. 1781	Capts. William Morris and William Rascoe	Marched to southeastern Va. and participated in reconnoitering the movement of British forces in the region—involved in no engagements with British forces

In March 1782 Gov. Thomas Burke appointed Maj. Thomas Hogg to lead a force of the state's troops on an expedition into the Deep River region of the Piedmont to subdue and suppress roving bands of Tories. Specifically, Hogg was to go into Randolph and Chatham counties, in which disaffected persons were most active and rebellious. Burke directed that militiamen from various counties across the state be included in the expeditionary force. On March 16 Burke ordered Colonel Campbell of Bertie County and the colonels of the others counties in the Edenton District to immediately dispatch the militiamen who had previously been drafted for the "State Corps" to join the body of troops under Major Hogg's command. At that time, the Edenton District tallied 3,380 militiamen potentially available for duty, 659 of whom were in Bertie County. The men raised pursuant to Burke's orders were to rendezvous at Hillsborough, where they would receive further orders.

In spite of the governor's orders for the troops to march immediately, the expedition was delayed as the result of a dispute between Maj. Bennett Crafton of the state militia and Burke. Crafton, who resided in the region in which the expedition was to be carried out, demanded to be given command of the force. According to Burke, "Major Crafton disputed, disobeying my orders, and thereby delayed the March of the Troops." On March 26 Burke wrote to Crafton and enclosed a copy of his (Burke's) orders to Major Hogg. The governor pointedly informed Crafton: "I expect you will obey my orders without disputing them. . . . Your . . . Commission in the State Troops neither entitles you to the Sole Command of those Troops nor to the Conduct of any Expedition in which they may be employed. . . . I, therefore, insist that upon receipt of this you Immediately proceed in your duty, agreeably to the rank you bear, under the orders of Major Hogg." Burke advised Crafton that if he chose not to abide by the orders, he was at "liberty to retire from the [militia] Service." Major Hogg presumably began the expedition soon thereafter. Moreover, it is presumed that some Bertie County troops were included in the force, in accordance with the governor's orders to Col. James Campbell. As of June the troops were "still operating against the Tories in the Deep River country."[69]

Peace talks between the Americans and the British began in Paris in April 1782. The Continental Congress named a five-member commission comprised of John Adams, Benjamin Franklin, John Jay, Thomas Jefferson, and Henry Laurens to negotiate with the British. Laurens was captured by a British warship and held in London until the end of the war and therefore did not participate in the negotiations. Jefferson did not depart the United States in time to take part. Therefore Adams, Franklin, and Jay conducted the talks. The treaty negotiations continued between the Americans and British for a year and a half. The war formally concluded on September 3, 1783, when the United States and Great Britain signed the final peace treaty in Paris.[70]

Notes

1. Worthington Chauncey Ford, ed., *Journals of the Continental Congress*, 34 vols. (Washington, D.C.: Government Printing Office, 1904–1937), 12:949–950.

2. Ford, *Journals of the Continental Congress*, 4:181, 12:951.

3. Hugh F. Rankin, *The North Carolina Continentals* (Chapel Hill: University of North Carolina Press, 1971), 189–190.

4. Henry Laurens to Richard Caswell, September 26, 1778, Paul H. Smith and Ronald M. Gephart, eds., *Letters of Delegates to Congress, 1774–1789*, 26 vols. (Washington, D.C.: Library of Congress, 1976–2000), 10:697–699.

5. Cornelius Harnett to Caswell, September 26, 1778, Smith and Gephart, *Letters of Delegates*, 10:695–696. Maj. Gen. Robert Howe had long been unpopular with certain South Carolina delegates because of his feud with Christopher Gadsden (South Carolina statesman, soldier, and principal leader of that state's Patriot movement during the Revolutionary War), and he had offended some Georgia delegates by his reluctance to cooperate with their state's expeditions against the British in East Florida. Harnett later claimed that the delegates from the two states were finally prompted to ask for Howe's removal from the southern military department by their disgust over a "ridiculous matter" in South Carolina involving a woman. See Harnett to Caswell, November 24, 1778. Smith and Gephart, *Letters of Delegates*, 11:251–252.

6. Walter Clark, ed., *The State Records of North Carolina*, 16 vols. (11–26) (Raleigh: State of North Carolina, 1895–1906), 13:245–246.

7. Ford, *Journals of the Continental Congress*, 12:1021; Clark, *State Records*, 13:242. On October 20, 1778, the Continental Congress resolved that the Continental Board of War transmit $150,000 to William Blount, deputy paymaster general of North Carolina, "for the pay and subsistence of the levies" to be sent from North Carolina to Charleston. See Ford, *Journals of the Continental Congress*, 12:1026.

8. Clark, *State Records*, 12:235, 13:245–246, 248, 249, 251, 252. General Vail died on June 5, 1777. See *Dictionary of North Carolina Biography*, s.v. "Vail, Edward."

9. Clark, *State Records*, 13:251. Skinner also served as North Carolina's treasurer for the Northern District, having been appointed to that position in December 1777. See Clark, *State Records*, 12:234.

10. Clark, *State Records*, 12:777, 832, 22:939. The General Assembly accepted Thomas Pugh's resignation on December 1, 1778, thereby leading the author to conclude that Pugh formally submitted the paperwork in November. The author found no orders or other records documenting Thomas Pugh's appointment or election as captain of the Bertie County militia company. No muster rolls exist for the company. The author determined that Pugh served as the captain of the company based on information from James Ward's Revolutionary War pension file. In November 1832 Ward, who had been a member of the company, stated that he "was under the command of Captain Thomas Pugh for a short period." Pugh apparently resigned the position since Ward further stated that he was "afterwards" under the command of Capt. John Wolfenden. James Ward, declaration dated November 15, 1832, Revolutionary War pension file for James Ward (S7819), Revolutionary War Pension and Bounty Land Warrant Files, 1800–1900, (microfilm, M804), Record Group 15, National Archives, Washington, D.C. (hereafter cited as Revolutionary War pension files). Besides James Ward, the author was unable to identify any other privates in the company. Likewise, while eighty-five men were reportedly members of the company, in the absence of company muster and/or pay rolls, the author was unable to determine the dates that they (1) were mustered at Windsor and (2) marched away from the town in route to the rendezvous site at Kinston.

11. Clark, *State Records*, 13:274.

12. Clark, *State Records*, 13:276–278, 292–293.

13. Clark, *State Records*, 13:288–289.

14. Clark, *State Records*, 13:290, 292–293; Rankin, *North Carolina Continentals*, 187; Ford, *Journals of the Continental Congress*, 12:949–950.

15. Clark, *State Records*, 13:297–198, 301–302.

16. William Brooks, declaration dated August 23, 1832, Revolutionary War pension file for William Brooks (S6705).

17. Clark, *State Records*, 14:7.

18. Clark, *State Records*, 13:332, 342.

19. Rankin, *North Carolina Continentals*, 189–191.

20. Rankin, *North Carolina Continentals*, 192–193; Clark, *State Records*, 14:271, 280; James Ward, declaration dated November 15, 1832, Revolutionary War pension file for James Ward (S7819).

21. Rankin, *North Carolina Continentals*, 194–195; Clark, *State Records*, 41, 280.

22. Rankin, *North Carolina Continentals*, 195; Clark, *State Records*, 14:41, 271.

23. James Ward, declaration dated November 15, 1832, Revolutionary War pension file for James Ward (S7819); Henry Halsey, declaration dated September 18, 1832, Revolutionary War pension file for Henry Halsey (S2597); Clark, *State Records*, 14:41, 278.

It is unclear how long the British held Capt. John Wolfenden as a prisoner of war. He had been released by August 1780, at which time he witnessed a deed in Bertie County court. See Weynette Parks Haun, comp., *Bertie County, North Carolina, Court Minutes, 1772–1780, Book IV* (Durham: the compiler, 1979), 119.

John Hancock, a militiaman from Bute County (present-day Franklin County), was captured at the battle. Hancock stated in July 1834 that several hundred of the Americans "were made prisoners" and "were carried down to Savannah Town and kept . . . [for] a few days." The prisoners were afterward transferred to prison ships lying at the mouth of the Savannah River. Hancock remained a prisoner aboard one of the ships for about six months, "suffering greatly for the want of wholesome provisions and sickness." He stated that the "continued confinement" caused him to partially lose the use of his limbs. He was then taken to Wilmington Island, Georgia. John Hancock, declaration dated July 24, 1834, Revolutionary War pension file for John Hancock (R4551).

24. Rankin, *North Carolina Continentals*, 196; Samuel Reed, declaration dated October 23, 1832, Revolutionary War pension file for Samuel Reed (S7372).

25. Clark, *State Records*, 14:271. On March 13 a court-martial of General Ashe was convened in which Brig. Gen. William Moultrie (South Carolina) served as president. On the sixteenth, Moultrie rendered the court's opinion: "The court having maturely considered the matter before them, are of opinion that Gen. Ashe did not take all the necessary precautions which he ought to have done to secure his camp, and obtain timely intelligence of the movements and approach of the enemy; but they do entirely acquit him of every imputation of a want of personal courage in the affair at Brier creek, and think he remained in the field as long as prudence and duty required." See Clark, *State Records*, 14:375–284.

26. James Ward, declaration dated November 15, 1832, Revolutionary War pension file for James Ward (S7819); William Brooks, declaration dated August 23, 1832, Revolutionary War pension file for William Brooks (S6705).

27. Clark, *State Records*, 13:625, 24:198–199.

28. Clark, *State Records*, 14:29–31.

29. Charles Rhodes, declaration dated January 26, 1829, Revolutionary War pension file for Charles Rhodes (S7386); Amos Rayner, declaration dated August 27, [1832], Revolutionary War pension file for Amos Rayner (S7355); John Rhodes, declaration dated November 23, 1832, Revolutionary War pension file for John Rhodes (S4084); Militia Troop Returns, Box 4, Folder 21, State Archives; Rankin, *North Carolina Continentals*, 203; Clark, *State Records*, 14:273.

30. Charles Rhodes, declarations dated January 26, 1829, and February 18, 1833, Revolutionary War pension file for Charles Rhodes (S7386); Amos Rayner, declaration dated August 27, [1832], Revolutionary War pension file for Amos Rayner (S7355). Captain Rhodes stated in his declaration that he made the trek on "horseback" (the common mode of travel for militia officers). Rankin, *North Carolina Continentals*, 201–203.

31. Rankin, *North Carolina Continentals*, 203–204.

32. Ibid.

33. Amos Rayner, declaration dated August 27, [1832], Revolutionary War pension file for Amos Rayner (S7355); Rankin, *North Carolina Continentals,* 204–205.

34. Clark, *State Records*, 15:751; Rankin, *North Carolina Continentals,* 205; John Rhodes, declaration dated August 23, 1832, Revolutionary War pension file for John Rhodes (S4084).

35. Amos Rayner, declaration dated August 27, [1832], Revolutionary War pension file for Amos Rayner (S7355); John Rhodes, declaration dated August 23, 1832, Revolutionary War pension file for John Rhodes (S4084); Esther Johnston (widow of Jonas Johnston), declaration dated November 23, 1839, Revolutionary War pension file for Jonas Johnston (W21470).

36. Scheme of a Draft for 2000 Men, New Bern, February 16, 1780, Military Collection, Troop Returns, Box 5, State Archives; Clark, *State Records*, 24:255–257; Rankin, *North Carolina Continentals*, 216.
   On July 7, 1779, Governor Caswell had notified the state's brigadier generals of militia that two thousand men were to be drafted, including an undisclosed number from the Edenton District. Caswell instructed Brig. Gen. Isaac Gregory that the Edenton District draftees were to rendezvous at Edenton on Sunday, August 1. The troops were to be immediately marched "Southward" [to South Carolina] and serve a three-month term, effective when they left the bounds of North Carolina. Caswell advised Gregory that Brig. Gen. Alexander Lillington would command the state's militia force sent to the aid of its southern neighbor. Despite the governor's explicit orders, General Gregory apparently was unable to assemble the district's quota of militiamen, presumably including the number from Bertie County. In December, Caswell called for another draft of militia from the Edenton District, but constituent militiamen apparently were not drafted, assembled, and marched from there. On March 8, 1780, General Gregory wrote to Governor Caswell, directly referring to "the militia that was drafted in July and December last [1779]." "I am sorry the Militia that was drafted in this Brigade hath delayed marching in the manner they have done," Gregory wrote. "I have done every thing in my power to hasten them on, there is more trouble with the Officers that is drafted to march them." A thousand-man militia contingent was marched from North Carolina to South Carolina in October 1779 under the command of General Lillington. Because of the lack of detailed military records, the author was unable to ascertain if any Bertie County militiamen were included in the contingent. Richard Caswell to Isaac Gregory, July 7, 1779, Gregory to Caswell, March 8, 1780, Richard Caswell, Governors Letter Books, State Archives; Clark, *State Records*, 19:995.

37. John Lednum, declaration dated November 15, 1832, Revolutionary War pension file for John Lednum (S7142); Cader Measles, declaration dated October 3, 1842, Revolutionary War pension file for Cader Measles (R7088); William Smith, declaration dated August 29, 1832, Revolutionary War pension file for William Smith (W17828).

38. Rankin, *North Carolina Continentals*, 216–217.

39. Clark, *State Records*, 14:x–xii.

40. Clark, *State Records*, 14:xii.

41. Josiah Harrell, declaration dated August 13, 1833, Revolutionary War pension file for Josiah Harrell (S8690); Isaac Hendrixen, declaration dated August 13, 1833, Revolutionary War pension file for Isaac Hendrixen (S8703); Arthur Wiggins, declaration dated February 13,1833, Revolutionary War pension file for Arthur Wiggins (S7952).

42. Clark, *State Records*, 14:xii, 809, 816; Rankin, *North Carolina Continentals*, 231–232; Josiah Harrell, declaration dated August 13, 1833, Revolutionary War pension file for Josiah Harrell (S8690); Isaac Hendrixen, declaration dated August 13, 1833, Revolutionary War pension file for Isaac Hendrixen (S8703); Kathleen B. Wyche, "North Carolina Militia Paroled by Lord Cornwallis in 1781," *North Carolina Genealogical Society Journal* 4 (August 1978): 150.

43. Clark, *State Records*, 15:399.

44. Clark, *State Records*, 15:399, 17:1054–1055, 1059–1061.

45. Clark, *State Records*, 15:v–vi; John Bentley, declaration dated November 14, 1850, Revolutionary War pension file for John Bentley (R784); Hosea Ball, declaration dated August 29, 1832, Revolutionary War pension file for Hosea Ball (S2365).
    On June 14, 1780, the Continental Congress selected Maj. Gen. Horatio Gates to succeed Maj. Gen. Benjamin Lincoln as commander of the Southern Department. Gates arrived at Coxe's Mill, North Carolina, on July 25, 1780, and took command of the forces that marched to Camden. Ford, *Journals of the Continental Congress*, 17:510–511; Rankin, *North Carolina Continentals*, 241.

46. Clark, *State Records*, 14:423, 661–662, 780, 15:74, 89–90.
    In early September the North Carolina General Assembly passed an act that established the state's Board of War. The assembly intended that the board handle military affairs and resources more effectually and expeditiously than it felt had been the case under the authority granted the governor, thus enabling the state's "generals and commanders to act with vigour and precision." The board convened its first meeting in Hillsborough on September 14, 1780. Minutes of the meeting for Tuesday, October 13, 1780, indicate that "Jarvis's and Exum's Regiments [are] almost all discharged." There is no indication that the board formally responded to General Sumner's letter of late September/early October. Clark, *State Records*, 14:376, 424, 24:355–357.

47. Clark, *State Records*, 13:757, 765; Solomon Barnes, declaration dated January 28, 1833, Revolutionary War pension file for Solomon Barnes (S6569).

48. Clark, *State Records*, 14:842.

49. Clark, *State Records*, 12:777, 14:847, 18:823, 825. James Moore was elected colonel of the Bertie County militia regiment in May 1779, succeeding Col. Thomas Whitmell.

50. Thomas Benbury to Abner Nash, June 12, 1780, Abner Nash, Governors Papers, State Archives.

51. Clark, *State Records*, 14:522–523.

52. Rankin, *North Carolina Continentals*, 242–243.

53. Rankin, *North Carolina Continentals*, 244–245; Clark, *State Records*, 14:xv.

54. Jesse Brown, declaration dated February 27, 1833, Revolutionary War pension file for Jesse Brown (S6719); Solomon Barnes, declaration dated January 28, 1833, Revolutionary War pension file for Solomon Barnes (S6569).

55. Solomon Barnes, declaration dated January 28, 1833, Revolutionary War pension file for Solomon Barnes (S6569). Without muster rolls or other primary documents, the author was unable to substantiate the specifics regarding the service of Private Barnes and/or other members (unidentified) of Capt. Francis Pugh's company.

56. John Rhodes, declaration dated November 23, 1832, Revolutionary War pension file for John Rhodes (S4084); William Brooks, declaration dated August 23, 1832, Revolutionary War pension file for William Brooks (S6705). Because of the very general nature of the information divulged by Rhodes in his declaration, the author was unable to identify the colonel of the regiment to which Capt. Thomas Rhodes's company was assigned.

57. William S. Powell, *North Carolina: A History* (Chapel Hill: University of North Carolina Press, 1977), 76–77.

58. Don Higginbotham, ed., *The Papers of James Iredell*, 2 vols. (Raleigh: Division of Archives and History, Department of Cultural Resources, 1976), 1:lxxx, 2:80–81, 248–251 (hereafter cited as *Iredell Papers*).

59. Francis B. Heitman, *Historical Register of Officers of the Continental Army during the War of the Revolution, April, 1775 to December, 1783* (Washington, D.C.: The Rare Book Shop Publishing Co., 1914), 456; Clark, *State Records*, 13:343–344, 15:475, 483, 518, 16:1141, 17:326, 19:524, 22:1030–1032.

60. *Iredell Papers*, 2:234–235, 239, 240.

61. John Lednum, declaration dated November 15, 1832, Revolutionary War pension file for John Lednum (S7142); Richard Dillon, declaration dated April 22, 1833, Revolutionary War pension file for Richard Dillon (R2959); James Ward, declaration dated November 15, 1832, Revolutionary War pension file for James Ward (S7819); Amos Rayner, declaration dated August 27, [1832], Revolutionary War pension file for Amos Rayner (S7355); Isaac Hendrixen, declaration dated August 13, 1833, Revolutionary War pension file for Isaac Hendrixen (S8703); Clark, *State Records*, 15:618–619.

62. Thomas Burke to Isaac Gregory, August 31, 1781, Thomas Burke, Governors Letter Books, State Archives (hereafter cited as Burke Letter Books).

63. Clark, *State Records*, 15:629–630, 635.

64. Burke to James Campbell, September 1, 1781, Burke to Campbell, September 3, 1781, Burke Letter Books.

65. Clark, *State Records*, 22:593–594.

66. Marybelle Delamar, "Transcriptions of Petitions to the General Assembly of North Carolina Relating to Revolutionary War Military Service, 1788–1833," 21–23, State Archives.

67. Clark, *State Records*, 22:593–594.

68. Burke to Gregory, September 5, 1781, Burke Letter Books.

69. Clark, *State Records*, 16:ix–xi, 43, 538–539, 544, 561–562; "Estimate of Militia, April 1782," *The North Carolinian: A Quarterly Journal of Genealogy and History* 6 (September 1960): 725. The author concluded that "drafted" militia from the Edenton District marched to the Piedmont region pursuant to Burke's orders, inasmuch as Thomas Walston, a Camden County militiaman, enlisted in the spring of 1782 for one year's service and "marched to Hillsboro," where he "remained . . . nearly the whole of the year." Thomas Walston, declaration dated November 13, 1833, Revolutionary War pension file for Thomas Walston (S11661).

70. Peace negotiations began in Paris in April 1782. The parties concluded a preliminary peace treaty on November 30, 1782; the accord was to become effective once Great Britain reached agreements with its other enemies. The United States Congress ratified the preliminary peace treaty on April 15, 1783. American peace commissioners Benjamin Franklin, John Jay, and John Adams signed the final treaty on September 3, ending the American Revolution. Alan Axelrod, *The Real History of the American Revolution: A New Look at the Past* (New York: Sterling Publishing Co., 2007), 344–347; Powell, *North Carolina*, 77.

EPILOGUE

America's successful prosecution of the Revolutionary War resulted in its people freeing themselves from established military and royal control and laying the foundation for self-governance. Throughout much of the conflict, a successful outcome likely seemed doubtful to many Americans as their military forces suffered a continuum of battle losses and setbacks. Indeed, had the outcome been favorable for Great Britain, the American Revolutionary leaders would have been viewed and treated as traitors rather than as founders and Patriots. Formal conclusion of the Revolutionary War in September 1783 with the signing of the Treaty of Paris affirmed the independence of the thirteen states, which had been declared more than seven years previously. As with most major conflicts, the cessation of hostilities led to the sorting-out of various business and affairs directly related to, or resulting from, the war.

In North Carolina one item of importance to certain of the victorious Whig leaders was the confiscation of lands owned by a number of influential and prestigious persons who maintained their loyalty to the Crown. During the state's November–December 1777 session of the General Assembly, the legislators passed an act that mandated confiscating the property of all persons residing in North Carolina who were "inimical" to the United States and who did not declare their allegiance to the state, thus becoming state citizens. The act stipulated that persons who "owned and possessed" lands, tenements, hereditaments, and moveable property as of July 4, 1776, and who had departed the state; "attached themselves to the Enemies of the United States of America"; relocated to places beyond the bounds of any of the thirteen states in order to avoid "bearing their proper and equal" part in the states' defense of freedom and independence; or been outside the United States at the commencement of the war and had "failed to return" and support the states' defense, were to have their properties confiscated by North Carolina. To avoid permanently losing their properties, any person subject to the law was authorized to appear before the next General Assembly (scheduled for October 1778) and declare his allegiance to the state, upon which the assembly would grant him "the Privilege of a Citizen of this State" and restore the "Possessions and Property to him." Persons charged with treason or misprision of treason were excluded from being allowed to recover their confiscated property.[1]

During the October–November 1779 session, the General Assembly passed another act to effectuate the 1777 law. The latter measure specifically identified 68 people and business partnerships whose properties were subject to confiscation. Included were Sir Nathaniel Duckenfield, Henry Eustace McCulloch, and Buchanan, Hastie and Company, which owned properties in Bertie County. The law further provided that each county court was to appoint commissioners authorized "to take possession of all lands, tenements, hereditaments, monies, debts, whether due by judgment, bond, bill, note, account, or otherwise, and all other personal property of the persons" named by the law. Additionally, the commissioners were permitted to order constables of their county to summon any of the county inhabitants to appear before them to give on oath an account of forfeited property. Commissioners were required to maintain a record of all lands, tenements, hereditaments, and personal property forfeited by persons, including their identities. In May 1780 Bertie County justices appointed Jonathan Jacocks, John Johnston, and John McGlaughon to act as "Commissioners of Confiscated Estates."[2]

By the spring of 1782 "many large and valuable tracts of land, as well as negroes and other personal property" had been confiscated throughout North Carolina and were being held under the authority and control of the county commissioners of confiscated estates. During the General Assembly session of April–May 1782, lawmakers concluded that selling the confiscated properties would raise "a considerable revenue" for the state. Accordingly, the legislators passed an act decreeing that properties held by the county commissioners were to be "considered as absolutely forfeited" and were to "be sold by the commissioners." Individuals whose properties had been confiscated could challenge the seizures by seeking trials in county courts; resulting verdicts were to be considered final determinations.[3]

The confiscation of Loyalists' lands and other properties was a contentious and divisive issue for North Carolina's legislators. Support for the confiscation measures was not unanimous. Certain lawmakers opposed the indiscriminate seizure of all Loyalists' land, and assemblymen from both the eastern and western regions of the state occasionally sought legislation to exempt their friends and families from the provisions of the confiscation statutes. North Carolina, very likely, was home to a greater number of Loyalists in proportion to its population than any other colony/state. Virtually every person in North Carolina was affected in some way by the Revolution, regardless of the person's status and affiliations during the war.[4] Nevertheless, despite the divisiveness and impact on numerous persons and families, confiscation was purposely carried out across the state.

Throughout North Carolina, confiscated properties were to be disposed (sold at public auctions) at central locations within seven specified districts. A commissioner was appointed for each district to superintend the sales of forfeited estates. Former North Carolina Continental Line officer Hardy Murfree of Hertford County was appointed commissioner for the Edenton District. The district commissioner's duty was to receive returns of all confiscated property from the county commissioners within the district, have surveys and plans made of land properties (each tract to be sold was to be limited in size to 640 acres), attend and oversee the public sales, and report the results of sales to the governor. Confiscated properties within the Edenton District were to be publicly sold at the courthouse in Edenton. County commissioners were required to give public notices at county courthouses one month before public sales (auctions) of forfeited properties were to be held.[5]

By the fall of 1783, substantial amounts of confiscated Loyalist properties had been sold in North Carolina. A November 1783 report indicates that property in the amount of nearly £584 had been publicly sold. Even so, significant holdings remained in the possession of the state. Between 1784 and 1790, additional properties in twenty-nine counties, including substantial tracts situated in Bertie County, were publicly auctioned, bringing more than £284 in revenue.[6]

Twenty-six land grants from Gov. Richard Caswell dated November 1787 conveyed ownership of more than 8,100 acres of confiscated lands in Bertie County. The tracts sold for more than £51,700. Eighteen of the properties, totaling 6,692 acres, had formerly belonged to Sir Nathaniel Duckenfield; they sold for £36,466. Duckenfield, forty-one years old in 1787, owned extensive land properties that he had inherited from his father, who died when Nathaniel was only about three years old. The Duckenfield estate was situated on the highly fertile lands along Salmon Creek in eastern Bertie County. In May 1768 Nathaniel, residing in England, had become the fifth Duckenfield baronet upon the death of his uncle Samuel. In 1769 he traveled to Bertie County to visit his mother and view his landholdings. While in North Carolina in November 1771, he was a member of the province's royal council, having been nominated by Gov. William Tryon. By the spring of 1772, Duckenfield had concluded that he was not a "good match" for residing in North Carolina and not suited for managing a large plantation.

After returning to England, Duckenfield acquired a coronet's commission in the royal army and resigned his seat on the North Carolina council. On May 27, 1773, the *Virginia Gazette* printed an ad by John Pearson, Duckenfield's stepfather, that announced that Pearson, by "Power [of attorney]" from his stepson, would sell, by bids, all of Duckenfield's lands that were "finely situated upon the Bay, opposite to Edenton, in Bertie County." (Obviously, the lands were not sold.) By 1775 and the outbreak of the Revolutionary War, Duckenfield, who had advanced to the rank of adjutant in a British army regiment, announced that he would not "serve happily" in America. He never did so serve. Nevertheless, in accordance with the North Carolina property confiscation statutes, his lands in Bertie County were seized and sold, despite January 1779 and January 1781 petitions from his mother to the North Carolina General Assembly seeking for Nathaniel an exemption from the confiscation statutes.[7]

Table 7 (pp. 182–183) presents summary information relating to the conveyances of confiscated lands in Bertie County. While the conveyances were recorded as grants, the persons receiving the grants had previously purchased the tracts at public sales.

TABLE 7
Grants of Confiscated Property in Bertie County Recorded
in the Office of the North Carolina Secretary of State[8]

Bertie County Deed*	Former Owner	Acres
P-325	Duckenfield, Nathaniel	462
N-82	Duckenfield, Nathaniel	333
S-680	Wallace & Company	166
O-139	Duckenfield, Nathaniel	475
P-433	McKitrick, [William]	.5
O-138	Duckenfield, Nathaniel	400
★★	Lother, William	100
O-141	Duckenfield, Nathaniel	213
R-185	McKitrick, [William]	.5
P-142	Duckenfield, Nathaniel	425
O-130	Duckenfield, Nathaniel	225
P-140	Duckenfield, Nathaniel	640
O-237	Duckenfield, Nathaniel	579
O-131	Duckenfield, Nathaniel	325
O-132	Duckenfield, Nathaniel	193
O-133	Buchannan, William & Co.	203
V-81	McCulloch, Henry E.	506
O-134	Duckenfield, Nathaniel	225
O-135	Duckenfield, Nathaniel	290
O-137	Duckenfield, Nathaniel	280
V-80	McCulloch, Henry E.	506
R-148	McKitrick, [William]	2
P-141	Duckenfield, Nathaniel	324
P-139	Duckenfield, Nathaniel	550
P-324	Duckenfield, Nathaniel	235
O-142	Duckenfield, Nathaniel	518

*All of the deeds bear the date November 15, 1787.

★★The author was unable to locate a deed in the records of the Bertie County Register of Deeds Office for this conveyance. He reviewed all grants from the state of North Carolina to George Ryan that were indexed in the register's records.

Table 7 (*continued*)
Grants of Confiscated Property in Bertie County Recorded
in the Office of the North Carolina Secretary of State

Purchaser (Deed)	Amount in pounds (£)
Jacocks, Jonathan (P-325)	332
Totevine, Simon (N-82)	3,335
Pouns, John (S-680)	260
Ashburn, William (O-139)	1,805
Pouns, John (P-433)	225
Hardy, Humphrey (O-138)	329
Ryan, George★★	451
Ashburn, William (O-141)	516
Bryer, Benjamin (R-185)	531
Ryan, George (P-142)	5,802
Pugh, Thomas W. (O-130)	75
Ryan, George (P-140)	766
Flectwood, Jeremiah (O-237)	427
Capehart, John (O-131)	310
Clark, Christopher (O-132)	1,120
West, George (O-133)	430
Johnston, John (V-81)	7,000
Ashburn, William (O-134)	104
Hagan, John (O-135)	123
Hardy, Humphrey (O-137)	102
Johnston, John (V-80)	6,021
Bryer, Benjamin (R-148)	363
Ryan, George (P-141)	4,955
Ryan, George (P-139)	9,191
Jacocks, Jonathan (P-324)	1,620
Ashburn, Elisha (O-142)	5,554

Arising from the war was a matter of business specific to Bertie County—the collection of taxes in arrears from county citizens. Arthur Brown was serving as sheriff of the county when the war started, and one of his duties was overseeing the collection of county taxes. The onset of war precluded him from collecting all amounts due. Brown, who also served as colonel of the Bertie County militia during part of the conflict, was impeded by the "well known situation of affairs" in Bertie County during "those days of difficulty and danger" that rendered "the almost impossibility of Collecting public taxes at that time." During 1779 and 1780 Brown collected a portion of the taxes due, but in greatly depreciated currencies (from the values of currencies in 1774 and 1775). As militia colonel, he applied the collections to paying bounties to county men who were drafted or volunteered for active military service and "other Public military uses."[9]

During the General Assembly session of April–June 1784, the lawmakers passed an act that authorized Arthur Brown, "late sheriff of Bertie County," to collect the arrears of taxes due for the years 1774 and 1775. The amount of unpaid taxes for the two years is not documented, but Brown surely began seeking payments from Bertie citizens upon passage of the act. Unfortunately, Brown died prior to February 1785 without having settled his accounts related to public taxes. In November 1788 Jesse Brown, Arthur's son and an executor of his will, petitioned the North Carolina General Assembly for payment of amounts due his father's estate related to the depreciated tax collections. The lawmakers ascertained that more than £4,512 was owed to Brown's estate. In early December both the state senate and the house of commons approved the payment.[10]

An additional issue to be addressed at the end of the war concerned claims by British merchants against American debtors. The peace treaty signed by the United States and Great Britain in September 1783 stipulated that creditors would not encounter legal obstacles to the collection of debts. Of course, special considerations to be confronted by British merchants lay in determining debtors' whereabouts years after the debts were incurred, as well as their ability to repay their debts. The merchants employed special agents and informants to locate such debtors. While no comprehensive accounting of all likely amounts owed by Bertie County citizens (including former county citizens who may have relocated during or after the war) is available, limited information has been published. The following table presents summary information from special agents' reports related to British merchants' claims against two Bertie County residents (deceased).

TABLE 8

British Merchants' Claims against Bertie County Residents (Deceased)[11]

British Merchant	Debtor	Amount(s) of Claim(s)	Description, comments, etc.
John Hay & Co.	Clarke, James	£9.9.4, £5.18.5	James Clark died in the year 1787. "James W. Clarke of Bertie County [is] his representative and only son. Estate is solvent."
John Hay & Co.	Johnson, John	£5.6.8	"John Johnson removed from Cumberland County in 1781 to the County of Bertie, where in the Spring follow-ing; he died leaving no estate whatsoever."

In the years following the war, the elder Bertie County Whig leaders of the Revolutionary period gradually passed away, and a younger generation of leaders, some who had been officers in the North Carolina Continental Line and the county's militia, ascended to positions of local prominence. Almost three decades later, sons and grandsons of Bertie County's Revolutionary War citizens would again be called forth to Windsor to enlist or possibly be drafted to march off in the regular army or detached militia companies—once again against the military forces of Great Britain. The United States would fight its "Second War of Independence" against Great Britain to sustain its existence, independence, and freedoms earned during the Revolutionary War.

Notes

1. Walter Clark, ed., *The State Records of North Carolina*, 16 vols. (11–26) (Raleigh: State of North Carolina, 1895–1906), 24:123–124.

2. Clark, *State Records*, 24:263–265; Weynette Parks Haun, comp., *Bertie County, North Carolina, Court Minutes, 1772–1780, Book IV* (Durham: the compiler, 1979), 116. Buchanan, Hastie

and Company owned stores in Halifax, Windsor, and Virginia. The business had purchased lot number 4 in the town of Windsor in 1769. See Deed M-34, Bertie County Register of Deeds Office, Windsor.

3. Clark, *State Records*, 24:424–425.

4. Don Higginbotham, ed., *The Papers of James Iredell* (Raleigh: Division of Archives and History, Department of Archives and History, 1976), lxxxv (hereafter cited as *Iredell Papers*); Jeffrey P. Lucas, "Cooling by Degrees: Reintegration of Loyalists in North Carolina, 1776–1790" (master's thesis, North Carolina State University, 2007), 4–5. The Treaty of Peace stipulated that "Congress shall earnestly recommend it to the legislatures of the respective states, to provide for the restitution of all estates, rights and properties, which have been confiscated, belonging to real British subjects, and also of the estates, rights and properties of persons residents in districts in the possession of his Majesty's arms, and who have not borne arms against the said United States." The treaty further provided that persons should be at "free liberty" to travel to any of the thirteen states and to remain for twelve months to "obtain the restitution of such of their estates, rights and properties, as may have been confiscated." Despite the treaty provisions, the British subjects failed to regain ownership of their confiscated properties, though numerous efforts were made. See Hugh T. Lefler, *History of North Carolina*, 4 vols. (New York: Lewis Historical Publishing Company, [1956]), 1:235.

5. Clark, *State Records*, 24:425–427; Deed R-2, Bertie County Register of Deeds Office.

6. Lefler, *History of North Carolina*, 1:235; Robert O. DeMond, *The Loyalists in North Carolina during the Revolution* (Baltimore: Genealogical Publishing Co., 1979), 58, 174.

7. *Dictionary of North Carolina Biography*, s.v. "Duckenfield, Nathaniel; *Virginia Gazette* (Williamsburg), May 27, 1793; DeMond, *Loyalists in North Carolina*, 240–241; *Iredell Papers*, 2:60–61, 203–204; Michael Hill, "The Historical Significance of the Batts-Duckenfield-Capehart Site, Bertie County: A Preliminary Report" (unpublished research report, Research Branch, Division of Archives and History, 1986), 7–8.

8. DeMond, *Loyalists in North Carolina*, 240–241; cited deeds, Bertie County Register of Deeds Office.

9. Marybelle Delamar, "Transcriptions of Petitions to the General Assembly of North Carolina Relating to Revolutionary War Military Service, 1788–1833," 21, State Archives.

10. Clark, *State Records*, 20:528, 597, 21:46, 181, 186, 24:628; Arthur Brown's will (C-13), Bertie County Office of the Clerk of Court; Delamar Transcripts, 21–22. Brown's will was probated during the February 1785 session of Bertie County Court.

11. Ransom McBride, "Claims of British Merchants after the Revolutionary War," *North Carolina Genealogical Society Journal* 17 (May 1991): 97, 101, (August 1991): 149.

Note on Appendixes

The author painstakingly prepared what he terms as "putative" rosters from a variety of sources, including available compiled service records, war rolls, pension files, army accounts, vouchers, North Carolina colonial and state records, secretary of state Revolutionary War military papers, treasurer's and comptroller's military papers, troop returns, county records, and secondary sources (books, periodicals, and genealogical and historical information sites from the Internet). Rank information given in brackets cannot be confirmed, but the author feels confident that the men were privates, for the most part, unless otherwise indicated.

In addition to the list of names and ranks, the author also prepared service histories for each soldier and officer. Due to the varied sources used in compiling this data, as cited above, the author prepared an endnote documenting the source(s) utilized for each person. Because of space limitations, those service histories and associated endnotes are not printed in this edition. Instead they are available in the Kindle e-book edition as a link to the data that is located at www.ncpublications.com/bertie.html.

In compiling these rosters, the author found that various records did not identify the places of birth, residence, and/or enlistment of individuals who served in North Carolina's Continental Line regiments. Therefore, the author was not able to identify all Bertie County residents who served in the state's Continental Line. The author further notes that due to the commonality of names in Bertie County with other communities in North Carolina, in certain cases there was no method of positively confirming that a soldier with the name of an individual who resided in Bertie County was indeed a county resident.

Finally, a significant challenge encountered in attempting to correctly identify and document the regiments and companies in which Bertie County's Continental Line troops served is embodied in the form of acknowledged, longstanding errors in the published roster of the state's army troops. The roster of North Carolina Continental Line troops is presented in volume 16 (pages 1002–1197) of Walter Clark's *State Records of North Carolina*, but the regimental information for hundreds of men (including tens of Bertie County soldiers) who, according to the published roster, were members of the Tenth North Carolina Regiment, is incorrect. The erroneous regimental information dates back almost 225 years. In 1790, when North Carolina was settling its share of the Revolutionary War debt with the federal government, it sent to the federal government all of the muster and pay rolls that could be found for the North Carolina regiments in the Continental Line. Then, in order to have a record against which to check claims for bounty land grants, the state had War Department clerks in Philadelphia copy all information from the muster and pay rolls. The result was a volume that is called "The Register of the North Carolina Line" (i.e., roster). The original records used by the clerks in Philadelphia when preparing the register were later destroyed when the British burned Washington in 1814. This is especially unfortunate because the clerks in Philadelphia mistakenly assigned to the Tenth North Carolina Regiment nearly thirty companies of soldiers belonging to the state's other nine regiments. The destruction of the original muster and pay rolls means that this error can never be corrected officially. Furthermore, in the early to mid-nineteenth century, North Carolina's Office of the Secretary of State was forced to cite the erroneous information in proving Revolutionary War veterans' service for pension and bounty land applications. Thus, the erroneous unit information was perpetuated into related records (pension documents, bounty land warrant records, Revolutionary War papers, etc.).

The regimental information for over 520 men who enlisted in Col. James Hogun's regiment at Halifax in July 1778 is erroneous in the "official" roster. Per the above explanation, the published roster lists the men as members of the Tenth North Carolina Regiment. The Tenth Regiment had been disbanded at Valley Forge in early June 1778. Colonel Hogun had previously commanded the Seventh North Carolina, which also had been disbanded at Valley Forge. Various records indicate that the regiment that Hogun organized at Halifax in July 1778, and subsequently commanded, was known as the Third North Carolina. While the Third Regiment was reduced to a cadre at Valley Forge, and its commander (Col. Jethro Sumner) was not "officially" transferred to another unit, within this study the author termed Hogun's unit as the Third North Carolina Regiment (Second Organization—Hogun's). A significant number of Bertie County men served in the regiment.

Among the men who fought in the war from Bertie County, the author identified 13 African Americans—12 were listed as mulatto—and 3 Native Americans. The African Americans are indicated by a single asterisk (*), and the Native Americans are indicated by a double asterisk (**). More detailed information is found in the service histories and endnotes mentioned above and found at www.ncpublications.com/bertie.html.

Despite all of the gaps and errors found in existing resources, the author has endeavored to present these rosters as accurately as possible, given the quantity, content, and veracity of available records.

APPENDIX 1

ROSTER OF BERTIE COUNTY CONTINENTAL LINE SOLDIERS

FIRST NORTH CAROLINA REGIMENT

Baker, Benjamin, private
Barksdale, Henry, sergeant
Barrow, John, private
Bates, James, private
Billups, Thomas, musician
Bonner, William, corporal
Bryant, John, private
Butler, Jethro, private
Butler, John, private
Byrd, William, [private]
Cale, John, private
Corbet, James, corporal
Dundelow, Henry, corporal
Dundelow, Hugh, private
Edwards, John, Jr., private
Farmer, James, private
Farmer, Jesse, private
Fort, Elias, sergeant
Fryar, Willis, private
Hedspeth, Marmaduke, private
Keel, Hardy, private
Kennedy, John, private

Lassiter, James, private
Ledenham, Isaac, private
Liscombe, Wilson, private
Lowe, William, musician
Mitchell, Oliver, private
Modlin, Ezekiel, private
Monk, Nottingham, private
Newbern, Thomas, private
Powell, Lewis, private
Pugh, Arthur, private★
Todd, William, corporal
Walton, William, captain
Ward, Thomas, private
Wharton, James, private
White, Ezekiel, private
White, George, private
White, William, sergeant
Williford, Archibald, private
Williford, James, private
Wilson, William, private
Woodward, John, private
Wren, William, corporal

Second North Carolina Regiment

Alexander, Benjamin, private
Billups, Thomas, musician
Chavis, Ceasar, private★
Cobb, Henry, private
Davidson, James, private
Evans, Charles, private
Freeman, Aaron, private
Fryar, Josiah, private
Fryar, William, private
Hoard, Micajah, musician
Hoggard, William, private
Howard, Solomon, private
James, Jeremiah, private
Ledenham, Isaac, private
Lewis, Hardy, private

Mitchell, William, private
Murter, John, private
Nichols, Henry, private
Nowell, Josiah, private
Oliver, John, ensign
Outlaw, James, private
Pierce, Hardy, private
Pugh, Whitmill, ensign
Richardson, Richard, private
Thomas, Amos, private
Thomas, Thomas, musician
Wiley, Absalom, private
Williford, Lewis, private
Wilson, Josiah, private

Third North Carolina Regiment

Baker, Dempsey, private
Billups, Richard, private
Case, Joseph, private
Champion, Thomas, private
Clemmons, John, private
Dunning, James, private
Fields, John, private
Fryar, William, private
Hall, James, private
Hedspeth, Marmaduke, private
James, William, private★
Johnson, William, private

Keel, Hardy, sergeant
Knight, Reuben, private
Morgan, Charles, sergeant
Page, Solomon, private
Smith, William, private
Sowell, William, private
Tennison, Matthew, private
Thurston, William, private
Tranton, John, private
Weston, John, private
Wiggins, Arthur, private
Wiggins, Matthew, private★

THIRD NORTH CAROLINA REGIMENT
(SECOND ORGANIZATION—HOGUN'S)

Anderson, William, corporal
Asbett [Asbell], James, private
Baker, William, musician
Barber, John, private
Blanchets, James, private
Boon, Lewis, private
Britt, Arthur, private
Butler, James, private
Butler, William, private
Cale, Job, private
Chamberlain, Malachi, private
Clanghorn, Timothy, private
Clark, Henry, private
Cobb, Nathaniel, private
Collins, John, private
Cook, Robert, private
Cooper, Nathaniel, private
Coward, Ephraim, private
Coward, Zadock, private
Doddriel, James, corporal
Dunning, Uriah, sergeant
Evans, Charles, private
Farmer, John, corporal
Fields, John, private
Freeman, William, private
Glisson, Arthur, private
Gregory, Robert, private
Heal, Elisha, private
Hoggard, John, private
Hoggard, Patrick, private
Hopkins, Daniel, corporal
Hubbard, James, private
James, David, private★
James, Jeremiah, private★

James, Thomas, private★
Kelly, William, private
King, Thomas, private
Lawrence, Joseph, private
Lee, Abraham, private
Leggett, Lewis, private
Newton, Jesse, private
Raby, Blake, private
Redditt, Constantine, sergeant
Robinson, Hardy, private
Robinson, John, private
Ryan, Thomas, corporal
Skinner, Thomas, private
Skinner, William, private
Smith, William, private
Sorrell, Thomas, private
Spencer, Solomon, private
Stone, Benjamin, private
Tart, Thomas, private
Thomas, Amos, private
Vann, Nathan, private
Watford, William, private
Weston, Amos, private
Wharton, Jacob, private★
White, Burrell, private
White, James, private
White, Peter, private
White, William, private
Wiggins, Edward, private★
Wiley, Absalom, corporal
Williams, John, private
Wilson, Edward, private
Woodward, Caleb, private

Fourth North Carolina Regiment

Adkinson, Richard, private
Barksdale, Henry, private
Barrow, John, private
Bird, Moses, musician
Boon, Joseph, private
Boyce, Jesse, private
Bryant, John, private
Butler, John, private★
Cooper, William, private
Donally, John, private
Gregory, James, private
Hale, Samuel, [private]
Hopkins, Daniel, private
Jenkins, Elijah, private
Knott, William, lieutenant

Liscombe, Willis, private
Lowe, William, musician
Manley, Moses, private
Morris, Abraham, musician
Newbern, Thomas, private
Pearce, Jacob, private
Pollock, Jacob, captain
Raby, Adam, private
Raby, Cader, private
White, Ezekiel, private
Whitmell, Thomas Blount,
    second lieutenant
Whitmell, Thomas West, sergeant
Wren, William, private

Fifth North Carolina Regiment

Bird, Moses, musician
Boon, Willis, private
Braveboy, Jacob, private★★
Broadwell, David, private
Carter, Zachariah, private
Cooper, Jeremiah, private
Dempsey, Squire, private★
Farmer, William, private
Green, John, private
Hedgpeth, Moses, [private]
Hicks, James, private★★
Hicks, John, private★★
Hill, Thomas, corporal
Hoggard, William, private
Holmes, Shadrack, private
Howard, Solomon, private
Hubbard, Warburton, sergeant
James, Edwin, private
Jenkins, Abraham, corporal

Jenkins, Robert, private
Johnson, William, private
Knott, William, lieutenant
McGlaughon, Jeremiah sergeant
McGuire, Michael, private
Mitchell, William, private
Morris, John, private
Pearce, William, private
Pugh, Thomas Whitmell,
    first lieutenant
Rhodes, Charles, sergeant
Rhodes, Elisha, ensign
Rhodes, Isaac, private
Ryan, Thomas, musician
Sholar, Isaac, private
Thomas, Thomas, private
West, Joseph, private
Williams, John Pugh, captain
Williams, Thomas, private

SIXTH NORTH CAROLINA REGIMENT

Coffield, Benjamin, adjutant
Hudson, Thomas, sergeant
Liscombe, John, ensign

SEVENTH NORTH CAROLINA REGIMENT

Alexander, Benjamin, private
Bennett, James, private
Billups, Thomas, musician
Bryer, Benjamin, lieutenant
Cale, Amos, private
Conner, Jacob, private
Conner, William, private
Cooper, John, private
Cooper, Josiah, private
Cowan, Robert, sergeant
Fort, Elias, corporal
Green, Abraham, private
Keel, Hardy, sergeant
Luton, Lemuel, corporal
McGlaughon, John, captain
Monk, Nottingham, private
Nichols, John, private
Oden, Robert, private
Ray, Stephen, private
Seals, John, private
Todd, Ephraim, private
Todd, James, private
Todd, Thomas, musician
Todd, William, private
Walton, William, second
    lieutenant
Watson, Thomas, first lieutenant
Wharton, James, private
White, James, private
White, John, private
White, William, sergeant

TENTH NORTH CAROLINA REGIMENT

Conner, John, private
Wiggins, Malachi, private

MISCELLANEOUS

Anderson, James, private
Bunoyer, William, [private]
Cale, Rice, [private]
Fryar, Bazemore, [private]
Harrison, James, private
Leigh, Lewis, sergeant
Lewis, William, [private]
Outhouse, Israel, [private]
Owens, John, [private]
Sowell, James, [private]
West, Robert, [private]
White, Paul, [private]

APPENDIX 2

ROSTER OF BERTIE COUNTY MINUTEMEN AND MILITIA

CAPT. CHARLES WORTH JACOCKS'S COMPANY (MINUTEMEN)

Anderson, James, private
Bardle, Henry, private
Bates, James, private
Billups, Richard, private
Brown, Arthur [Jr.], private
Bryant, John, private
Cale, John, private
Cherry, James, private
Cherry, Solomon, Jr., private
Collins, David, private
Collins, John, private
Fellow, William, private
Flood, John, private
Fort, Elias, private
Harrell, Adam, private
Howard, Solomon, private
Hubbard, Warburton, private
Hurst, William, private
Jacocks, Charles Worth, captain
Kelly, William, private
Knott, William, sergeant
Leggett, John, private
Lewis, Samuel, private

Liscombe, Wilson, private
Lowe, William, private
Murray, William, private
Oden, Robert, private
Oliver, Andrew, private
Perkins, William, private
Pollock, Jacob, lieutenant
Redditt, Job, corporal
Redditt, Samuel, private
Rhodes, Elisha, sergeant
Rhodes, James, private
Rhodes, John, private
Rhodes, Jonathan, private
Simmons, James, drummer
Simmons, Mallekiah, private
Turner, Amos, private
Urqhuart, Alexander, private
Walton, Timothy, private
Watson, Thomas, corporal
Watson, William, private
Whitmell, Thomas Blount, ensign
Whitmell, West, private
Wynants, Wynant, private

CAPT. SOLOMON CHERRY'S COMPANY (MILITIA)

Cherry, Solomon, Jr., captain
Cook, William, [private]
Lednum, John, private
Measles, Cader, private
Rhodes, Thomas, ensign
Smith, William, private
Watford, Hardy, lieutenant

CAPT. JOHN FOLK AND CAPT. DEMPSEY COOK'S COMPANY (MILITIA)

Byrd, William, [private]
Cook, Dempsey, lieutenant/captain
Dillon, Richard, [private]
Folk, John, captain
Higgs, John, [private]
Lednum, John, private
Ward, James, private

CAPTAINS WILLIAM MORRIS AND WILLIAM RASCOE'S COMPANY (MILITIA)

Hendrickson, Isaac, private
Morris, William, captain
Rascoe, William, captain
Rayner, Amos, private

CAPT. ANDREW OLIVER'S COMPANY (MILITIA)

Freeman, William, private
Oliver, Andrew, captain

CAPT. FRANCIS PUGH'S COMPANY (MILITIA)

Barber, Charles, lieutenant
Barnes, Solomon, private
Pugh, Francis, captain

CAPTAINS THOMAS PUGH AND JOHN WOLFENDEN'S COMPANY (MILITIA)

Davis, William, lieutenant
Pugh, Thomas, captain
Ward, James, private
Wolfenden, John, captain

CAPT. ALLEN RAMSAY'S COMPANY (MILITIA)

Butler, Jethro, [private]
Calend, Robert, [private]
Carter, Benjamin, [private]
Deans, Samuel, [private]
Dymond, James, [private]
Farmer, James, [private]
Fields, John, [private]
Fryar, William, [private]
Harrell, Josiah, private
Hedgpeth, Joseph, [private]
Hedgpeth, Josiah, [private]
Hendrickson, Isaac, private
Horton, William, [private]
James, Frederick, [private]★
Jernigan, William, [private]
Lloyd, Jesse, [private]
Lowe, William, [private]
Minton, Thomas, [private]
Ramsay, Allen, captain
Wiggins, Arthur, private
Wilson, Josiah, private

CAPT. CHARLES RHODES'S COMPANY (MILITIA)

Goodman, William, ensign
Rascoe, William, lieutenant
Rayner, Amos, private
Rhodes, Charles, captain
Rhodes, John, private
Williams, George, Sr., private

Capt. Elisha Rhodes's Company (Militia)

Bass, Jacob, private
Buck, Stephen, ensign
Cochran, John, private
Duers, John, private
Grover, James Swinhow,
  lieutenant
Harrell, Christ[opher], private
Harrell, Shad[rack], private
Harrison, George, private
Holland, Frederick, private
Holland, Henry, private
Johnson, Levi, private
McDuel, St. [McDowell,
  Stephen], private
Pilant, Peter, corporal
Raby, Blake, private
Rhodes, Elisha, captain
Sanderson, Joseph, ensign
Sorrell, Ben[jamin], private
Thomas, Thomas, fifer
Wilks, James, private
Wilson, Edward, private

Capt. Thomas Rhodes's Company (Militia)

Rhodes, John, private
Rhodes, Thomas, captain

Capt. John Walton's Company (Militia)

Harrell, Josiah, private
Walton, John, captain

Miscellaneous

Airs, John, [private]
Airs, Thomas, [private]
Ashburn, William, captain
Barker, John, [private]
Bazemore, Thomas, [private]
Billups, Richard, private
Brown, Arthur, colonel
Butler, Curry, private
Campbell, James, colonel
Chavis, Ceasar, [private]
Cherry, John, [private]
Cherry, Robert, [private]
Clark, Abraham, [private]
Cook, Dempsey, [private]
Cross, Stephen, [private]
Davis, William, lieutenant
Everitt, Jesse, [private]
Freeman, William, [private]
Hall, Nathan, drummer
Hendrickson, John, private
Hinton, Reuben, [private]
Hopkins, Joseph, [private]
Howard, Elijah, [private]
Hunter, Hardy, [private]
Hunter, William, [private]
Hust [Hurst], John, [private]
Jacocks, Charles Worth, [officer]
Jenkins, Abraham, [private]

MISCELLANEOUS (*continued*)

Johnston, John, [private]
Jones, Thomas, [private]
Knott, Absalom, ensign
Knott, James, [private]
Knott, William, lieutenant
Lednum, John, private
Liscombe, Willis, ensign
McDonald, James, [private]
Miller, Steven, [private]
Mitchell, Jeremiah, [private]
Monk, Jacob, [private]
Moore, James, colonel
Morris, Abraham, [private]
Page, Solomon, lieutenant
Perry, Lewis, [private]
Powell, Willis, [private]
Pugh, John, [private]
Pugh, Shadrach, private
Pugh, Thomas, lieutenant colonel

Reed, Christian, ensign
Ryan, George, captain
Seay, John, [private]
Smith, William, [private]
Stone, William, [private]
Sumerlin, Elisha, [private]
Tennison, Matthew, [private]
Thomas, Josiah, [private]
Thomas, Thomas, [musician?]
Tomlinson, James, [private]
Tromble, Jethro, [private]
Vanburan, William, [private]
Weston, Solomon, [private]
Whitmell, Thomas, colonel
Williams, John Pugh, lieutenant
  colonel
Williams, Nathan, private
Williams, William, captain
Williford, James, [private]

BERTIE COUNTY MILITIA CAPTAINS (Not Detached)

Captain Askew
Capt. John Campbell
Capt. Charles Everitt
Capt. Solomon Freeman
Capt. Moses Gillam
Capt. Timothy Hunter
Capt. John Moore
Capt. Henry Speller
Captain Worley

Capt. Thomas Ballard
Capt. Christopher Clark
Capt. John Freeman
Captain Garrett
Captain Hardy
Captain King
Capt. Cader Powell
Capt. Hardy Watford
Capt. William Watkin Wynns

APPENDIX 3

BRITISH SOLDIERS FROM BERTIE COUNTY

During the Revolutionary War significant numbers of North Carolinians, including certain Bertie County citizens, maintained their loyalty to the British Crown. Numbers of Loyalists were exiled from the state and had their land-holdings and other properties confiscated by Whig authorities. Some North Carolinians joined the British military forces as soldiers and sailors, including the two individuals listed below, who—as prisoners of war—decided to enlist in the British army.

Hust [Hurst], John, [private]
Jones, Thomas, [private]

Bibliography

PRIMARY SOURCES

BERTIE COUNTY COURTHOUSE, WINDSOR, N.C.

Deeds. Bertie County Register of Deeds Office.

Wills. Bertie County Office of the Clerk of Court.

NATIONAL ARCHIVES, WASHINGTON, D.C.

Compiled Service Records of Soldiers Who Served in the American Army during the Revolutionary War (microfilm, M881). Record Group 94.

First Census of the United States, 1790: Bertie County, North Carolina, Population Schedule, National Archives, Washington, D.C. (microfilm, State Archives, Office of Archives and History, Raleigh).

Military Service Records: A Select Catalog of National Archives Microfilm Publications. Washington, D.C.: National Archives Trust Fund Board, National Archives and Service Administration, 1985.

Revolutionary War Pension and Bounty Land Warrant Files, 1800–1900 (microfilm, M804). Record Group 15.

Revolutionary War Rolls, 1775–1783 (microfilm, M246). Record Group 93.

NORTH CAROLINA STATE ARCHIVES, OFFICE OF ARCHIVES AND HISTORY, RALEIGH

Bertie County Criminal Action Papers, C.R.010.326, folder 1771–1780.

Bertie County Estate Records, 1730–1920.

Bertie County Lists of Taxables, 1755–1860.

Bertie County Miscellaneous Records, Revolutionary War Papers.

Chowan County Papers, XV, 1772–1777, March–October.

Comptrollers Records, State of North Carolina—Vouchers

Duplin County Court of Pleas and Quarter Sessions, Duplin County: Minutes, County Court, 1823–1828, 1832–1837 (microfilm).

Edenton District Superior Court. Depositions Relative to Llewelyn Conspiracy, 1777.

Edenton District Superior Court. Minute Docket, April 1769–November 1781, D.C.R. 2.001.

Edenton District Superior Court. Papers, 1774–1779.

English Records. "Brimage, William."

English Records. State Papers—Domestic—Military Commissions.

General Assembly Session Records

Governors Letter Books: Thomas Burke, Richard Caswell.

Governors Papers: Richard Caswell, Abner Nash.

List of North Carolina Militia Parole (Z.5.176P, microfilm), Foreign Archives, British Records, PRO 30/11/5 (1781).

Military Collection, Troop Returns.

Militia Troop Returns.

"North Carolina Pension Roll." (Publication facts missing; bound volume available at the North Carolina State Archives Search Room).

Secretary of State Revolutionary War Military Papers.

Treasurer's and Comptroller's Papers, Military Papers.
1776–1792, Service Records and Final Settlements.
1782, Receipts, Accounts and Orders for Clothing.
1782–1783, Receipts, Orders, Accounts for salt, corn, etc.

TYRRELL COUNTY COURTHOUSE, COLUMBIA, N.C.

Deeds. Tyrrell County Register of Deeds Office.

Wills. Tyrrell County Office of the Clerk of Court.

NEWSPAPERS

North Carolina Gazette (New Bern).

Virginia Gazette (Williamsburg).

INTERVIEW

Lange, William, park ranger, Valley Forge National Historic Park, telephone conversation with author, December 10, 2011.

BOOKS, PAMPHLETS, ARTICLES, AND OTHER PUBLISHED MATERIAL

Abbott, W. W., et. al., eds. *The Papers of George Washington*. 20 vols. to date. Charlottesville and London: University Press of Virginia, 1985–2010.

Axelrod, Alan. *The Real History of the American Revolution: A New Look at the Past*. New York: Sterling Publishing Co., 2007.

Bennett, William Doub. "Some Revolutionary War Service Veterans in Bertie County, NC." *North Carolina Genealogical Society Journal* 12 (February 1986).

Bigelow, Barbara, and Linda Schmittroth. *American Revolution Almanac.* Stacy A. McConnell, ed. Detroit, San Francisco, London, Boston, Woodbridge, Conn.: UXL, imprint of the Gale Group, 2000.

Bradley, Stephen E., Jr., comp. *The Deeds of Bertie County, North Carolina, 1757–1772.* Keysville, Va.: the compiler, 1992.

_____. *The Deeds of Bertie County, North Carolina, 1772–1785.* Keysville, Va.: the compiler, 1993.

Camin, Betty J. "Revolutionary War Pension Applications at the NC Archives." *North Carolina Genealogical Society Journal* 11 (August 1985).

Clark, Walter, ed. *The State Records of North Carolina.* 16 vols. numbered 11 through 26. Raleigh: State of North Carolina, 1895–1906.

Connor, R. D. W. *History of North Carolina: The Colonial and Revolutionary Periods (1584–1783).* Chicago and New York: Lewis Publishing Company, 1919.

Corbitt, David Leroy. *The Formation of the North Carolina Counties, 1663–1943.* Raleigh: Division of Archives and History, North Carolina Department of Cultural Resources, 1987.

Crow, Jeffrey J. *A Chronicle of North Carolina during the American Revolution, 1763–1789.* Raleigh: Department of Cultural Resources, Division of Archives and History, 1975.

_____. "Tory Plots and Anglican Loyalty: The Llewelyn Conspiracy of 1777." *North Carolina Historical Review* 55 (January 1978).

Daughters of the American Revolution. *Roster of Soldiers from North Carolina in the American Revolution.* Durham: North Carolina Daughters of the American Revolution, 1932; Baltimore: Genealogical Publishing Company, 1967, 1972, 1977, 1984, 1988.

Delamar, Marybelle. "Transcriptions of Petitions to the General Assembly of North Carolina Relating to Revolutionary War Military Service, 1788–1833." State Archives.

DeMond, Robert O. *The Loyalists in North Carolina during the Revolution.* Baltimore: Genealogical Publishing Co., 1979.

The Episcopal Church in Bertie County, 1701–1990, From Its Anglican Roots to the Twentieth Century. Windsor, N.C.: St. Thomas' Episcopal Church, 1990.

"Estimate of Militia, April 1782." *The North Carolinian: A Quarterly Journal of Genealogy and History* 6 (September 1960).

Ford, Worthington Chauncey, ed. *Journals of the Continental Congress.* 34 vols. Washington, D.C.: Government Printing Office, 1904–1937.

Hannings, Bud. *Chronology of the American Revolution*. Jefferson, N.C., and London: McFarland and Company, Publishers, 2008.

Hathaway, J. R. B., ed. *North Carolina Historical and Genealogical Register II* (1901).

Haun, Weynette Parks, comp. *Bertie County, North Carolina, County Court Minutes, 1763 thru 1771, Book III*. Durham: the compiler, 1978.

_____. *Bertie County, North Carolina, County Court Minutes, 1781 thru 1787, Book V*. Durham: the compiler, 1982.

_____. *Bertie County, North Carolina, County Court Minutes (Court of Pleas & Quarter Sessions) 1778 thru 1792, Book VI*. Durham: the compiler, 1984.

_____. *Bertie County, North Carolina, Court Minutes, 1772–1780, Book IV*. Durham: the compiler, 1979.

_____. *North Carolina Revolutionary Army Accounts, Accounts of the United States with North Carolina [Treasurer, State], Book C, [Part XIV]*. Durham: the compiler, 1999.

_____. *North Carolina Revolutionary Army Accounts, Military Land Warrant Book, 1783–1841, Continental Line 1783–1841, Secretary of State: SS.981.1:S.108.264 [Part XV]*. Durham, the compiler, 1999.

_____. *North Carolina Revolutionary Army Accounts, Secretary of State, Treasurer's & Comptroller's Papers, Journal "A" (Public Accounts), 1775–1776*. Durham: the compiler, 1988.

_____. *North Carolina Revolutionary Army Accounts, Secretary of State, Treasurer's & Comptroller's Papers, Vol. I, Vol. II, Part II*. Durham: the compiler, 1990.

_____. *North Carolina Revolutionary Army Accounts, Secretary of State Treasurer's & Comptroller's Papers, Vol. III, Vol. IV, Part III*. Durham: the compiler, 1991.

_____. *North Carolina Revolutionary Army Accounts [Treasurer's and Comptroller's Papers], Volume XI, [Part X]*. Durham: the compiler, 1999.

_____. *North Carolina Revolutionary Army Accounts [Treasurer, State], Book B [Part XIII]*. Durham: the compiler, 1999.

_____. *North Carolina Revolutionary Army Accounts, Treasurer, State, Books: E–G, H, J, Part XVII*. Durham: the compiler, 2004.

_____. *North Carolina Revolutionary Army Accounts, Treasurer, State, Book K, Part XVIII*. Durham: the compiler, 2004.

Heinegg, Paul. *Free African Americans of North Carolina and Virginia*. Second Edition. Baltimore: Clearfield Company, by Genealogical Publishing Co., 1994.

Heitman, Francis B. *Historical Register of Officers of the Continental Army during the War of the Revolution, April, 1775 to December, 1783*. Washington, D.C.: Rare Book Shop Publishing Co., 1914.

Higginbotham, Don, ed. *The Papers of James Iredell*, 2 vols. Raleigh: Division of Archives and History, Department of Cultural Resources, 1976.

"Index to N.C. Revolutionary War Pay Vouchers." *The North Carolinian: A Quarterly Journal of Genealogy and History* 6 (March 1960).

Lefler, Hugh T. *History of North Carolina*, 4 vols. New York: Lewis Historical Publishing Company, [1956].

Linn, Jo White. "Revolutionary War Claims: Abstracts from the Delamar Transcripts." *North Carolina Genealogical Society Journal* 5 (February 1979).

McBride, Ransom. "Claims of British Merchants after the Revolutionary War." *North Carolina Genealogical Society Journal* 17 (May, August 1991).

_____. "Revolutionary War Service Records and Settlements." *North Carolina Genealogical Society Journal* 9 (February 1983), 12 (May 1986), 14 (May, November 1988), 15 (May, November 1989), 16 (May 1990), 17 (May 1991), 18 (May, November 1992).

North Carolina Revolutionary War Records of Primary Interest to Genealogists. Archives Information Circular No. 13 (1975; revised March 2002). http://www.archives.ncdcr.gov/FindingAids/Circulars/AIC13.pdf.

Powell, William S., ed. *Dictionary of North Carolina Biography*. 6 vols. Chapel Hill: University of North Carolina Press, 1979–1996.

_____. *North Carolina: A History*. Chapel Hill and London: University of North Carolina Press, 1977.

Rankin, Hugh F. *The North Carolina Continentals*. Chapel Hill: University of North Carolina Press, 1971.

"Revolutionary War: Final Settlements." *The North Carolinian: A Quarterly Journal of Genealogy and History* 6 (December 1960).

Roberts, James A. *New York in the Revolution as Colony and State*. Albany: Press of Brandow Printing Company, 1898.

Saunders, William L., ed. *The Colonial Records of North Carolina*. 10 vols. Raleigh: State of North Carolina, 1886–1890.

Schmittroth, Linda, and Mary Kay Rosteck. *American Revolution Biographies*. Stacy A. McConnell, ed. Detroit, San Francisco, London, Boston, Woodbridge, Conn.: UXL, imprint of the Gale Group, 2000

Smith, Paul H., and Ronald M. Gephart, eds. *Letters of Delegates to Congress, 1774–1789*. 26 vols. Washington, D.C.: Library of Congress, 1976–2000.

Speidel, Frederick G. *North Carolina Masons in the American Revolution*. Oxford, N.C.: Press of Oxford Orphanage, 1975.

Thompson, Harry Lewis. "The Lost Town of 'Cashy.' " Unpublished research report dated October 1961, Search Room, State Archives, Raleigh.

Troxler, Carole Watterson. *Farming Dissenters: The Regulator Movement in Piedmont North Carolina.* Raleigh: Office of Archives and History, North Carolina Department of Cultural Resources, 2011.

Watson, Alan D. *Bertie County: A Brief History.* Raleigh: North Carolina Division of Archives and History, 1982.

_____. "The Committees of Safety and the Coming of the American Revolution in North Carolina, 1774–1776." *North Carolina Historical Review* 73 (April 1996).

Winslow, Raymond A., Jr. "North Carolina Apprentice Indentures through 1850." *North Carolina Genealogical Society Journal* 13 (August 1987).

_____. "Two Lists of North Carolinians Serving in British Armies during the American Revolution." *North Carolina Genealogical Society Journal* 16 (August 1990).

World Book Encyclopedia. 2000 edition.

Wright, Robert K., Jr. *The Continental Army.* Washington, D.C.: Center of Military History, United States Army, 1963.

Wyche, Kathleen B. "North Carolina Militia Paroled by Lord Cornwallis in 1781." *North Carolina Genealogical Society Journal* 4 (August 1978).

OTHER SOURCES

Brier, Marc, park ranger, Valley Forge National Historic Park. "Revolutionary Resting Place" (undated information paper).

Hill, Michael. "The Historical Significance of the Batts-Duckenfield-Capehart Site, Bertie County: A Preliminary Report." Unpublished research paper, Research Branch, Division of Archives and History, Raleigh, 1986.

The History Place, American Revolution. www.historyplace.com/unitedstates/revolution. Website.

Lucas, Jeffrey P. "Cooling by Degrees: Reintegration of Loyalists in North Carolina, 1776–1790." Master's thesis, North Carolina State University, 2007.

"Marriage Bonds of Tyrrell County, North Carolina." www.ncgenweb.us/tyrrell/TYRMARBB.HTM. Website.

McKown, Harry. "November 1765: The Stamp Act Crisis in North Carolina." www.lib.unc.edu/ncc/ref/nchistory/nov2006/. Website. University of North Carolina at Chapel Hill Libraries.

The North Carolina History Project. www.northcarolinahistory.org. Website. John Locke Foundation, Raleigh.

Index

C